Excel 2013 and 2010 for Seniors

Studio Visual Steps

Excel 2013 and 2010
for Seniors

Learn step by step how to work with Microsoft Excel

Summit Free Public Library

www.visualsteps.com

This book has been written using the Visual Steps™ method.
Cover design by Studio Willemien Haagsma bNO

© 2014 Visual Steps
Author: Studio Visual Steps

First printing: May 2014
ISBN 978 90 5905 180 5

Do you have questions or suggestions?
Email: info@visualsteps.com

Would you like more information?
www.visualsteps.com

Website for this book:
www.visualsteps.com/excel2013

Subscribe to the free Visual Steps Newsletter:
www.visualsteps.com/newsletter

Table of Contents

Foreword

Nowadays, being able to work with *Excel* from *Microsoft's Office* suite is one of the standard skills required for many computer users. Employees, high school students and college students alike are expected to know the program and be able to use it to organize and display various types of data.

With *Excel's* collection of built-in functions for financial and mathematical calculations, the program has become a powerful tool that can be used for many different purposes. This book will show you step by step how to work with *Excel 2013* or *2010*.

We hope this book will be helpful for you,

Studio Visual Steps

P.S.
We welcome all your comments and suggestions regarding this book.
Our email address is: info@visualsteps.com

Newsletter

All Visual Steps books follow the same methodology: clear and concise step-by-step instructions with screenshots to demonstrate each task. A complete list of all our books can be found on our website **www.visualsteps.com**

You can also sign up to receive our **free Visual Steps Newsletter**.
In this Newsletter you will receive periodic information by email regarding:
- the latest titles and previously released books;
- special offers, supplemental chapters, tips and free informative booklets.
Also, our Newsletter subscribers may download any of the documents listed on the web page **www.visualsteps.com/info_downloads**

When you subscribe to our Newsletter you can be assured that we will never use your email address for any purpose other than sending you the information as previously described. We will not share this address with any third-party. Each Newsletter also contains a one-click link to unsubscribe.

Introduction to Visual Steps™

The Visual Steps handbooks and manuals are the best instructional materials available for learning how to work with the computer, mobile devices and software applications. Nowhere else will you find better support for getting started with a *Windows* or *Mac* computer, an iPad or other tablet, iPhone, the Internet or various other software applications such as *Picasa*.

Characteristics of the Visual Steps books:
- **Comprehensible contents**
  Every book takes into account the wishes, knowledge and skills of computer users, beginners as well as more advanced users.
- **Clear structure**
  Every book is set up as an entire course, which you can easily follow, step by step.
- **Screenshots of every step**
  You will be guided by simple instructions and screenshots. You will immediately see what to do next.
- **Get started right away**
  All you have to do is place the book next to your keyboard and perform each operation as indicated on your own computer.
- **Layout**
  The text is printed in a large size font and is clearly legible.

In short, I believe these manuals will be excellent guides for you.

Dr. H. van der Meij
Faculty of Applied Education, Department of Instructional Technology, University of Twente, the Netherlands

Website

This book is accompanied by the website **www.visualsteps.com/excel2013**
Be sure to check this website from time to time, to see if we have added any additional information or errata for this book.
You can also download the practice files used throughout this book from this website.

What You Will Need

To be able to work through this book, you will need a number of things:

The main requirement for working with this book is to have **Microsoft Excel 2013** or **Microsoft Excel 2010** installed on your computer.
It does not make a difference if you use the stand alone *Excel* application or *Excel* as part of the *Office* suite. You can also use this book if you are a subscriber to *Office 365*, the subscription-based online service from *Microsoft Office*.

Your computer needs to have *Windows 8.1* or *Windows 7* installed.
Excel 2013 will only work on computers with the *Windows 8.1* or *Windows 7* operating system. *Excel 2010* is suitable for *Windows 8.1*, *7* and *Vista*.

You will need to have an active Internet connection in order to download the practice files from the website that accompanies this book.

Some of the exercises require the use of a printer. If you do not own a printer you can skip these exercises.

Your Basic Knowledge

This book has been written for computer users who already have some experience using *Windows* and have acquired basic text editing skills. To work through this book successfully, you should be able to do the following:

***Windows*:**
- start and stop *Windows*;
- click, right-click, double-click, and drag with the mouse;
- open and close programs;
- use a scrollbar;
- use tabs.

Basic text editing skills:
- type a text;
- correct errors;

- create and delete a new line;
- move the cursor;
- select text;
- save a document and open it again;
- create a new document.

If you do not have these skills, you can use one of our beginner's books. For more information about our current titles, visit the catalog page on our website: **www.visualsteps.com**

How to Use This Book

This book has been written using the Visual Steps™ method. The method is simple: just place the book next to your computer or laptop and perform each task step by step, directly on your own device. With the clear instructions and the multitude of screenshots, you will always know exactly what to do next. This is the quickest way to become familiar with the many features and options in *Excel 2013* or *Excel 2010*.

In this Visual Steps™ book, you will see various icons. This is what they mean:

Techniques
These icons indicate an action to be carried out:

     The mouse icon means you need to do something with the mouse.

     The keyboard icon means you should type something on your keyboard.

     The hand icon means you should do something else, for example, turn on the computer or carry out a task previously learned.

In some areas of this book additional icons indicate warnings or helpful hints. These help you to avoid making mistakes and alert you when a decision needs to be made.

Help
These icons indicate that extra help is available:

The arrow icon warns you about something.

The bandage icon will help you if something has gone wrong.

1   Have you forgotten how to do something? The number next to the footsteps tells you where to look it up at the end of the book in the appendix *How Do I Do That Again?*

The following icons indicate general information or tips about *Excel 2013* and *Excel 2010*. This information is displayed in separate boxes.

Extra information

Information boxes are denoted by these icons:

The book icon gives you extra background information that you can read at your convenience. This extra information is not necessary for working through the book.

The light bulb icon indicates an extra tip for using a program or service.

Test Your Knowledge

After you have worked through this book, you can test your knowledge online, on the **www.ccforseniors.com** website. By answering a number of multiple choice questions you will be able to test your knowledge of *Excel*. If you pass the test, you can also receive a free *Computer Certificate* by email.
Participating in the test is **free of charge**. The computer certificate website is a free service from Visual Steps.

For Teachers

This book is designed as a self-study guide. It is also well suited for use in a group or a classroom setting. For this purpose, we offer a free teacher's manual containing information about how to prepare for the course (including didactic teaching methods) and testing materials. You can download the teacher's manual (PDF file) from the website which accompanies this book: **www.visualsteps.com/excel2013**

More about Other Office Programs

Excel is one of the programs included in the *Microsoft Office* suite. One of the other programs in this suite is the *Word* text editing program, for which the same type of step-by-step book is available. See **www.visualsteps.com/word2013**

The Screenshots

The screenshots used in this book indicate which button, folder, file or hyperlink you need to click on your computer screen. In the instruction text (in **bold** letters) you will see a small image of the item you need to click. The black line will point you to the right place on your screen.
The small screenshots that are printed in this book are not meant to be completely legible all the time. This is not necessary, as you will see these images on your own computer screen in real size and fully legible.

Here you see an example of an instruction text and a screenshot. The black line indicates where to find this item on your own computer screen:

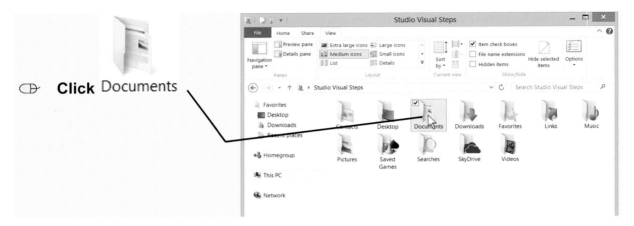

Sometimes the screenshot shows only a portion of a window. Here is an example:

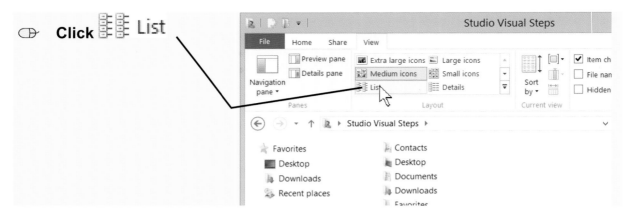

It really will **not be necessary** for you to read all the information in the screenshots in this book. Always use the screenshots in combination with the image you see on your own computer screen.

1. Cells and Formulas

Microsoft Excel is a spreadsheet program used for calculating figures. The word *spread* indicates that the text is spread out over multiple columns, and even multiple sheets. A spreadsheet is actually a large sheet of squared paper. You can write down something in each box (cell). This can be a number, an amount or text. It can also be an underlying formula that performs a certain calculation.

A spreadsheet is an ideal tool for creating a summary of calculations. For example, you can use the program to keep track of your monthly or weekly household expenditures or the annual costs of your car, or to compute the profitability of your investments, or provide an overview of the annual membership fees of a club.

These various types of data analyses do not really differ with regard to the nature of the data and the calculations, only the actual values change. If you create a data summary in a spreadsheet program and enter the correct formulas, the totals will be quickly and automatically computed without any errors. This can save you a lot of work when preparing annual reports or estimates for a company or a club. There are plenty of other useful tasks that can be done at home with this program too.

In this chapter you will learn how to:

- set up the *Quick Access* toolbar and adjust the ribbon;
- distinguish between columns, rows, and cells;
- select cells;
- move the cursor;
- enter numbers and text;
- change the column width;
- add up numbers and enter formulas;
- copy formulas;
- use *Sum* for automatic additions;
- save workbooks.

 Please note:

In order to perform the exercises in this book, you need to download the practice files from the website accompanying this book and save them to the (*My*) *Documents* folder on your computer. In *Appendix A Downloading the Practice Files* you can read how to do this.

1.1 Opening Excel

This is how you open *Microsoft Excel*:

In *Windows 8*, on the Start screen:

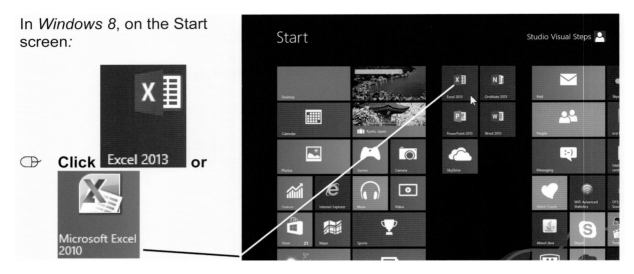

☞ **Click** Excel 2013 **or**

Microsoft Excel 2010

HELP! I do not see the Excel tile.
If you do not see the *Excel* tile, you can also open it from the apps list:
☞ **Move the pointer at the bottom left side of the screen**
☞ **Click**
☞ **Click the *Excel* tile**

In this example in *Windows 7* or *Windows Vista Excel 2010* is opened. Opening *Excel 2013* works the same way.

☞ **Click**

☞ **Click** ▶ **All Programs**

☞ **Click**
   Microsoft Office

☞ **Click**
   Microsoft Excel 2010

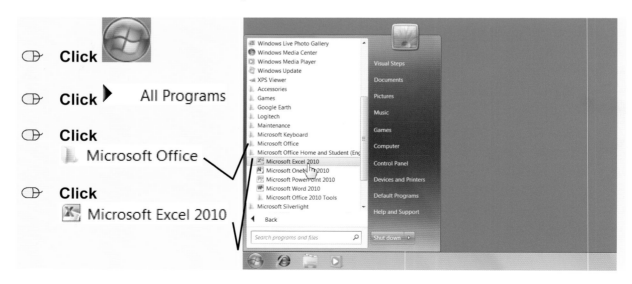

HELP! I see different windows.

When you open an *Office* suite program for the first time, you will see a number of different windows.

Only in *Excel 2010*:

☞ **Click the radio button** ⦿ **by** **U̲se Recommended Settings**

☞ **Click** OK

You can choose whether you want to send information:

☞ **Click the radio button** ⦿ **by** N̲o thanks

☞ **Click** Accept

Select the default file format. **Office Open XML formats** is the one most frequently used:

☞ **Click the radio button** ⦿ **by** **Office Open XML formats**

☞ **Click** OK

Close the welcome window that is displayed:

☞ **Click** ✕

When you open *Excel 2013* you will see this window:

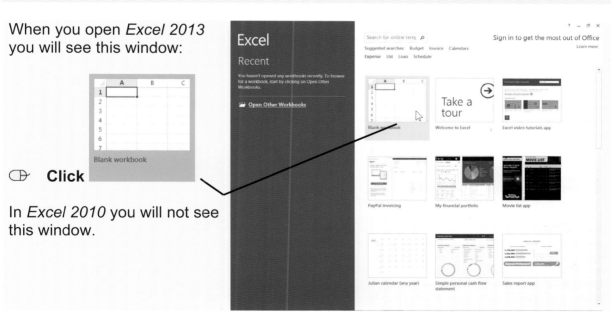

☞ **Click**

In *Excel 2010* you will not see this window.

Now you see the *Excel* window:

In the title bar you can see the name of the document:

Furthermore, you will see:
- the *Quick Access* toolbar
- the ribbon
- the tabs

Here you see the blank worksheet:

At the bottom of the window you see the status bar:

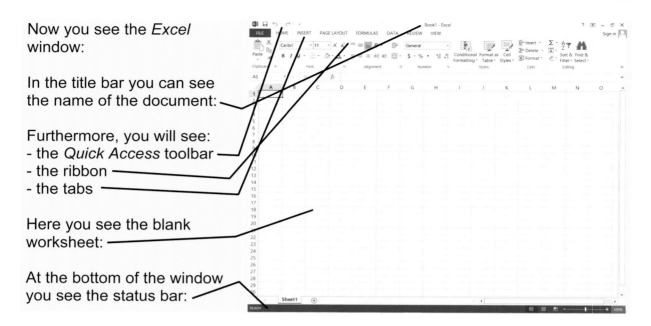

1.2 The Ribbon

The ribbon has been designed to help you quickly find the commands you need while editing your documents. The commands have been arranged into logical groups on separate tabs. Each tab refers to a specific type of activity, such as designing or formatting.

The ribbon contains a number of tabs. Each tab has several groups, where similar tools and features can be found.

By clicking a tab, the corresponding groups and their commands are displayed. You can temporarily minimize the ribbon by collapsing it, if you need more work space.

In the upper left-hand corner of the window:

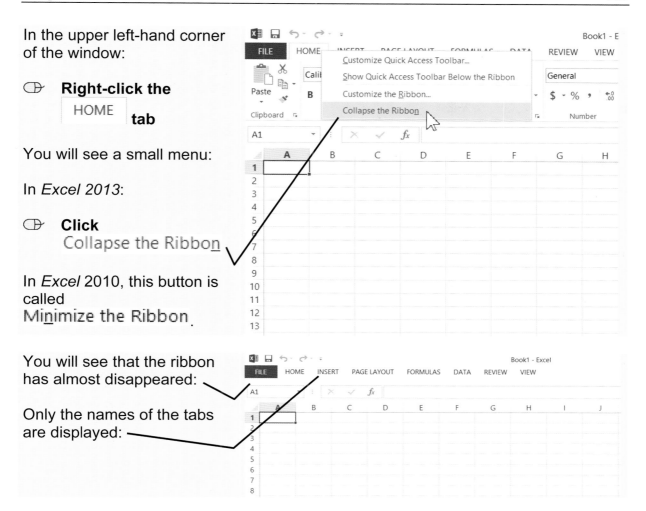

☞ **Right-click the** HOME **tab**

You will see a small menu:

In *Excel 2013*:

☞ **Click** Collapse the Ribbon

In *Excel* 2010, this button is called Minimize the Ribbon.

You will see that the ribbon has almost disappeared:

Only the names of the tabs are displayed:

You can also restore the ribbon:

☞ **Right-click the** HOME **tab**

☞ **Click** ✓ Collapse the Ribbon **(Excel 2013)** / ✓ Minimize the Ribbon **(Excel 2010)**

Now the ribbon is restored to its original and default size.

HELP! The ribbon looks different on my screen.

The buttons that are displayed on the tabs may vary; this also depends on the settings and the size of your screen. On a high resolution screen they can look like this:

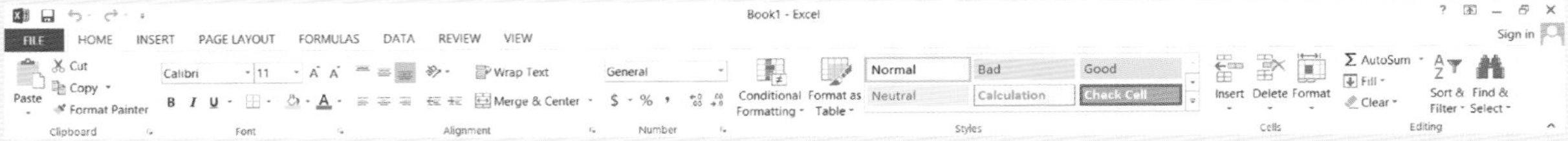

With a lower resolution, they may look like this:

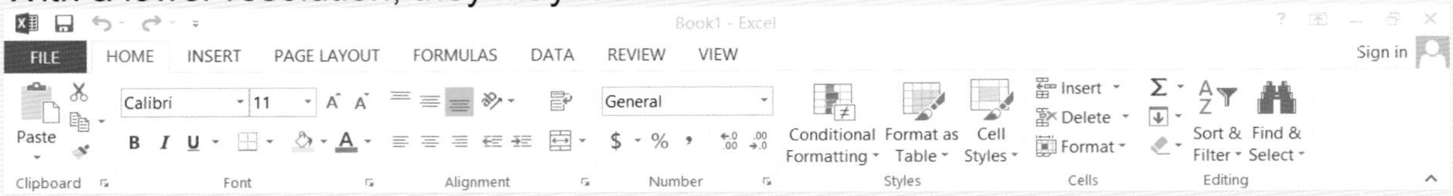

If it is hard to see an entire button with its icon and text, just look for the icon and click it.

1.3 Adjusting the Quick Access Toolbar

If you want to use a command on the ribbon, you usually need to click twice: first you click the tab, and then the command. This can get a little tiresome, if you use some of these commands very often. There is a special toolbar you can use that is very useful, called 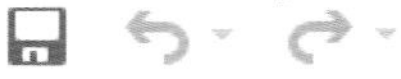. By adding frequently used commands to this toolbar, you can access them with just one mouse-click.

You can see the *Quick Access* toolbar at the top of the *Excel* window:

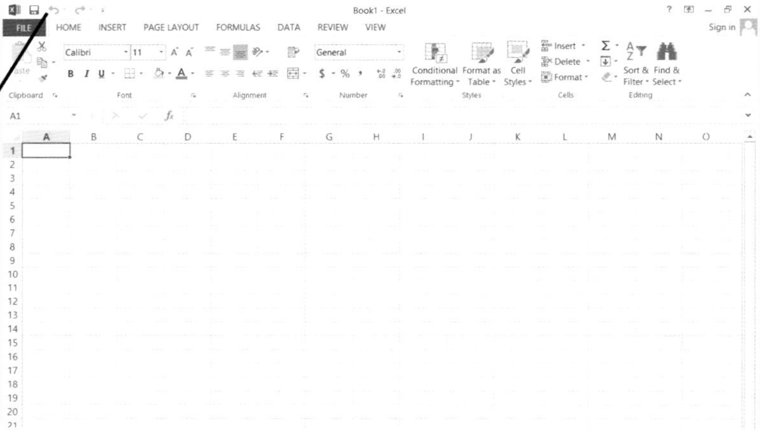

You can decide which commands to add to the *Quick Access* toolbar. You can also remove a command that you do not use very often, if you want:

🖰   **Click** ▼

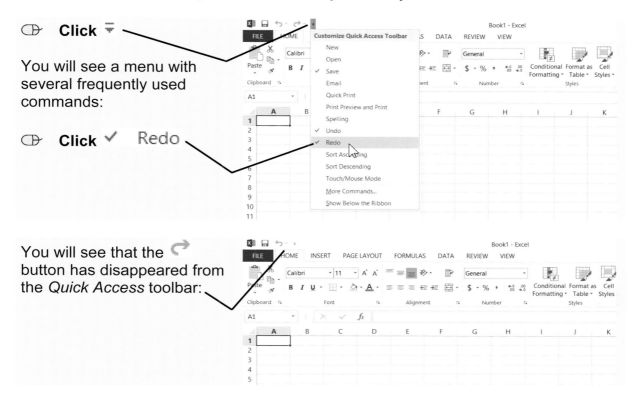

You will see a menu with several frequently used commands:

🖰   **Click** ✓   Redo

You will see that the ↻ button has disappeared from the *Quick Access* toolbar:

In the same way, you can add a button to the *Quick Access* toolbar:

🖰   **Click** ▼, Open

Now the *Quick Access* toolbar looks like this: 🖫 ↺ ▾ 📁 ▼.

You can also change the location of the *Quick Access* toolbar, that is to say, you can display the toolbar above or below the ribbon:

🖰   **Click** ▼, Show Below the Ribbon

Now you see the *Quick Access* toolbar below the ribbon:

You can revert back to the *Quick Access* toolbar's original position like this:

☞ **Click** ⬱ , S̲how Above the Ribbon

Now the *Quick Access* toolbar is displayed above the ribbon in its original position.

1.4 Adjusting the Ribbon

The ribbon can also be adapted to better fit the way you work. For instance, you can create your own tab and group the commands you frequently use on this tab:

☞ **Click the FILE tab**✓
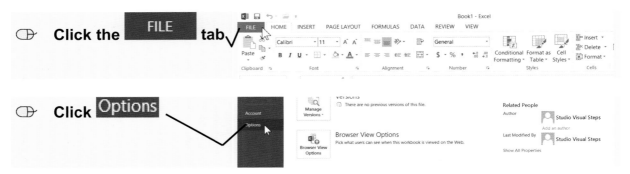

☞ **Click Options**

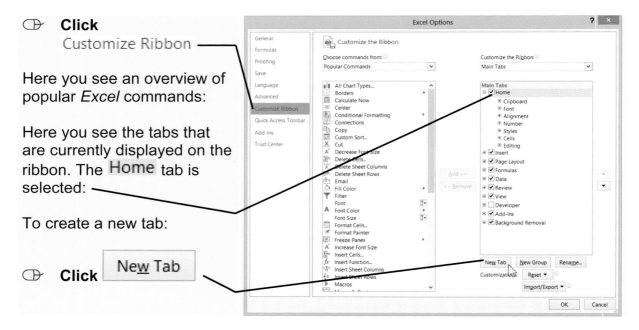

The *Excel Options* window will be opened. This is where you can change all sorts of settings for *Excel*. If you would like to customize the ribbon, for instance:

☞ **Click** Customize Ribbon

Here you see an overview of popular *Excel* commands:

Here you see the tabs that are currently displayed on the ribbon. The Home tab is selected:

To create a new tab:

☞ **Click** New̲ Tab

The new tab called New Tab (Custom) has been added, below the Home tab:

Also, a new group has been added to the tab, called New Group (Custom):

With the Rename... button you can change the name of a selected tab:

For now this will not be necessary.

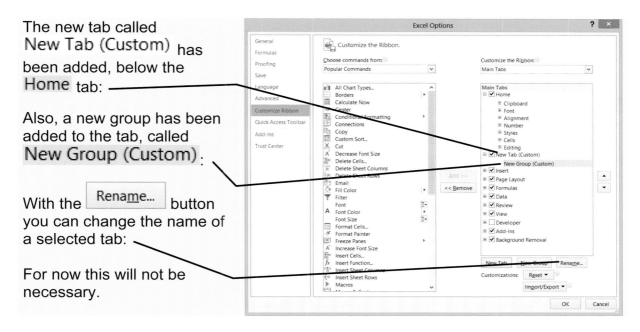

This is how you add a command to the new tab:

👉 **Drag the scroll bar downwards**

👉 **For example, click** 🖥️ **Pictures...**

👉 **Click** Add >>

👉 **Click** OK

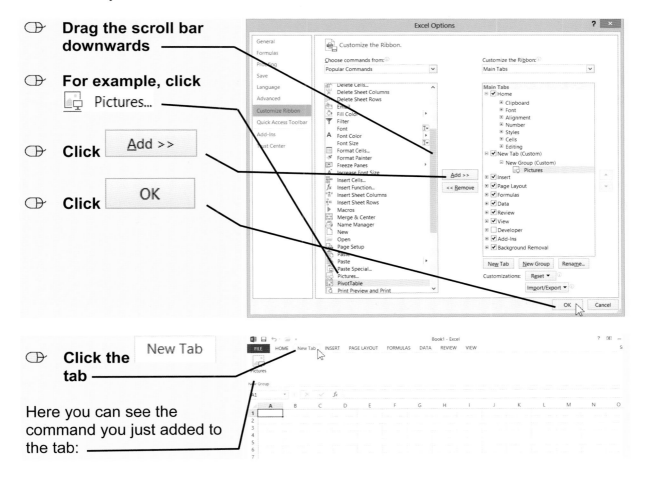

👉 **Click the** New Tab **tab**

Here you can see the command you just added to the tab:

You can just as easily delete the new tab. This is also another way of opening the *Excel Options* window:

☞ **Right-click the** New Tab **tab**

☞ **Click** Customize the Ribbon...

This is how you delete the new tab:

☞ **Right-click** New Tab (Custom)

☞ **Click** Remove

☞ **Click** OK

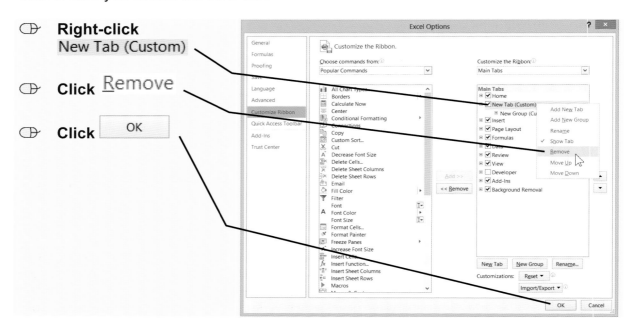

Now the ribbon has been restored to its original again.

1.5 Selecting Cells

Below the ribbon you see the *Excel* worksheet:

The worksheet is divided into boxes. These boxes are called cells.

The first cell has a thicker border: ────

This is the cell that is currently selected.

A worksheet consists of vertical columns and horizontal rows. The columns are indicated by letters and the rows are indicated by numbers:

Above the selected cell you see [**A**]. This cell is located in column A: ──────

To the left of the cell you see [1]. This tells you that the selected cell is in row 1: ──

So, the selected cell is called cell A1. This is also known as the *cell reference* or *cell address*.
You can also see this on the toolbar, in the *Name Box*: ──

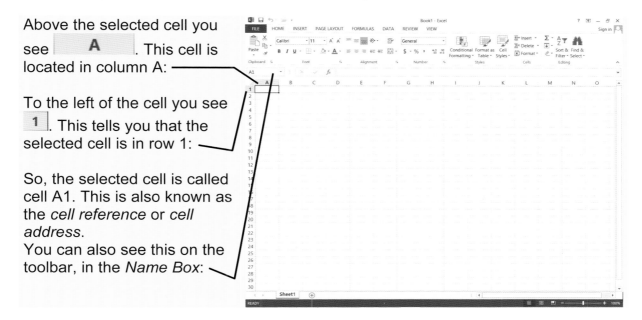

You can use the arrow keys to select a different cell:

Arrow keys: ──

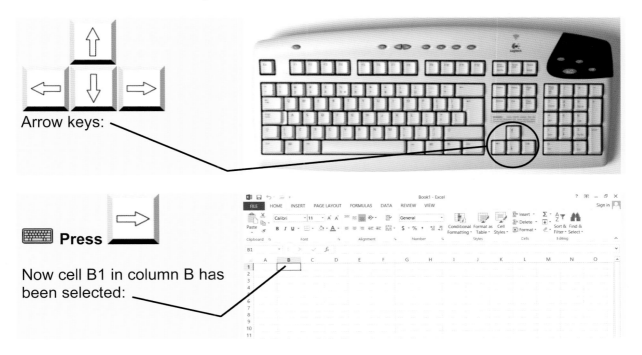

Press

Now cell B1 in column B has been selected: ──

Press

Now cell B2 in column B2 has been selected:

Tip
Use other keys

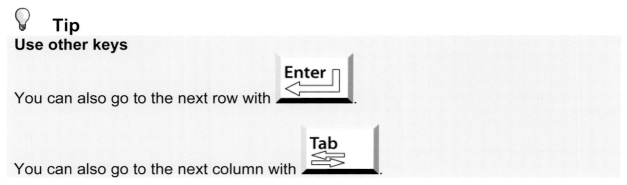

You can also go to the next row with **Enter**.

You can also go to the next column with **Tab**.

And you can also select a cell by clicking it with the pointer ✛ :

Click in cell C4

Now cell C4 is selected:

Please note:
Do not forget to click the cell. If you just place the pointer on the cell, hovering over it as you will, you will not have selected the cell. Only after you have clicked it, the cell will get a dark border, indicating that it has been selected.

There are even more ways of quickly selecting a specific cell. With this key you can jump to the first cell in the same row:

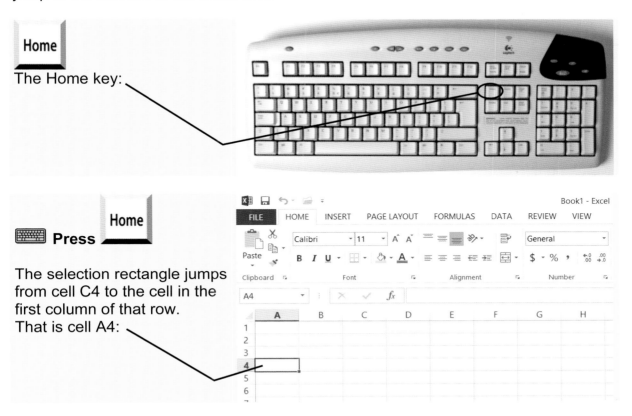

The Home key:

Press

The selection rectangle jumps from cell C4 to the cell in the first column of that row. That is cell A4:

You can also select cell A1 right away. You can do this with the following key combination:

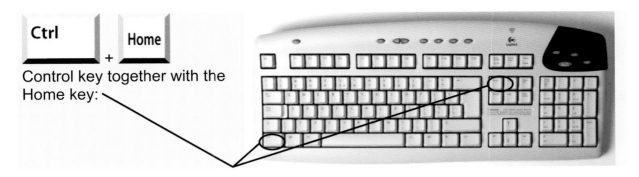

Control key together with the Home key:

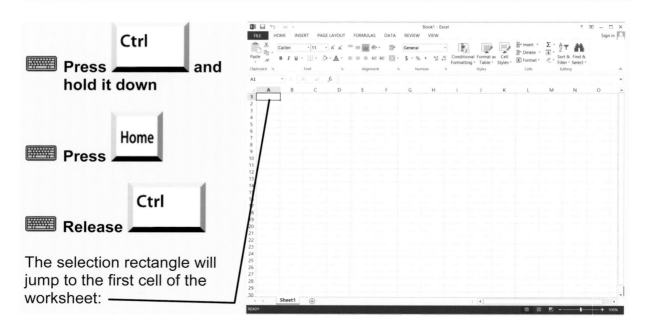

Press **Ctrl** and hold it down

Press **Home**

Release **Ctrl**

The selection rectangle will jump to the first cell of the worksheet:

1.6 Entering Text

You can enter various types of data in a cell, for example:

- numbers to be used in calculations;
- text for names, comments, or descriptions;
- dates.

In the following exercise you will be creating a simple household recordkeeping book. In this way you will learn how to enter data in *Excel* and how to use it in various calculations.

Press →

Now the cursor is in cell B1:

Type: bank

HELP! I have made a typing error.

Typing errors can be corrected with **Backspace**. **Please note:** do not press

or **Enter**. By doing this you will move the cursor to another cell.

Has the cursor already moved to another cell?

☞ **Click the correct cell**

⌨ **Type the correct text**

Now you can select the cell next to cell B1 and type text in this cell too:

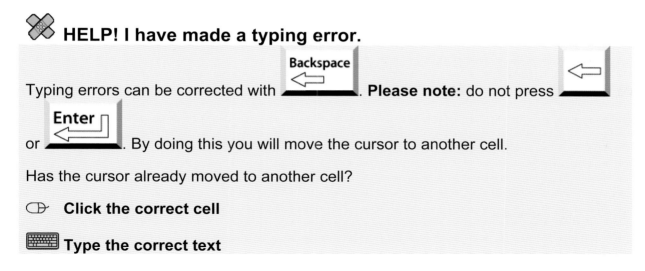

⌨ **Press** →

⌨ **Type:** `cash`

⌨ **Press** →

⌨ **Type:** `total`

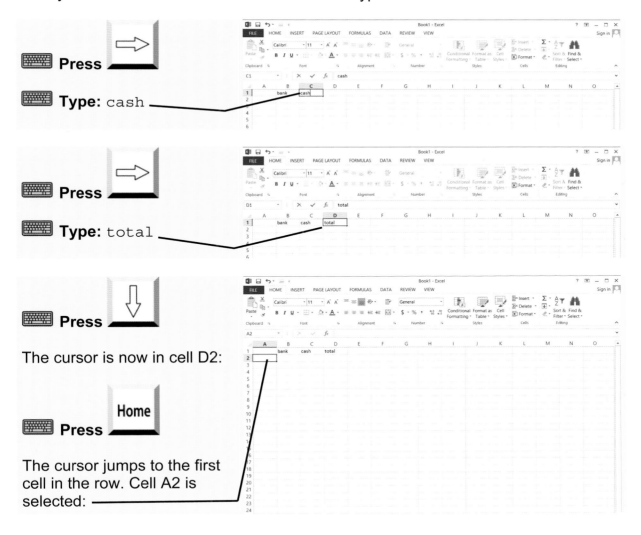

⌨ **Press** ↓

The cursor is now in cell D2:

⌨ **Press** Home

The cursor jumps to the first cell in the row. Cell A2 is selected:

1.7 Changing the Column Width

The first column often contains descriptions. If the description does not fit the cell, you can change the width of the column:

Type:
`food / groceries`

Press ⬇

The words *food / groceries* are too long for the cell:

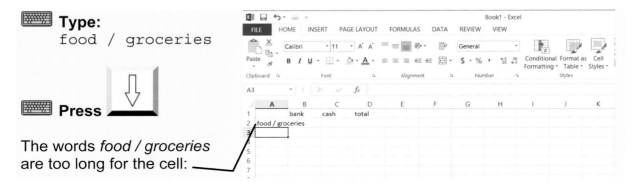

You can change the width of the column by dragging the mouse:

Place the pointer ✛ between the column headers

The pointer turns into ✛:

Press and hold the mouse button down

Drag the pointer to the right

You will see a vertical line in the worksheet moving along to the right:

Release the mouse button when the line is to the right of the words `food / groceries`

Please note: in *Excel 2010* you will see a dotted line.

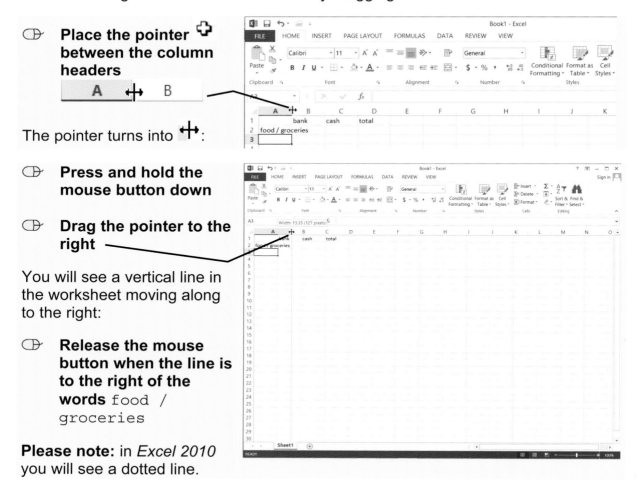

Now the width of the entire column has been adjusted. In this way you do not just change the width of a single cell, but of the whole column. The other columns will remain unchanged. They will move to the right a bit. You can type the other descriptions:

Type: rent

Press

Type: car expenses

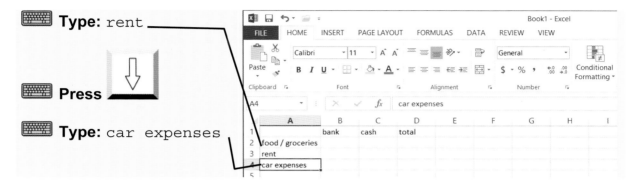

1.8 Entering numbers

Entering numbers is done in the same way as entering text:

Click in cell B2

Type: 200

Press

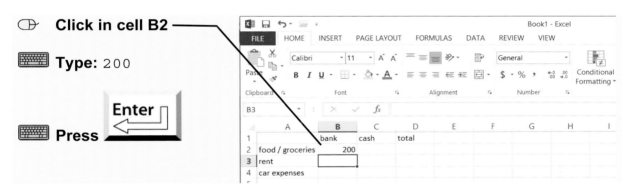

Tip

Go to the next cell

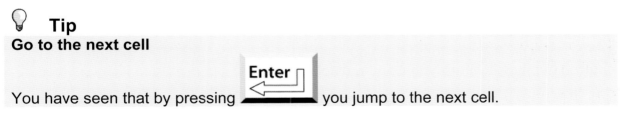

You have seen that by pressing _Enter_ you jump to the next cell.

Excel distinguishes between text and numbers. This can be seen by how it positions the data in a cell:

A number is aligned to the right-hand side of the cell:

Text is aligned to the left-hand side of the cell:

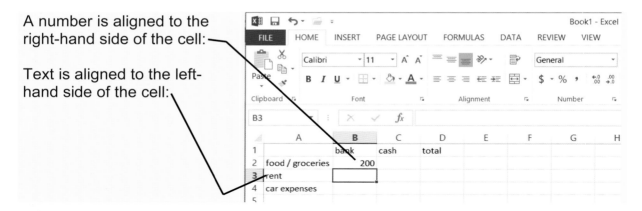

Now you can enter the necessary data that will be used in this practice workbook:

⌨ **Type the data in the workbook**

	A	B	C	D
1		bank	cash	total
2	food / groceries	200	350	
3	rent	1100		
4	car expenses	50	175	

The numbers have been entered. Now you can use these numbers in calculations. For example, you can add up numbers in a row or column.

1.9 Adding

The amounts in the *food / groceries* and *car expenses* rows are paid through the bank account, but also in cash. You can compute the total amount spent on groceries and on the car. In order to do this you need to enter a formula. This formula is entered in the cell where you want to display the sum.

In order to calculate the total amount spent on *food / groceries*, you need to select cell D2.

☞ **Click cell D2**

You want the total amount for the groceries to be displayed in cell D2. In *Excel*, a formula always begins with =.

⌨ **Type:** =

Excel is now ready to construct a formula. By clicking another cell you can indicate you want to use the number in that cell for a calculation. In cell B2 you find the amount paid for groceries through a bank account. You want to include this cell in the formula:

🖱 **Click cell B2**

You will see that B2 is added to the formula in cell D2:

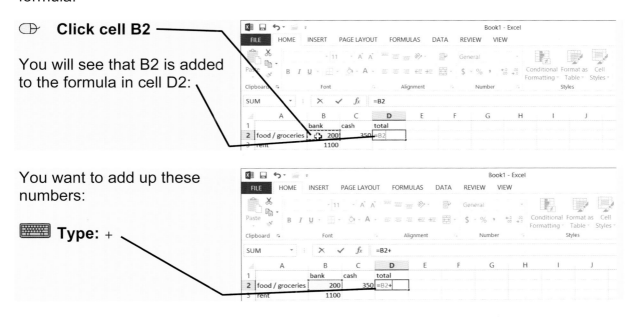

You want to add up these numbers:

⌨ **Type:** +

Next, you can select another cell. In this case it will be cell C2. This cell contains the amount for groceries paid in cash:

🖱 **Click cell C2**

Cell C2 is added to the formula:

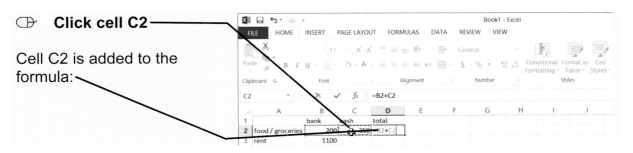

You can insert the formula by pressing the Enter key:

Press

The addition will be inserted in cell D2:

Since cell D2 now contains a formula, each time one of the cells in this formula is altered, the total in cell D2 will also be recalculated.

Click cell B2

Type: 180

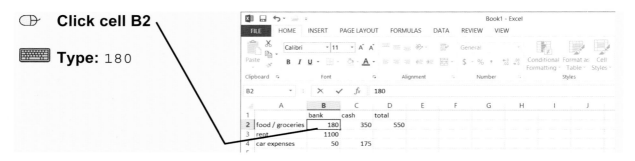

💡 **Tip**

Change content of a cell

In order to change the content of a cell you do not need to delete the old content first. Just type the new data directly in the cell.

Press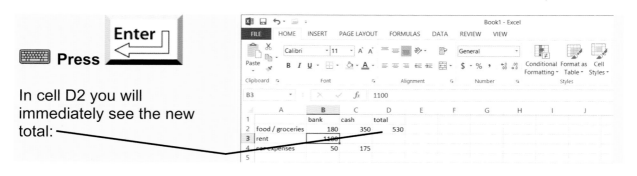

In cell D2 you will immediately see the new total:

Tip

Which formula does the cell contain?

If you want to know what the formula of a cell is, you need to do this:

☞ **Click the cell**

☞ **Look at the *Formula Bar***

There you will see the formula $=B2+C2$:

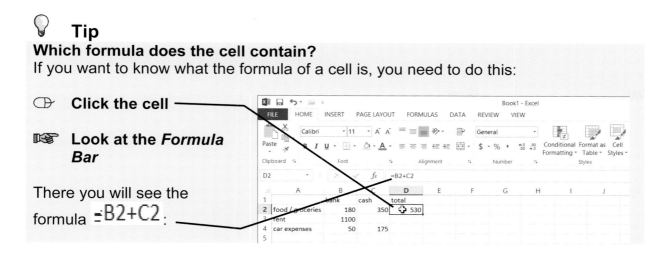

1.10 Copying Formulas

You also want to calculate the totals for the rows with *rent* and *car expenses*. The formulas you use for them are basically the same as the other calculations. The only difference is that the amounts you want to add up are in the rows below the first one. In this case you can copy the formula. It is quick to do and it will prevent you from making typing errors. Here is how you do it:

☞ **Click cell D2**

☞ **Place the pointer on the handle of cell D2**

The pointer turns into ➕:

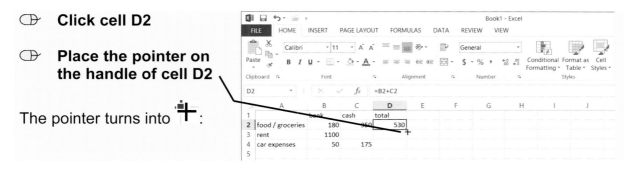

You can drag the mouse:

☞ **Press and hold the mouse button down**

☞ **Drag the pointer to cell D4**

☞ **Release the mouse button**

The formula has been automatically copied to cells D3 and D4:

![bandaid icon] **HELP! I have dragged the pointer the wrong way.**

The easiest way of undoing an error is by clicking the ↶ button in the top left-hand corner of the window. Your last action will be undone. Afterwards you can try again.

Excel has automatically adjusted the formulas to the row in which the cursor has been placed:

☞ **Click cell D3**

In the *Formula Bar* you will see this formula =B3+C3:

☞ **Click cell D4**

In the *Formula Bar* you will see this formula =B4+C4:

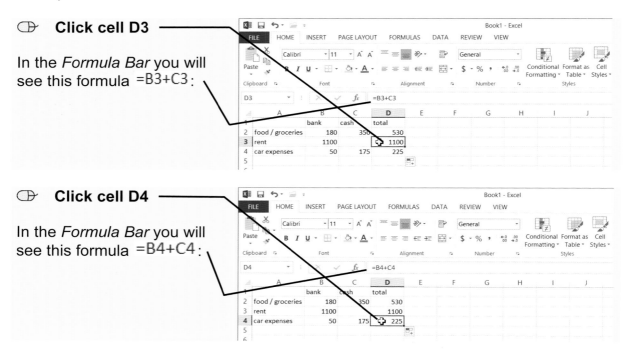

1.11 Sum

You can enter a formula to add up a whole column or row with numbers. But if you want to add up lots of numbers, constructing the formula will be a lot of work. Also, the formula will become difficult to read and you run a greater risk of making mistakes. Fortunately, *Excel* has a function which lets you automatically add up a column or row of numbers. This function is called *Sum*.

Click cell D2

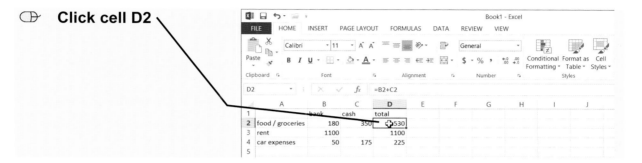

First you select the cells you want to add up:

Press and hold the mouse button down

Drag the pointer to cell D4

Release the mouse button

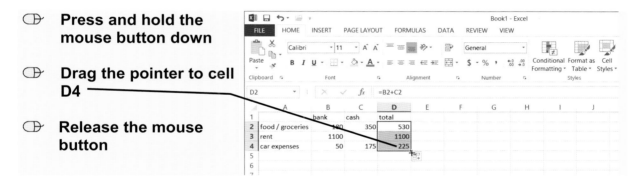

 Please note:

You need to start dragging when the pointer turns into ＋. You will see that the mouse pointer can take on different shapes in *Excel*. These shapes all have a different meaning.

Now you can add up the selected cells with the *Sum* function:

The **HOME** tab is already open:

Click Σ

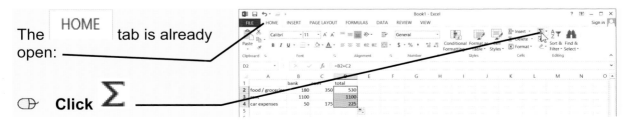

Below the selected column, the total (1855) of this column will appear:

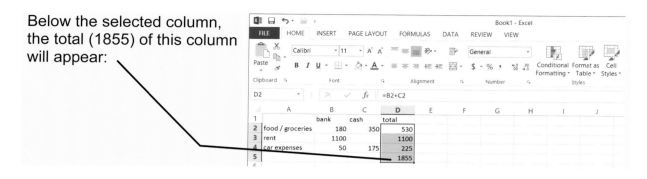

1.12 Saving

Your first *workbook* is finished. A completed workbook with its formulas is sometimes also called a *(calculation) model*. In one of the next chapters you will develop this model even further. It is important to save the workbook on your computer at regular intervals. Saving a file in *Excel* is done in the same way as in other *Windows* programs:

In the top left-hand corner of the window:

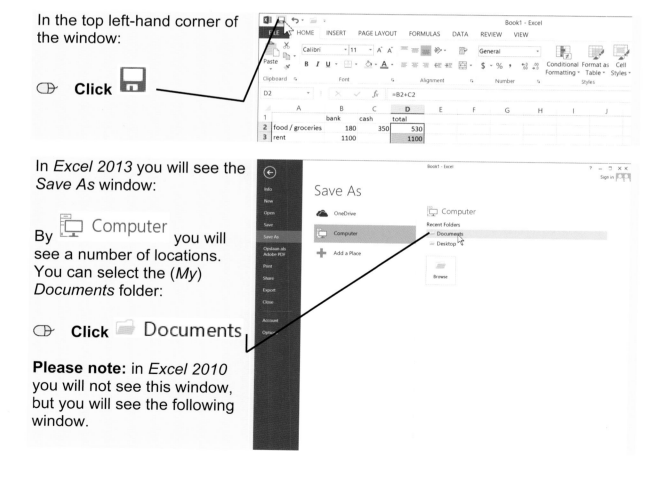

Click 💾

In *Excel 2013* you will see the *Save As* window:

By 🖥 Computer you will see a number of locations. You can select the (*My*) *Documents* folder:

Click 📁 Documents

Please note: in *Excel 2010* you will not see this window, but you will see the following window.

You will see the folder in which the document is saved:

You can type the name:

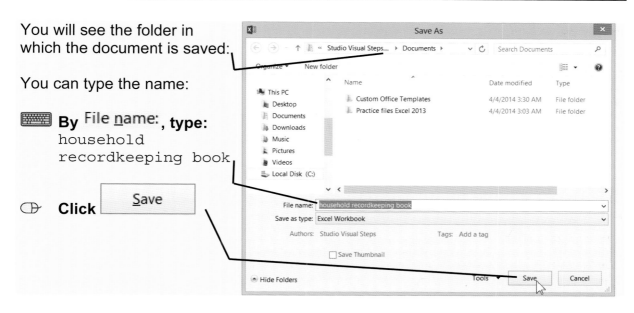

⌨ **By** File name:, **type:**
household
recordkeeping book

👆 **Click** Save

The household recordkeeping book has now been saved in the (*My*) *Documents* folder on your computer.

1.13 Testing

Testing the calculation model is very important, because you want to be able to rely on the results later on. You can test the model by changing some of the amounts. This is the only way of finding out whether all the formulas have been entered correctly.
After you have tested the model, you still need to check the results now and then. If the results do not seem to be logical, you should check the model again.

👆 **Click cell B3**

⌨ **Type:** 1200

⌨ **Press** Enter

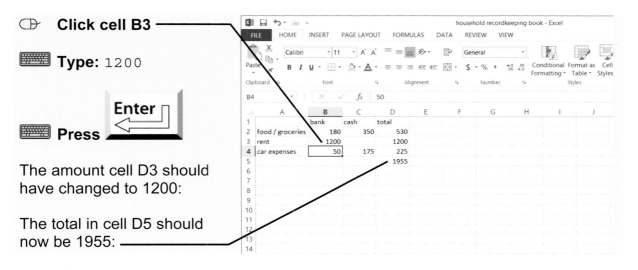

The amount cell D3 should have changed to 1200:

The total in cell D5 should now be 1955:

In this way you can change all the amounts and check if the model correctly computes the formulas.

 Please note:

Do not change any cells that contain a formula. Since *Excel* automatically overwrites the cells you will lose your formula and any subsequent changes will no longer be computed correctly.

 HELP! I have typed something in the wrong cell.

You may occasionally type an entry in the wrong cell. This can easily be corrected.

If you notice there is something wrong while you are typing, and the cursor is still placed in this cell:

 Press

If you have already moved the cursor to another cell:

⊕ **Click** ↰

1.14 Closing the workbook

You can now close the workbook. You do not need to save the changes you made while testing:

⊕ **Click the**  **tab**

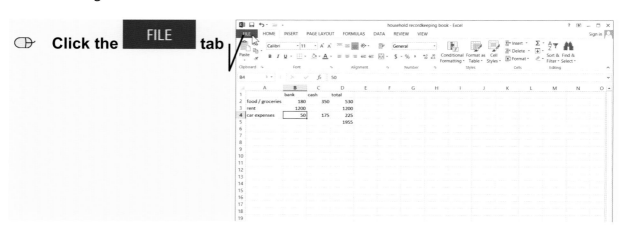

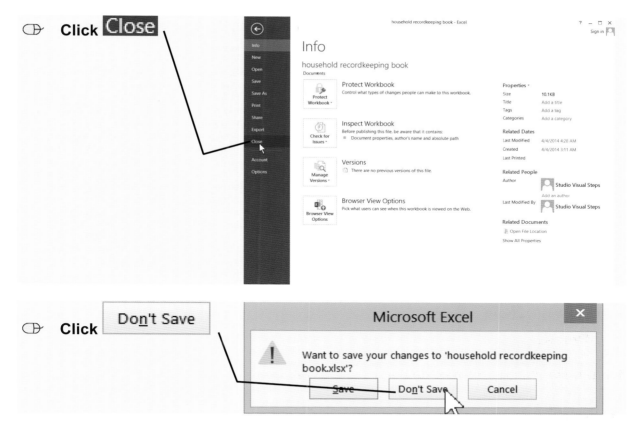

Now you will see a blank window.

In this chapter you have been introduced to *Excel*. In the next couple of exercises you can repeat the operations.

1.15 Exercises

In this chapter you have already executed quite a few operations that are essential to working with a spreadsheet. That is why it is good to repeat some of the main operations at this stage.

Have you forgotten how to do something? Use the number beside the footsteps to look it up in appendix *B How Do I Do That Again?* at the end of this book.

Exercise 1: Calculating Totals

For this exercise you need to use a blank workbook. *Excel* is still open:

☞ Click the **FILE** tab

☞ Click **New**, **Blank workbook**

In *Excel 2010*:

☞ Click **Create**

A new, blank workbook appears:

☞ Type these data in the workbook:

	A	B	C	D
1				
2	youngsters and juniors			
3	seniors			
4	veterans			
5	total			

☞ Widen column A to fit the longest text entry. 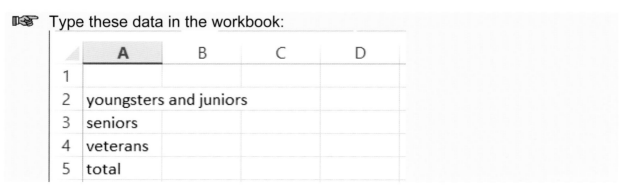²

☞ Enter the following data:

	A	B	C	D
1		men	women	total
2	youngsters and juniors	38	31	
3	seniors	25	22	
4	veterans	16	19	
5	total			

☞ Type the formula to calculate the total number of *youngsters and juniors* in cell D2. 👣**3**

☞ Copy the formula from cell D2 to cells D3 and D4. 👣**4**

☞ Use *Sum* to calculate the total number of men in cell B5. 👣**5**

☞ Copy the formula from cell B5 to cells C5 and D5. 👣**4**

☞ Check the model:

	A	B	C	D
1		men	women	total
2	youngsters and juniors	38	31	69
3	seniors	25	22	47
4	veterans	16	19	35
5	total	79	72	151

☞ Save the workbook and name the file *members*. 👣**6**

The numbers of members have changed.

☞ Edit the numbers as shown in this example:

	A	B	C	D
1		men	women	total
2	youngsters and juniors	(42)	(30)	
3	seniors	(28)	(26)	
4	veterans	(18)	19	
5	total	88	75	

If the formulas have been entered correctly, the total number of members in cell D5 should be: 163.

☞ Save the changes. ⁷

Exercise 2: Overwrite a Formula

In this exercise you will see what happens when you overwrite a formula in a calculation model. For example, when you change a cell that contains a formula to a number.

☞ In cell D2, type: `72`

Now you have overwritten the formula in this cell, but you do not yet see the consequences.

☞ In cell B2, type: `100`

	A	B	C	D
1		men	women	total
2	youngsters and juniors	100	30	72
3	seniors	28	26	54
4	veterans	18	19	37
5	total	88	75	163

Cell D2 no longer contains a formula, so the total results are not accurate.

☞ Restore the formula in cell D2 by clicking ↶ twice.

☞ Close *Excel* without saving the changes. ⁸

1.16 Background Information

Dictionary

Alphanumeric data	Text or numbers that cannot be used in calculations in *Excel*.
Calculation model	A set of formulas used to perform various calculations. Example: mortgage payments can be computed by using a calculation model.
Cell	The smallest unit in a table.
Column	A vertical series of cells.
Formula	A sequence of values, cell references, names, functions or operators within a cell, that together produce a new value. A formula always begins with an equal sign (=).
Formula Bar	A bar at the top of the *Excel* window, where you can enter or edit the values or formulas in the cells.
Handle	Also called the fill handle. A little block in the bottom right-hand corner of a cell. The fill handle allows you to fill cells with data that originates from one or more source cells. By clicking and dragging the handle you can copy the content of a cell, or range of cells, to adjacent rows or columns.
Name box	The box on the left-hand side of the *Formula Bar*, indicating the selected cell.
Numeric data	Numbers that can be used in calculations.
Ribbon	The ribbon is the toolbar at the top of the *Excel* window. The ribbon is organized into different tabs. Each tab has several groups, where similar tools and features are found.
Row	A horizontal series of cells.
Spreadsheet	Another word for calculation sheet. A calculation program such as *Excel* is also called a spreadsheet program.
Sum	Function to add up all the numbers in a series of cells.
Workbook	A workbook consists of cells, arranged in columns and rows. The workbook is used to edit and save data.
Zoom factor	Percentage that indicates the degree of enlarging or diminishing the view of a workbook on the screen.

Source: Microsoft Excel Help

Numeric and alphanumeric data

You have already noticed that *Excel* distinguishes between text and numbers. Text is aligned to the left-hand side of a cell. Numbers are aligned to the right-hand side of a cell.

This matches the way in which we usually work with text or numbers in everyday life. Just take a look:

text	numbers
Car	25
Bus	1215
Airplane	3
Train	197

If you would do it the other way round, it would look very strange and be more difficult to read:

text	numbers
Car	25
Bus	1215
Airplane	3
Train	197

Numbers that can be used in calculations are also called *numeric data*. Numeric data can only consist of the digits 0 up to and including 9, sometimes supplemented by a comma or a period, as a decimal point. Or with a minus sign, to indicate a negative number.

Text or numbers that cannot be used in calculations are called *alphanumeric data*. Alphanumeric data can consist of letters, numbers and special characters. An example of a number that cannot be used in a calculation is a Social Security Number: it consists of numbers but it is not used in calculations.

Neither is a *phone number*, so this is also an alphanumeric number. You can clearly see this, because some numbers contain hyphens to separate the area code and the home number. The area code and country code may also appear in parentheses.

1.17 Tips

 Tip

Regularly test your spreadsheet

Be alert when looking at the results of your calculation model, even if you have used the model for a long time. Check if the model still functions correctly, once in a while. It happens quite often that an underlying formula in a cell is accidentally replaced by a number that is entered. This is not something you will notice at once. Test the model by replacing all the variables one by one. In this way you can check whether the calculations are correctly executed. And it may help to find other potential errors.

 Tip

Enlarge or reduce the view

With larger workbooks you will not be able to see all the columns and rows on your screen. If this is the case, you can adjust the zoom factor. Usually it is set to 100%. If you lower this percentage, everything will be displayed a bit smaller and you will be able to fit more data on the screen. But make sure the workbook is still large enough for you to read the data.

Here is how you change the zoom factor:

In the bottom right-hand corner of the window:

☞ **Click 100 %**

You will see this window:

☞ **Click the radio button ⊙ by the desired percentage**

☞ **Click OK**

If you do not like this view you can set it back to 100% in the same way.

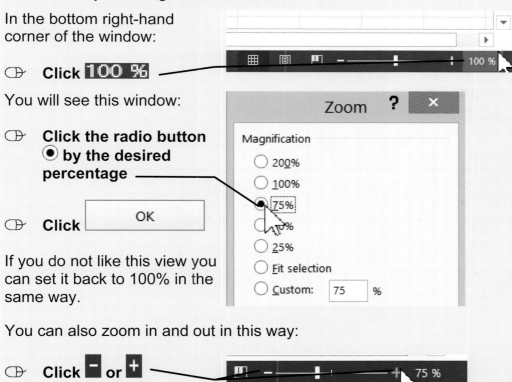

You can also zoom in and out in this way:

☞ **Click ▬ or ➕**

- Continue on the next page -

☞ **Drag the slider to the left or to the right**

Please note: enlarging or reducing the view in this way only affects the view on the screen. It does not affect the size of the workbook when you print it.

 Tip

Save in another file format

Sometimes you may want to save an existing *Excel* file that you have opened and store it in a different file format. In this way, someone who does not yet have *Excel 2013, 2010* or *2007* will also be able to view the file. Here is how to do that:

☞ **Click the** FILE **tab**
☞ **Click**  Save As

You will see the *Save As* window. In this example, the file is saved in the (*My*) *Documents* folder.

☞ **Click** 📁 Documents

By default, the file is saved as an *Excel Workbook*. You can change that like this:

☞ **By** Save as type: **, click**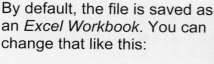

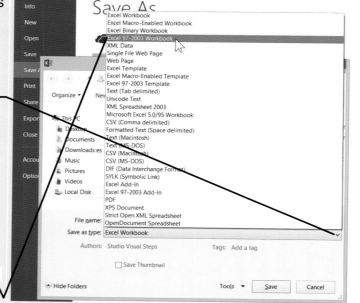

Now you will see a menu with various file types.
For example, you can select a file format that can also be edited in older versions of *Excel* or other programs:

☞ **Click** Excel 97-2003 Workbook

If you wish, you can also enter a different file name and location. After you have finished, click ⌊ <u>S</u>ave ⌋.

2. Worksheets and Workbooks

When you work with data in *Excel* the type of file you are using is called a *workbook*. A workbook can contain multiple *worksheets*. Just to simplify things a bit, we have used the term *workbooks* in the first chapter, while we were actually using a single *worksheet*.

From now on we will use the correct terminology:
• *worksheet* when we mean a single, specific sheet;
• *workbook* when we mean the entire file, which may include several worksheets.

By using multiple worksheets you can arrange and order your data within a workbook. For example, you can enter a company's turnover, costs, and profits in different sheets and save them all within one workbook.
You can also distribute the various categories of a club's members among multiple worksheets within a single workbook.
Until now you have only used *Sheet1*. In this chapter you will be using the other sheets as well.

A household recordkeeping book will often contain expenses that are not paid on a monthly basis but only annually. You can add up these annual costs on a separate worksheet, so you can set aside a certain monthly amount for these expenses. Then you can add them to the monthly expenses on *Sheet1*.

In this chapter you will learn how to:

• open worksheets;
• distinguish between worksheets and workbooks;
• subtract, multiply, and divide;
• round off figures;
• use data from another worksheet;
• enter formulas yourself;
• give worksheets a name;
• move worksheets;
• add extra worksheets;
• delete worksheets;
• save workbooks.

Please note:

In this chapter you will continue using the *household recordkeeping book* file from *Chapter 1 Cells and Formulas*. If you have not created this file, you can use the file called *household recordkeeping book - ch 2* from the folder with the practice files. If you have not copied this folder to your computer, you can read how to do that in *Appendix A Downloading the Practice Files*.

2.1 Opening a Workbook

☞ Open *Excel* 🥿🥿⁹

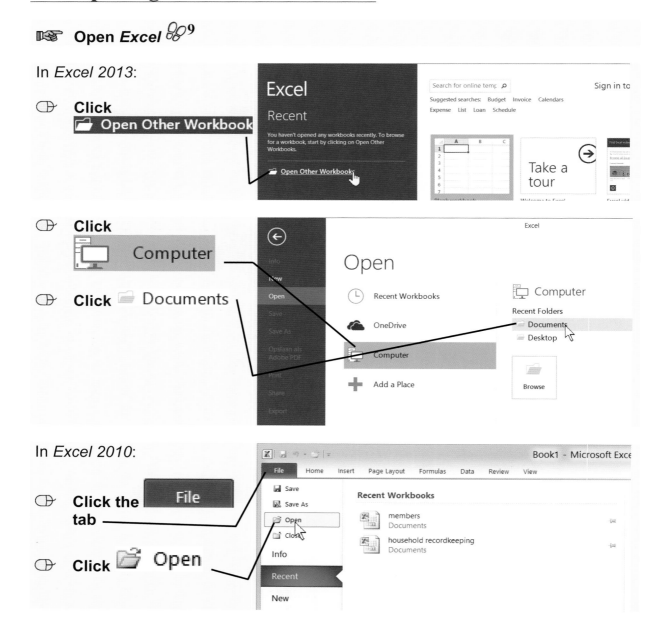

You will see the content of the (*My*) *Documents* folder:

In the address bar of this window you can see which folder is opened:

Please note: the content of this folder may look different on your computer.

☞ **Click**

🗎 household recordkee

☞ **Click** Open

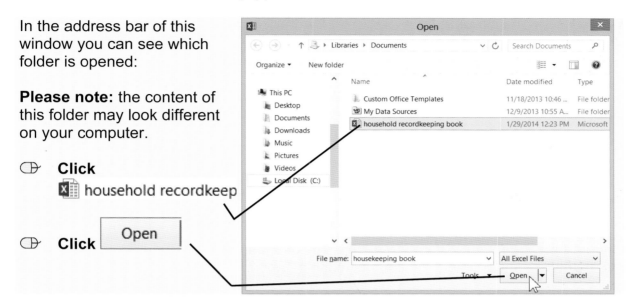

2.2 Go to Another Worksheet

By default, there is always one open worksheet in *Excel 2013*. But in *Excel 2010* there are three worksheets by default. When you open a workbook you will always see *Sheet1*. Until now this is the only worksheet you have used. But you can also use one of the other worksheets:

At the bottom you see the tabs of the open worksheets:

To create a new sheet in *Excel 2013*:

☞ **Click** ⊕

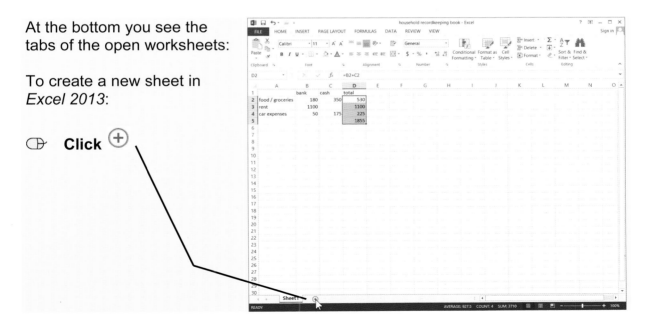

You will see a blank worksheet. At the bottom you see that *Sheet2* has been opened:

In *Excel 2010*, the second tab has already been inserted:

☞ **Click** Sheet2

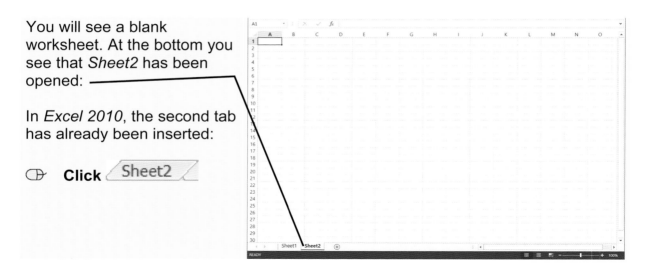

On this worksheet you can create a summary of all the amounts you do not pay on a monthly basis but in other installments, such as annual installments, for example.

⌨ **Type the data in the worksheet**

☞ **Widen column A** ℘2

	A	B	C	D
1		number	amount	total
2	insurance premium	4	120	
3	taxes	6	80	
4	vacations	1	1400	

You can calculate the totals by multiplying the number with the amount.

2.3 Multiplication

You have already seen how to add up numbers in *Excel*. Multiplying works the same way. The only things you will need to get used to is the * symbol that is used to multiply numbers. You can use the asterisk symbol above the 8 (numeric key). Or you can use the asterisk symbol on the key of your numeric keypad.

A multiplication formula also begins with an = too.

🖱️ **Click cell D2**

⌨️ **Type:** =

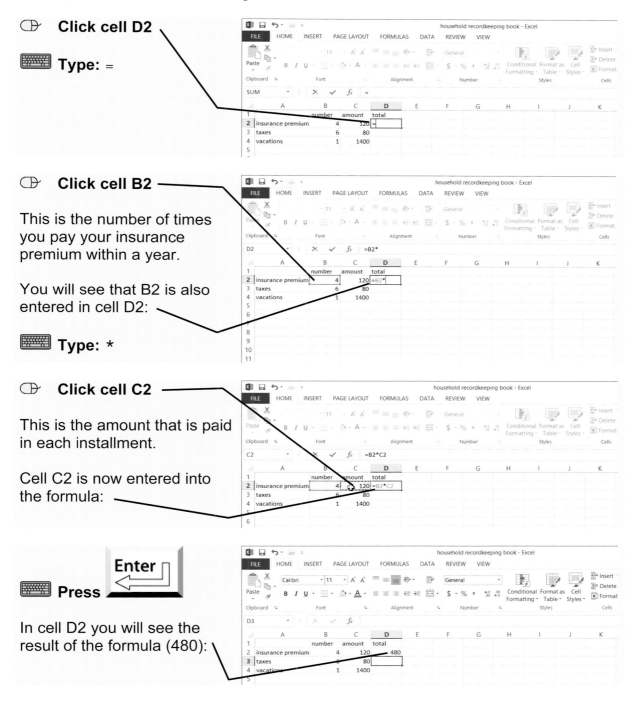

🖱️ **Click cell B2**

This is the number of times you pay your insurance premium within a year.

You will see that B2 is also entered in cell D2:

⌨️ **Type:** *

🖱️ **Click cell C2**

This is the amount that is paid in each installment.

Cell C2 is now entered into the formula:

⌨️ **Press** Enter

In cell D2 you will see the result of the formula (480):

You can copy this formula to the next rows in the same way you did as in *Chapter 1 Cells and Formulas*:

⊕ **Click cell D2**

⊕ **Place the pointer on the handle of cell D2**

The pointer turns into ➕:

⊕ **Drag the handle to cell D4**

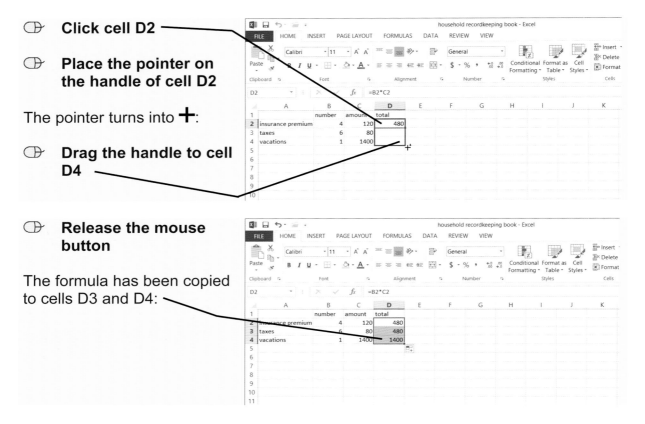

⊕ **Release the mouse button**

The formula has been copied to cells D3 and D4:

Excel has automatically inserted the right cells into the formula. The next step is adding up the totals. This way, you can calculate how much your annual expenses are with regard to recurring expenses.

The correct cells have already been selected.

⊕ **Click Σ**

At the bottom you will see the total amount of this column:

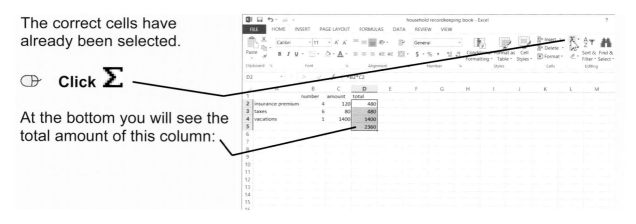

2.4 Division

Now that you have calculated the annual expenses, you can calculate the average expenses per month. In order to divide numbers you need to use the / character. You can find this character on one of the keys of the numeric keypad, and also on the key with the question mark ? on it.

First enter a text description for the monthly amount:

Click cell A7

Type: per month

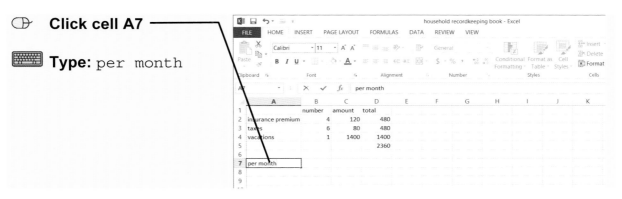

Then you can enter the formula for calculating the monthly amount. The formula always begins with =, for divisions as well.

Click cell D7

Type: =

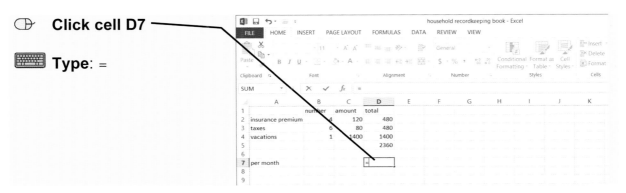

Enter the total amount of annual expenses:

☞ **Click cell D5** ———————

Cell D5 will be inserted into the formula. You can divide this annual amount by twelve months:

⌨ **Type:** /12

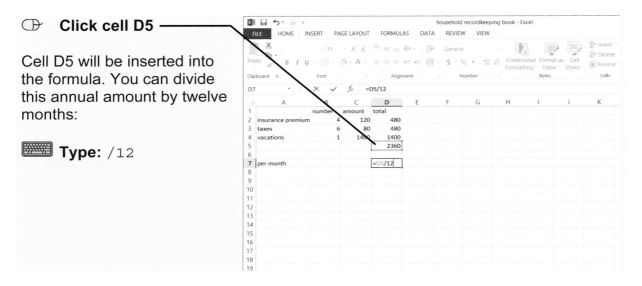

You can calculate this:

⌨ **Press** **Enter**

In cell D7 you will see the result of the formula:

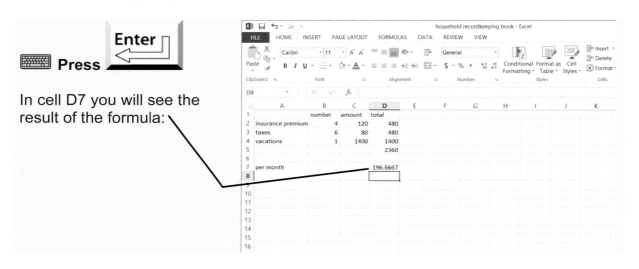

2.5 Rounding Off Amounts

The result that has been calculated is very detailed: no less than four decimals. In this case it is better to round off the amount and display a number without decimals. *Excel* has a specific button for this: .00 →.0 . You can find this button on the ribbon of the HOME tab.

☞ **Click cell D7**

Here is the number you want to round off.

The HOME tab is already open:

☞ **Click** .00 →.0

One of the decimals disappears:

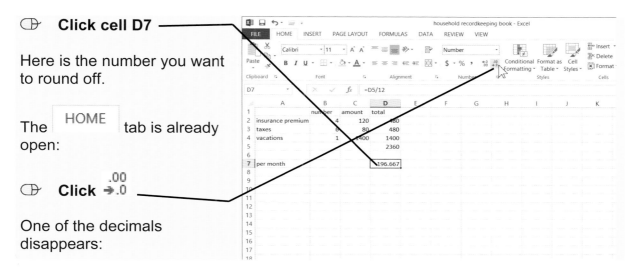

Every time you click this button, a decimal will disappear.

☞ **Click** .00 →.0 **three times**

All decimals have disappeared. You will only see the rounded off number 197:

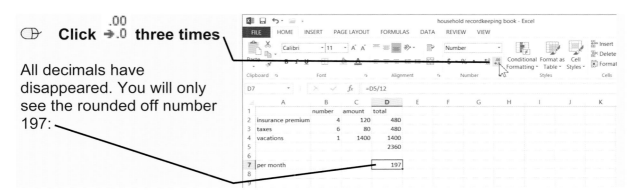

🔖 **Please note:**

The decimals are no longer displayed in the window. Even though *Excel* has now made these decimals invisible, they will still be used in the calculations. This may result in slight differences if you use the rounded off number in other calculations.

Now you have calculated the monthly amount of all other recurring expenses, and rounded off the resulting figure.

2.6 Using Data from Other Worksheets

The amount you have just calculated needs to be added to the monthly expenses on *Sheet1*. This way, you will have a complete summary of your average monthly expenses.

In the bottom left corner of the window:

☞ **Click** | Sheet1

Here you can type a text to describe this amount:

☞ **Click cell A6**

⌨ **Type:** set aside for recurring expenses

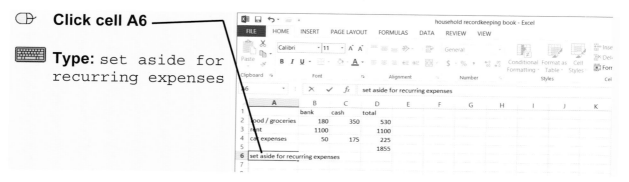

The text is too long to fit in the first column. This is not a problem. In this case there are no entries in column B. You only need to widen column B if you want to enter something on the same row. First you select the cell where you want the amount:

☞ **Click cell D6**

⌨ **Type:** =

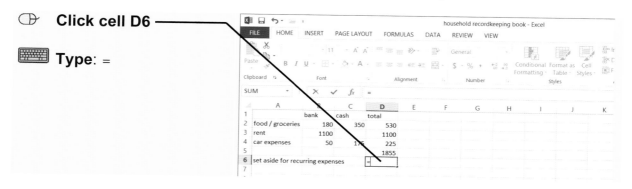

The amount of the monthly recurring expenses cannot be found on this worksheet, but on *Sheet2*. That is why you need to go to *Sheet2* first:

In the bottom left corner of the window:

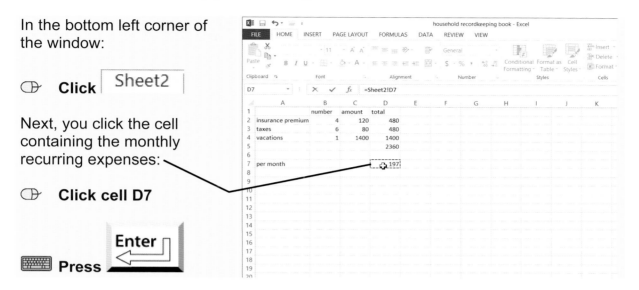

Click | Sheet2 |

Next, you click the cell containing the monthly recurring expenses:

Click cell D7

Press **Enter**

Excel will automatically jump back to *Sheet1*.

Now the amount of the recurring expenses has also been entered in cell D6 on *Sheet1*:

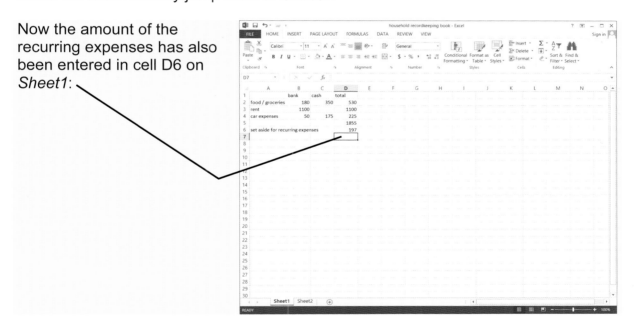

Since you have used a formula to refer to the amount on *Sheet2*, the amount on *Sheet1* will automatically be recalculated whenever you change the amount on *Sheet2*. Just try it:

At the bottom left-hand side of the window:

☞ **Click** Sheet2

☞ **Click cell C3**

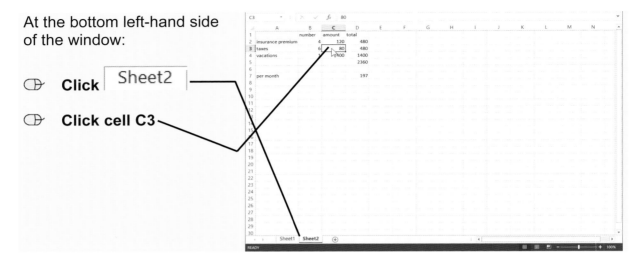

Try increasing this amount to 85, just to see what happens:

⌨ **Type:** 85

⌨ **Press** Enter ⏎

You see that the new monthly amount has been calculated right away:

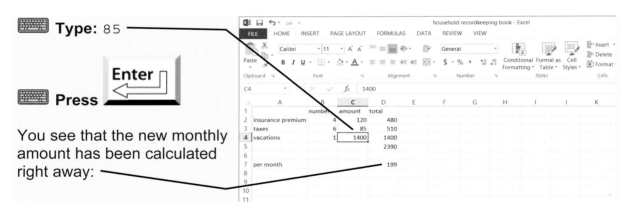

And the changes have also been applied to *Sheet1*:

At the bottom left side of the window:

☞ **Click** Sheet1

On *Sheet1* you see that the amount set aside for recurring expenses in cell D6 has changed too:

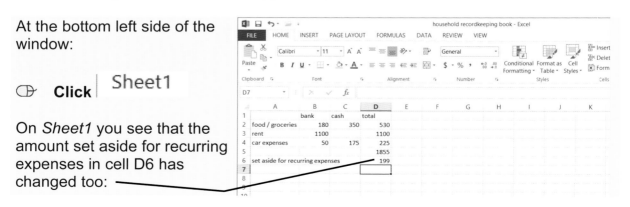

You have not yet completed the model. You can still add up the amounts for *total* and *set aside for recurring expenses*, so you will know exactly what your average monthly expenses are. You can do this by typing the formula.

2.7 Typing Formulas

Until now you have been clicking the cells with which you wanted to execute calculations. This is not necessary. Sometimes it is more convenient to type the formula on the keyboard:

If necessary, click cell D7

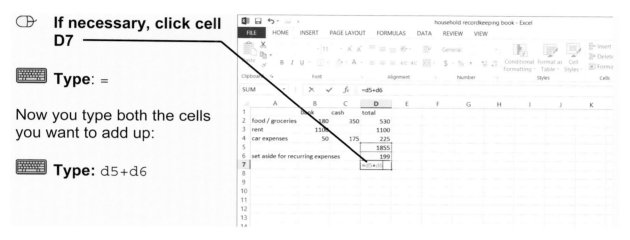

Type: =

Now you type both the cells you want to add up:

Type: d5+d6

Tip
Capital letters and lowercase letters
When typing the names of cells in formulas you can use both capital letters and lowercase letters.

Press Enter

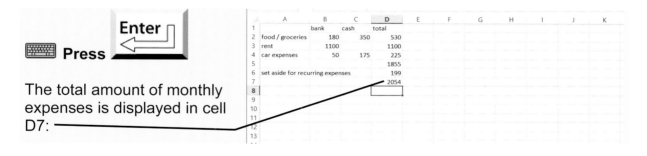

The total amount of monthly expenses is displayed in cell D7:

In order to completely finish the model, you can create a summary of your financial position on *Sheet3*:

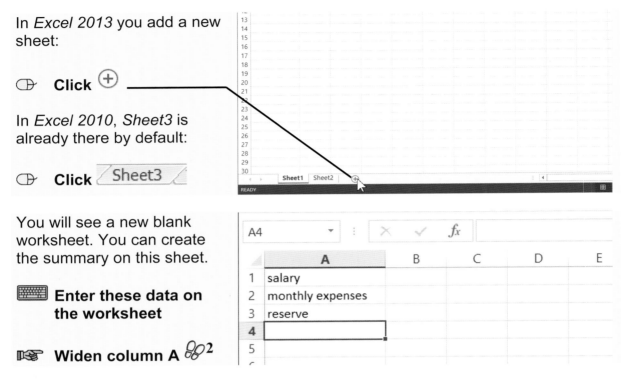

In *Excel 2013* you add a new sheet:

⟴ **Click** ⊕

In *Excel 2010*, *Sheet3* is already there by default:

⟴ **Click** ⟋ Sheet3 ⟍

You will see a new blank worksheet. You can create the summary on this sheet.

⌨ **Enter these data on the worksheet**

☞ **Widen column A** ⥁²

First, you type the salary:

⟴ **Click cell B1**

⌨ **Type:** 2100

⌨ **Press** ⟵ Enter

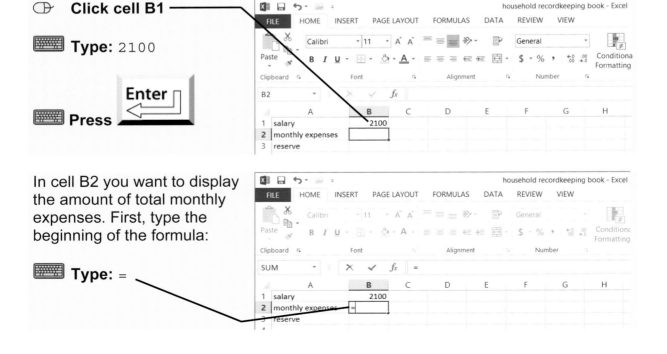

In cell B2 you want to display the amount of total monthly expenses. First, type the beginning of the formula:

⌨ **Type:** =

You will need to get the total monthly expenses from *Sheet1*:

👉 **Click** | Sheet1

You can click the cell containing the total expenses on *Sheet1*:

👉 **Click cell D7**

⌨ **Press** Enter

Excel will automatically go back to *Sheet3*.

The total amount will appear in cell B2, on *Sheet3*:

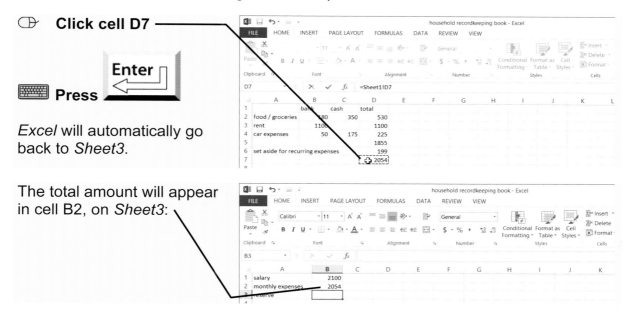

If you subtract the *monthly expenses* from the *salary* you will know how much money you have left.

2.8 Subtraction

By now you have already added, multiplied, and divided numbers. All you have yet to do now is subtract numbers. This is done in the same way as the other calculations. Try to do this by entering a formula instead of clicking the cells.

⌨ **Type:** = b1-b2

⌨ **Press** Enter

You have a monthly reserve of 46:

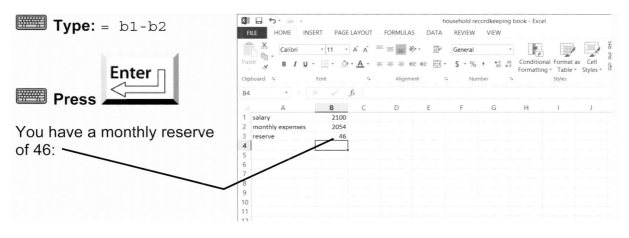

The model is finished. You can give each of the worksheets a different name.

2.9 Worksheet Names

You have created three worksheets:

- *Sheet1* contains the total of all household expenses;
- *Sheet2* contains the recurring expenses;
- *Sheet3* contains the calculation of your monthly reserve.

If you want to clarify the content of a worksheet, you can enter different names for the worksheets. This can be very useful, especially if you use a lot of worksheets. This is how you do it:

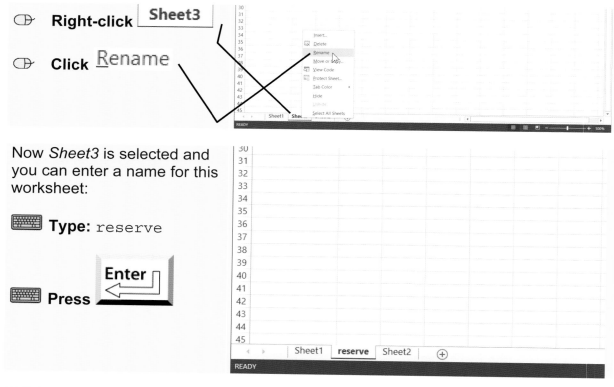

Now *Sheet3* is selected and you can enter a name for this worksheet:

⌨ **Type:** reserve

⌨ **Press** Enter

☞ **Enter the name *recurring expenses* for Sheet2** 〽️18

☞ **Enter the name *household recordkeeping* for Sheet1** 〽️18

Now all three worksheets have a clear name.

2.10 Saving Worksheets

By saving a single worksheet you will automatically save the entire workbook too. You cannot save the worksheets separately.

At the top left-hand side of the window:

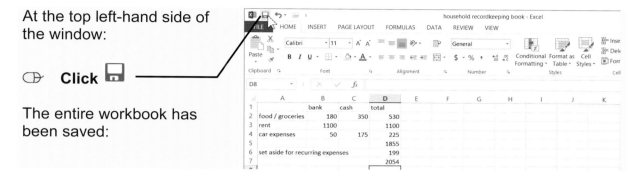

☞ **Click** 🖫 ——————

The entire workbook has been saved:

2.11 Moving Worksheets

After you have created the worksheets, they may not always be arranged in the correct order. You can change the order yourself. For instance, in order to move the *reserve* worksheet to the far left, you need to do this:

☞ **Place the pointer on**

    reserve ——————

☞ **Press and hold the mouse button down**

You can drag the worksheet:

☞ **Drag the worksheet to the location you have chosen**

The black triangle indicates where the worksheet will be placed: ——————

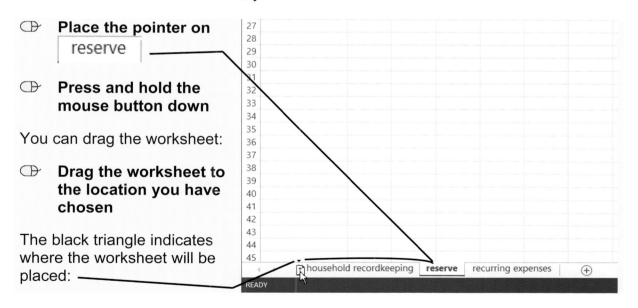

☞ **Release the mouse button**

Now the *reserve* worksheet has moved to the left:

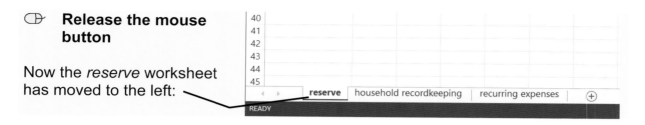

2.12 Creating Extra Worksheets

In *Excel 2010*, a new workbook will automatically have three worksheets. The default setting for *Excel 2013* is to have just one worksheet when you open a new blank file. If this is not enough for you, you can add extra worksheets yourself, like this:

☞ **If necessary, click the** HOME **tab**

☞ **By** ⊞ Insert **, click** ▾

☞ **Click** Insert Sheet

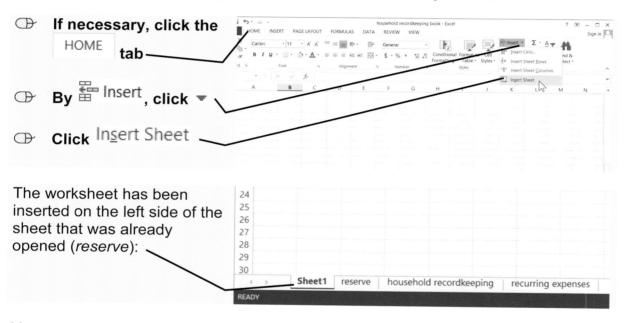

The worksheet has been inserted on the left side of the sheet that was already opened (*reserve*):

You can rename or move this worksheet just like you did with the others.

💡 **Tip**

Quickly create extra worksheets

You can also use the ⊕ button that appears to the right of the last tab to create a new worksheet right away. In that case, the new worksheet will be placed at the end of the row in *Excel 2010*. In *Excel 2013* the worksheet is inserted to the right of the active worksheet.

2.13 Deleting Worksheets

If you no longer need a worksheet, you can delete it. This is how you delete the new worksheet:

☞ **By ▤ Delete , click ▼**

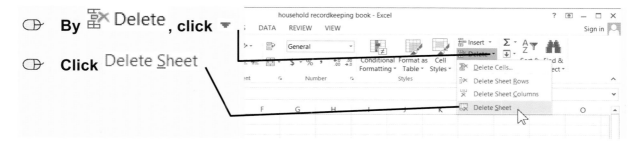

☞ **Click Delete Sheet**

You can close this workbook:

☞ **Close the workbook and save the changes** ✂ 17

In the next few exercises you can repeat the actions needed to work with formulas and data in a worksheet.

2.14 Exercises

Have you forgotten how to do something? Use the number beside the footsteps to look it up in appendix *B How Do I Do That Again?* at the end of this book.

 Please note:

In this exercise you will continue to work on the *members* workbook that you used in the exercises for *Chapter 1 Cells and Formulas*. If you have not completed these exercises, you can use the file named *members - ch 2* from the folder with the practice files. If you have not copied this folder to your computer, you can read how to do that in *Appendix A Downloading the Practice Files*.

Exercise 1: Copying Data from Other Worksheets

☞ Open the *members* workbook. 🦶²²

☞ Change the name of *Sheet1* to *2011*. 🦶¹⁸

☞ Add a new worksheet 🦶⁷³ and, if necessary, go to that sheet. 🦶¹⁹

☞ Change the name of the new worksheet to *2012*. 🦶¹⁸

☞ Enter these data on the *2012* worksheet:

	A	B	C
1		total	
2	youngsters and juniors	66	
3	seniors	55	
4	veterans	29	
5			

☞ Calculate the total with *Sum*. 🦶⁵

☞ Add a new worksheet 🦶⁷³ and, if necessary, go to that sheet. 🦶¹⁹

☞ Change the name of the new worksheet (or of *Sheet3*) to *membership development.* ⚐**18**

☞ Enter the following data:

	A	B	C
1		2011	2012
2	youngsters and juniors		
3	seniors		
4	veterans		

☞ Use a formula to enter the total number of *youngsters and juniors* from sheet *2011* (cell D2) in cell B2 .⚐**20**

	A	B	C
1		2011	2012
2	youngsters and juniors	72	
3	seniors		
4	veterans		
5			

☞ Copy this formula from cell B2 to cells B3 and B4. ⚐**4**

☞ Display the total of cells B2 to B4 in cell B5. ⚐**5**

☞ Insert the total number of *youngsters and juniors* from cell B2 on sheet *2012* in cell C2 by using a formula. ⚐**20**

	A	B	C
1		2011	2012
2	youngsters and juniors	72	66
3	seniors	54	
4	veterans	37	
5		163	

☞ Copy this formula from cell C2 to cells C3 and C4. ⚐**4**

☞ Display the total of cells C2 to C4 in cell C5. ⚐**5**

☞ Go to the *2011* sheet. ✂¹⁹

☞ Change the number of *senior women* to *32*.

The total number of members in cell D5 should be changed to 169.

☞ Go to the *membership development* sheet. ✂¹⁹

☞ Check whether the total number of members (for 2011) here has changed to 169 as well:

	A	B	C	D
1		2011	2012	
2	youngsters and juniors	72	66	
3	seniors	60	55	
4	veterans	37	29	
5		169	150	
6				

☞ Close this workbook and save the changes. ✂¹⁷

☞ Close *Excel*. ✂¹¹

2.15 Background Information

Dictionary

Result	A number that is the result of a calculation.
Round off/up	Rounding up or off a number, so it does not include any decimals.
Workbook	The entire file, consisting of one or more worksheets.
Worksheet	A single specific sheet within a workbook.

Source: Microsoft Excel Help

Keep things manageable

An *Excel* worksheet is extremely large. There are a lot of columns and rows. In general, you will often use just a small part of this worksheet. Nevertheless, the size of the worksheet ensures flexibility and enables you to create the model you need. There are hardly any limitations regarding the space you can use. Because the worksheet is much longer than it is wide, it is often better to create a vertical display of your data.

Keep in mind that the model needs to be practical. It is technically possible to create a list containing 20,000 items, but this will be difficult to manage when you need to work with it. If you need to process large amounts of data it may be easier to use a database program, such as *Microsoft Access*, for example.

You can try to split up larger worksheets in *Excel* into individual sections and save each section as a separate worksheet. For example, you can create separate worksheets for:
- income/earnings and expenses;
- different periods (years, quarters, months);
- budgets, materials, personnel, post-calculation;
- different departments, etc.

Try to keep your worksheets neat and well-ordered. It is better to create three smaller worksheets that are easy to read and print, instead of one big comprehensive overview that cannot be viewed in a single glance.

2.16 Tips

 Tip

Set the number of worksheets

By default, *Excel 2013* creates one worksheet per workbook (in *Excel 2010* there are three default worksheets). You can increase this number by adding new worksheets, like you have learned in this chapter. But if you often need new worksheets, you can also change the default number of worksheets. Then, every new workbook will immediately contain the number of worksheets you have set. You can set the option like this:

☞ **Click the** FILE **tab**

☞ **Click** Options

You will see the *Excel Options* window:

☞ **If necessary, click** General

To increase or reduce the number of sheets:

☞ **Click** ▲▼

☞ **Click** OK

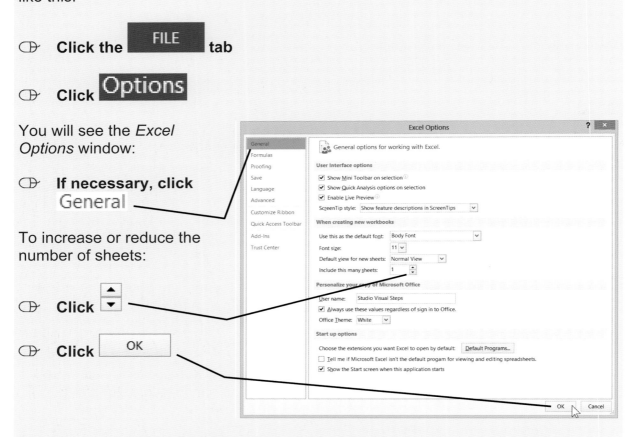

When you open a new workbook you will immediately see the number of sheets you have set.

💡 Tip

Protect worksheet

To prevent others from editing your worksheet, you can protect it:

☞ **Click the** REVIEW **tab**

☞ **Click** Protect Sheet

You will see a window where you can enter a password, if you wish:

☞ **Click** OK

Now the worksheet is protected from edits.

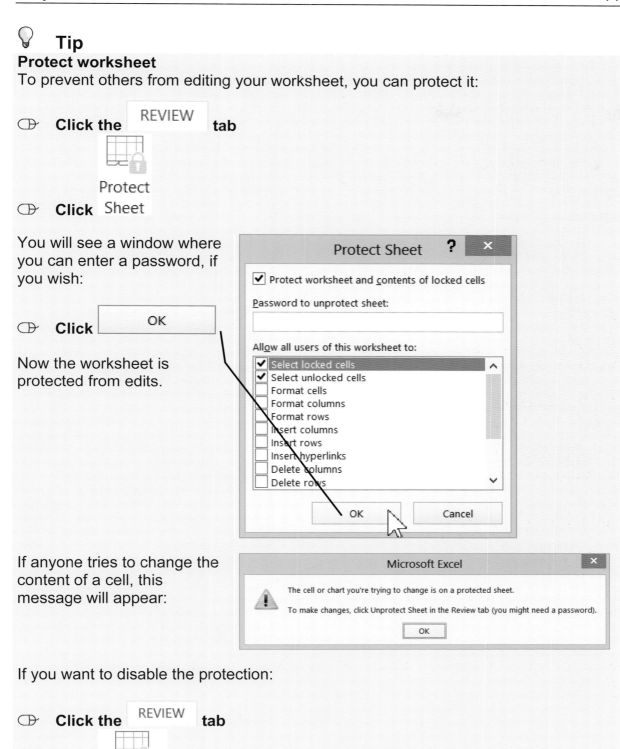

If anyone tries to change the content of a cell, this message will appear:

If you want to disable the protection:

☞ **Click the** REVIEW **tab**

☞ **Click** Unprotect Sheet

Tip

Protect part of a worksheet

In a protected worksheet you can exclude certain cells from being protected, for example the cells in which variable data needs to be entered. All the other cells will still be protected. This will prevent others from accidentally changing the cells containing the formulas while entering data.

Before you protect the worksheet you need to indicate which cells can be edited. This is how you do it:

☞ **Select the cells that can be edited**

☞ **Right-click the selected cells**

☞ **Click** Format Cells...

You will see the *Format Cells* window:

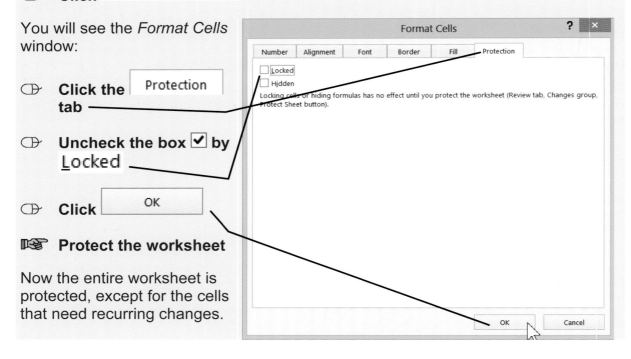

☞ **Click the** Protection **tab**

☞ **Uncheck the box** ☑ **by** Locked

☞ **Click** OK

☞ **Protect the worksheet**

Now the entire worksheet is protected, except for the cells that need recurring changes.

3. Printing

In many cases, you will want to print your calculation models on paper as well. If the entire worksheet does not fit on your screen, it may be necessary to print it out on paper, since this will provide a better overview. Besides, you can also use a printed worksheet to save a paper copy of a certain point in time for your records. And printouts can be used for reports or written presentations as well.

If you have a color printer you can make full use of the color options offered by *Excel*. If you print an *Excel* file with a black-and-white printer you need to take into account that the colors will be replaced by gray shades. The clear view you have on your screen will not be as clear when you print the worksheet on paper. In that case it is better to use various formatting options, such as bold, italic, underlined, or different fonts.

When you print a worksheet you also need to take into account the size of the model. If the worksheet is very large, it may not fit on legal or letter-sized paper. Before you start printing you can check the print preview and adjust the printer settings as needed.

In this chapter you will learn how to:

- view the print preview;
- print horizontally or vertically;
- create a grid;
- print worksheets;
- print selected parts of a worksheet;
- set the print area;
- hide rows and columns;
- display hidden rows and columns;
- insert rows and columns;
- delete rows and columns;
- enlarge and diminish prints;
- print titles on all of the pages;
- block titles on the screen.

 Please note:

Some of the exercises in this chapter require a printer. If you do not have a printer, you can skip these exercises.

3.1 Print Preview

Before you print your worksheet it is wise to take a look at the print preview first. Once you are satisfied with the print preview, you can print the worksheet. The print preview displays a smaller view of the page.
You do not use this window to read the text, but just to check whether the page layout is correct, and whether the data is neatly arranged on the page.

 Please note:

In this chapter you will continue to use the *household recordkeeping book* file that you used in *Chapter 2 Worksheets and Workbooks*. If you have not created this file, you can use the file named *household recordkeeping book - ch 3* from the folder with the practice files. If you have not copied this folder to your computer, you can read how to do that in *Appendix A Downloading the Practice Files*.

☞ **Open *Excel*** 🦶⁹

☞ **Open the *household recordkeeping book* workbook** 🦶²²

☞ **Go to the *household recordkeeping* worksheet** 🦶¹⁹

👆 **Click the** FILE **tab**

👆 **Click** Print

You will see what your worksheet looks like when it is printed on paper:

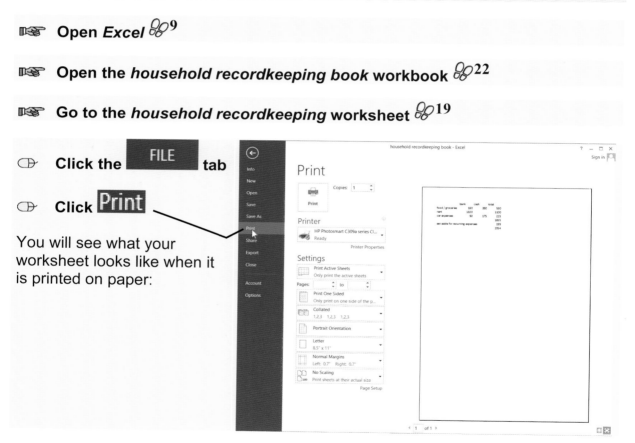

This is what you need to do in order to zoom in:

In the bottom right corner of
the window:

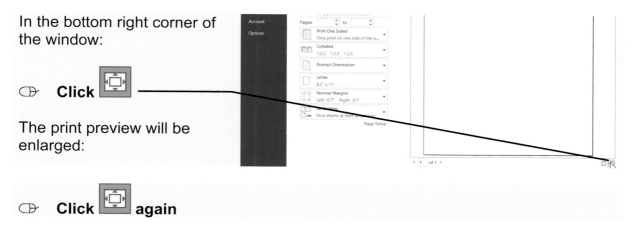

⊕ **Click**

The print preview will be
enlarged:

⊕ **Click** again

Now the print preview has become smaller again.

💡 **Tip**

Number of pages
When looking at the print preview, always check the number of pages that is

displayed at the bottom of the window: ◄ 1 of 1 ► . You may have accidentally
typed something in a distant cell, which is not clearly displayed on the screen. If this
is the case, *Excel* will print all the sheets, including that one cell, which may result in
lots of blank pages coming out of your printer. If this happens, try to locate the cell
and clear the content. Or select the print range first. You be learning more about this
a little later on this chapter.

You can close the print preview again:

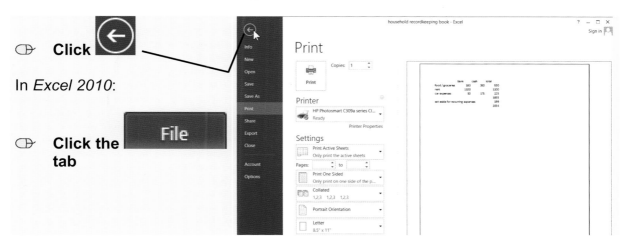

⊕ **Click**

In *Excel 2010*:

⊕ **Click the** **File** **tab**

You will see the normal view of the worksheet again.

After you have looked at the print preview, you will see a dotted line, indicating which parts will fit on a sheet of paper:

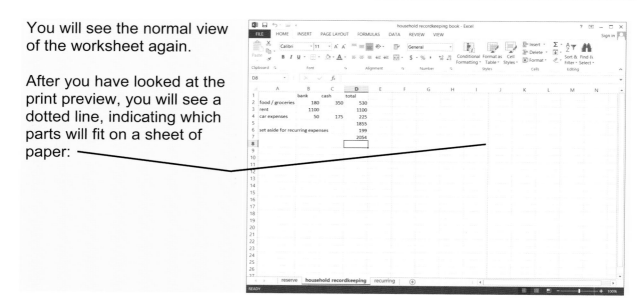

You can take this into account when you are arranging your worksheet. For example, you can try to enter the data within the dotted line and fit it all on a single page. The line indicating the page margin (the white space between cells) is also present at the bottom of the page.

3.2 Printing Horizontally or Vertically

In the print preview you have seen that the page is printed in portrait mode. But many workbooks are created in such a way that it is better to print them in landscape mode. You can change this setting while you look at the print preview:

☞ **Open the print preview** ✂²⁸

⊕ **Click**
 Portrait Orientation

⊕ **Click**
 Landscape Orienta

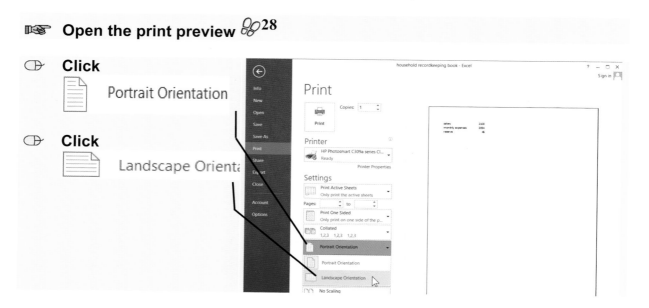

Now you will see a page in horizontal mode:

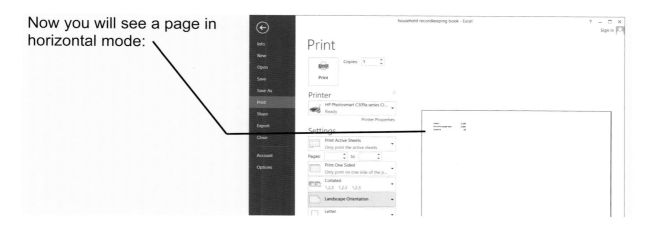

3.3 Gridlines

When the page is printed, the gridlines between the cells will not be printed. This results in a calmer image. Although it may sometimes be hard to see on which line a certain entry is placed, especially if there are a couple of blank cells between the columns. *Excel* has some options for printing lines of different width on paper. If you want to see the default lines between the cells that will be printed, you can do this:

☞ **Click** Page Setup

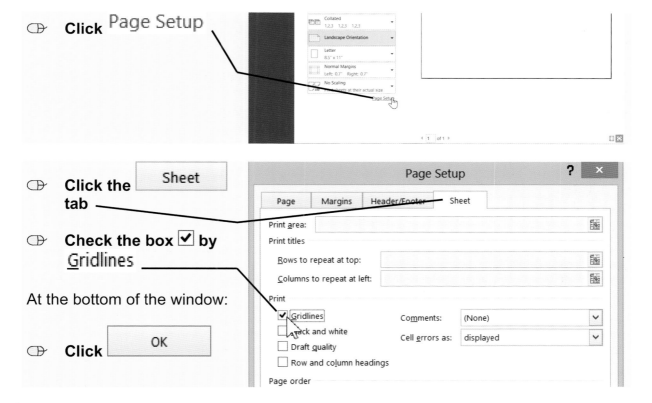

☞ **Click the** Sheet **tab**

☞ **Check the box** ☑ **by** Gridlines

At the bottom of the window:

☞ **Click** OK

Now you will see lines
between the cells:

☞ **Click**

In *Excel 2010*:

☞ **Click the
tab**

3.4 Printing a Worksheet

You can print the sheet by clicking the **FILE** tab first, and then click **Print**. But you can do this faster by adding the Quick Print 🖨 button to the *Quick Access* toolbar. It is a good idea to do this now:

☞ **Add the Quick Print button to *Quick Access* toolbar** 🦶**1**

The button has been added to the *Quick Access* toolbar: 🖫 ↩ ▾ 🗀 🖨 ▾.

☞ **Click** 🖨

The worksheet is printed. By default, *Excel* only prints the active worksheet, in other words, where the cursor is currently placed. The other worksheets in the workbook will not be printed.

If you have a color printer, all the colors will be printed. A monochrome printer will print the colors in shades of grey.

3.5 Printing Selections

If you just want to print a certain section of a worksheet (or several sections), first you need to select the area you want to print. This is called the *print area*.

For example, if you do not want to print the *set aside for recurring expenses* heading, this is what you do:

☞ **Select cells A1 to D5**
  ✂10

☞ **Click the**

  PAGE LAYOUT **tab**

☞ **Click** Area ▾

☞ **Click**
  🖫 Set Print Area

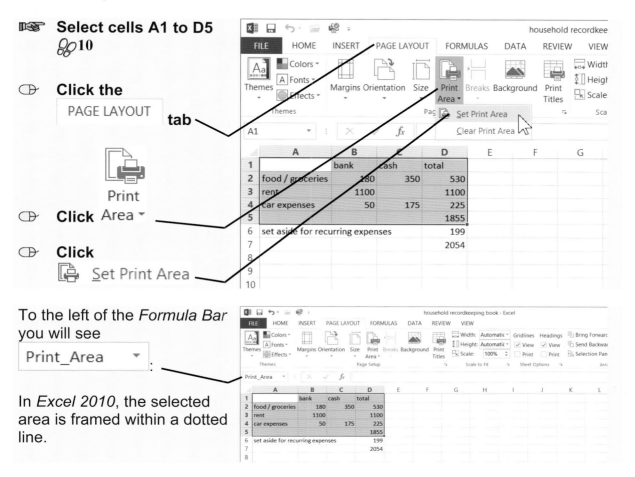

To the left of the *Formula Bar* you will see

Print_Area ▾ :

In *Excel 2010*, the selected area is framed within a dotted line.

This is the only area that will be printed. Take a look at the print preview:

☞ **Open the print preview** ✂28

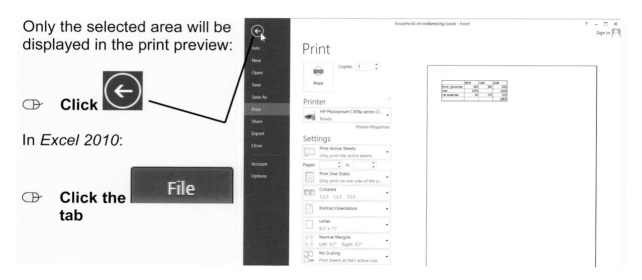

Only the selected area will be displayed in the print preview:

☞ **Click**

In *Excel 2010*:

☞ **Click the File tab**

You needed to click twice to open the print preview. You can do this faster by adding the Print Preview and Print [icon] button to the *Quick Access* toolbar:

☞ **Add the Print Preview and Print button to the *Quick Access* toolbar** 🦶[1]

The button has been added to the *Quick Access* toolbar: 💾 ↩ ▾ 📂 🖨 🔍 .

If you use *Excel* on a regular basis, it can you save time if you add the command buttons you most frequently use to this toolbar.

3.6 Hiding Columns and Rows

Things become a little more difficult when you want to exclude columns or rows between a selected section from being printed. If you try to select different areas and set these as a print area, the separate areas will be printed on separate pages.
You can prevent intermediary columns and rows from being printed by hiding them temporarily. If you only want to print the column containing the *descriptions* and the *total* heading, you can hide the *bank* and *cash* columns:

☞ **Select columns B and C** 🦶[10]

You can hide both columns:

👉 **If necessary, click the** HOME **tab**

👉 **Click** 📋 Format ▾

A menu appears:

👉 **Click** Hide & Unhide

You will see a submenu:

👉 **Click** Hide Columns

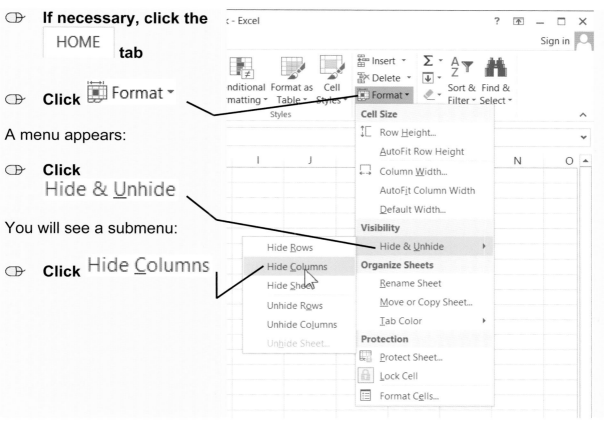

The B and C have been hidden:

Because you have hidden the B and C columns, the description *set aside for recurring expenses* is also cut off, since this text continued in column B.

In this case it does not matter, because this row was already outside the print area:

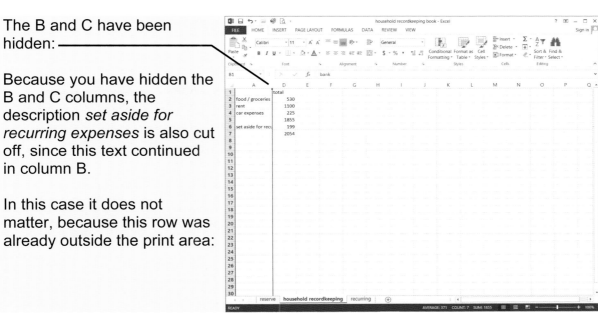

Rows can be hidden in this way as well. Instead of columns you select rows. View the result in the print preview:

☞ **Open the print preview** 🐾**28**

Here, the columns *cash* and *bank* are hidden too:

↪ **Click**

In *Excel 2010*:

↪ **Click the tab**

3.7 Display Hidden Columns and Rows

In order to continue working on your model, you are going to display the hidden columns again:

☞ **Select columns A and D** 🐾**10**

↪ **Click** 📋 Format ▾

↪ **Click** Hide & Unhide

↪ **Click** Unhide Columns

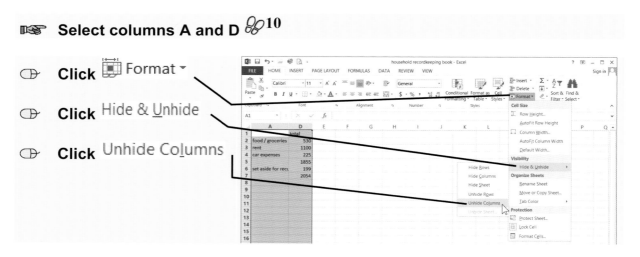

Now the *cash* and *bank*
columns have been restored:

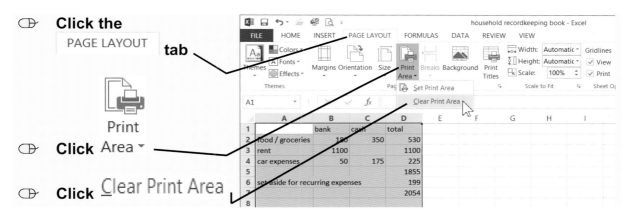

 Tip

Hiding rows or columns

You can also use this hide rows or columns option to execute intermediate
calculations (for example, profit percentages) or operations.

3.8 Clearing the Print Area

If you want to print the entire worksheet again you will need to clear the print area:

☞ **Click the**

PAGE LAYOUT **tab**

☞ **Click** Print Area ▾

☞ **Click** Clear Print Area

Now the entire worksheet will be printed when you click the Print button.

3.9 Inserting Columns and Rows

Instead of hiding something you might also want to insert extra items sometimes. You
can insert blank rows or columns for these items. In *Excel* you can use the
commands called *Insert Sheet Rows* or *Insert Sheet Columns*.

☞ **Click cell A4**

By default, a new row will be inserted above the row of the selected cell. Since you want to insert an entire row, it does not matter which cell you click in the current row. The default setting for columns is to be inserted to the left of the selected cell or column. If you want to insert a column you place the cursor in the column where you want to insert a new column to the left of the current column.

Click the HOME **tab**

By Insert **, click**

Click
Insert Sheet Rows

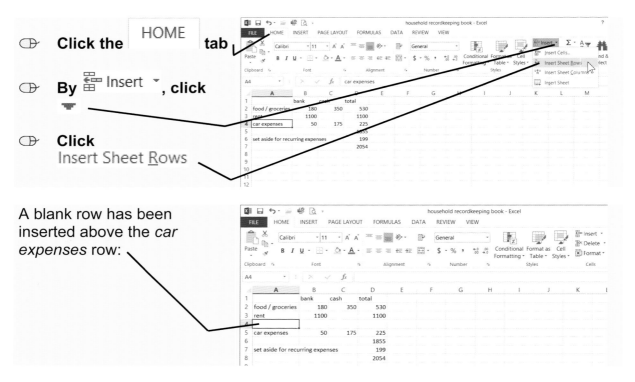

A blank row has been inserted above the *car expenses* row:

This row is actually empty. This means it does not contain any formulas or data.

 Tip

No rows or columns at the beginning or end of a table
It is better not to insert rows or columns at the beginning or end of your table. If you decide to do this, you will need to enter your *Sum* formula all over again. But if you insert rows or columns in between existing rows or columns, the *Sum* formulas will automatically be adapted.

3.10 Deleting Columns and Rows

In order to delete a row or a column, you need to select this row or column first. After that, you can delete the row. The *Home* tab is still opened. You can find the command to delete sheet rows on the ribbon of this tab.

☞ **If necessary, click cell A4**

☞ **By Delete ▾, click**

☞ **Click Delete Sheet Rows**

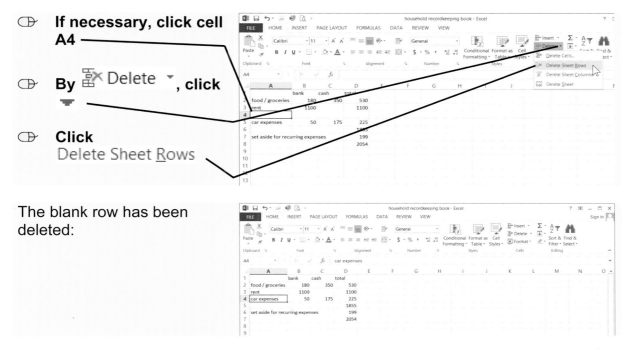

The blank row has been deleted:

You can close this workbook.

☞ **Close the workbook without saving the changes** 🐾²¹

☞ **Open a new workbook** 🐾¹²

3.11 Make a Worksheet Fit the Printed Page

It is usually very convenient if you can print your data on a single page. Although this will not be possible if the worksheet is very large. Sometimes, the worksheet is just a little bit too big. In this case you can diminish the print a bit, in order to fit the data on a single page.

First you are going to create a worksheet with lots of rows and columns:

⌨ **In cell B1, type:**
   section 1

☞ **Place the pointer on the handle of cell B1**

The pointer turns into ✚:

☞ **Drag the handle to cell I1, to** section 8

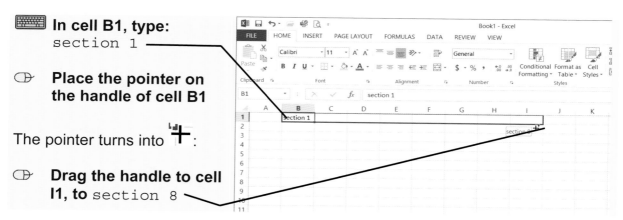

Next, you create the rows:

⌨ **In cell A2, type:**
   01/01/2010

Please note: in *Excel*, the default separator for dates is a slash /.

☞ **Place the pointer on the handle of cell A2**

The pointer turns into ✚:

☞ **Drag the handle to cell A60**

☞ **Widen column A** ⚿²

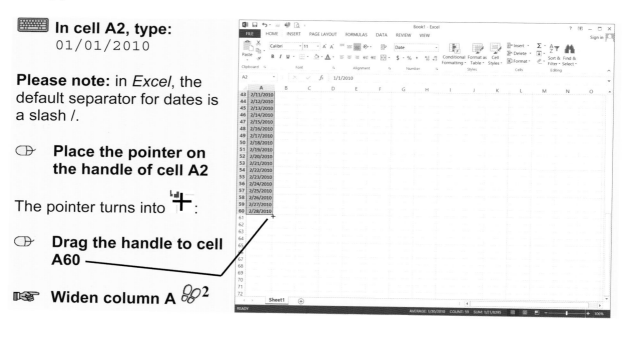

With the Ctrl and Home key combination, *Excel* will jump back to cell A1 at once:

 Simultaneously press **Ctrl** **Home** **and**

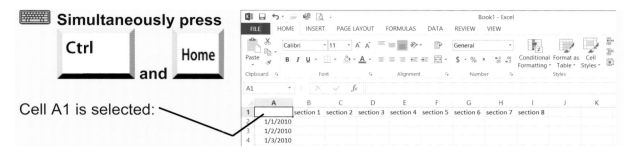

Cell A1 is selected:

You can take a look at the print preview:

☞ **Open the print preview** ✂**28**

At the bottom of the window you can see that the total number of pages is two:

🠮 **Please note:**

Maybe you will see more or fewer columns or rows on your own computer. This may depend on your computer or printer settings. This will not affect the operations you are going to execute afterwards.

You can view the second page. At the bottom of the window:

☞ **By** of 2 **, click** ▶

You will see page 2, that contains a small part of the overview:

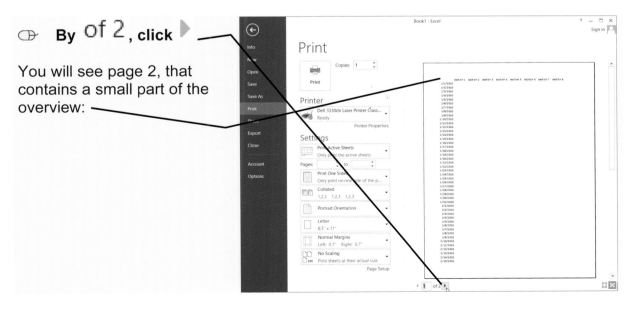

You just have a few rows too many to be able to fit the print on a single sheet of paper. You can let *Excel* fit the overview on a single page:

⊕ **Click** Page Setup

⊕ **If necessary, click the** Page **tab**

⊕ **Click the radio button** ⊙ **by** Fit to:

The number of pages is already set to 1:

At the bottom of the window:

⊕ **Click** OK

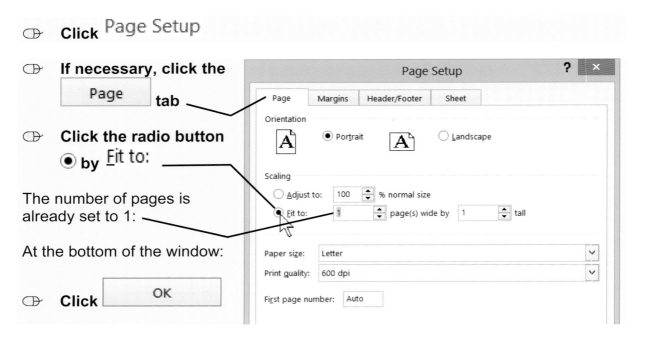

Excel will adjust the worksheet so that it fits on a single sheet of paper.

At the bottom of the window you can see that all the data fit on a single page:

⊕ **Click** ⬅

In *Excel 2010*:

⊕ **Click the** File **tab**

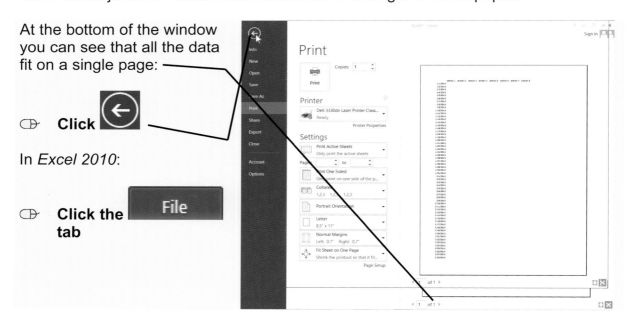

Excel has reduced the size of the data in order to fit it all on one page. Be careful when using this option. If the worksheet is very large, the data may be shrunk so much that it can become unreadable.

3.12 Enlarging or Diminishing a Print Output

Instead of letting *Excel* reduce the size of the print output, you can also set a percentage yourself. You can reduce the print output (as you did previously) or enlarge it by means of scaling. Scaling to a larger size can be useful for presentations or reports.

☞ **Open the print preview**  **28**

☞ **Click** Page Setup

You can enlarge the page to 150%, for example:

☞ **By** Adjust to: **, click ▲ until you reach 150**

At the bottom of the window:

☞ **Click** OK

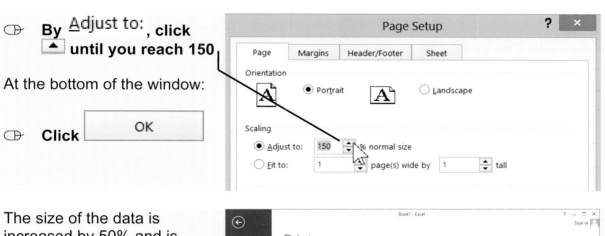

The size of the data is increased by 50% and is clearly legible in the print preview:

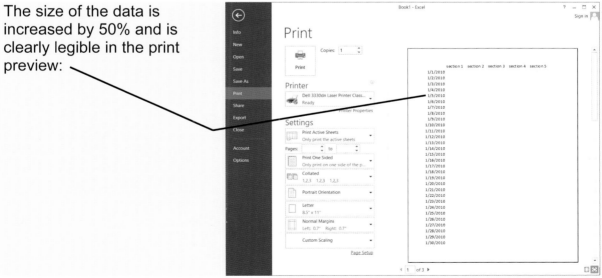

3.13 Print Titles on All Pages

If your columns are very long, the next pages often do not have a title. Just take a look:

☞ **By** of 3**, click** ▶

On page 2 you will see the column with the dates, but it would be easier to read and understand if the sections were shown at the top of every page:

In *Excel 2013*:

☞ **Click**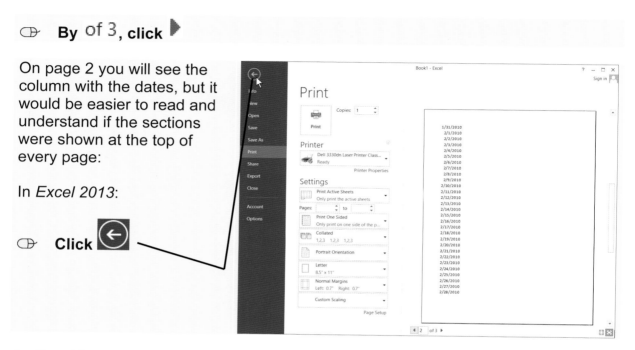

In *Excel 2013* and *2010*:

☞ **Click the tab** PAGE LAYOUT

☞ **Click** Print Titles

In *Excel 2010* the button

looks like this Print Titles.

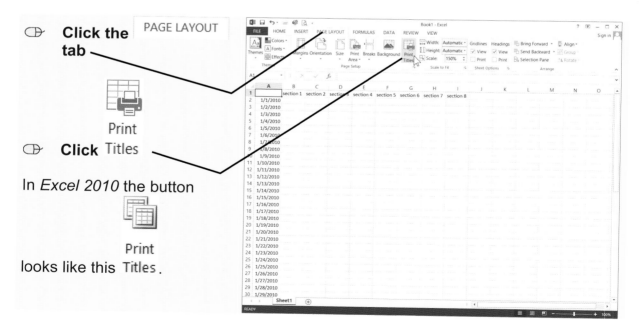

You will see the *Page Setup* window:

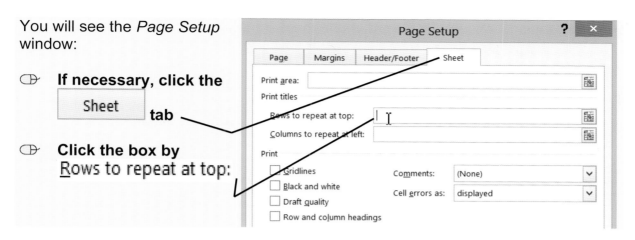

☞ **If necessary, click the**

Sheet **tab**

☞ **Click the box by**
Rows to repeat at top:

You want to repeat the top row on every page. The top row often contains your column headings or titles (also called labels). You can do this by clicking this row:

☞ **Click a spot in row 1**

Excel will copy the data in this row to the window, and insert a code

Rows to repeat at top: **$1:$1**

You can view the result in the print preview:

☞ **Click**

Print Preview

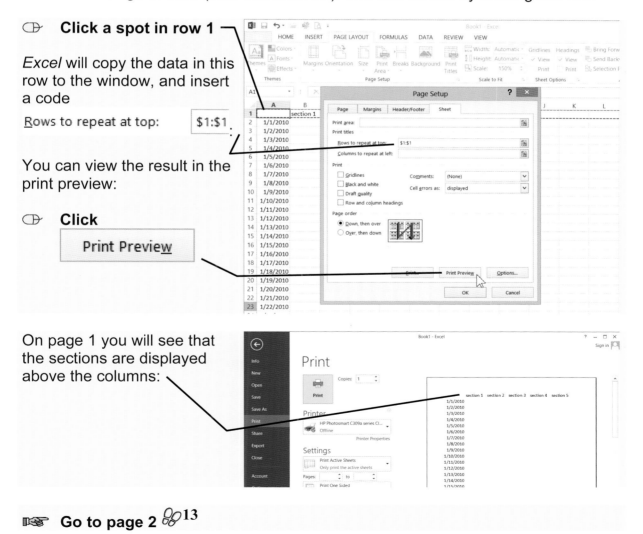

On page 1 you will see that the sections are displayed above the columns:

☞ **Go to page 2** 📑¹³

Here too, the sections are displayed above the columns:

☞ **Go to page 3** ¹³

On page 3 you will see that the sections are shown above each sheet. But what if you want to show the columns with dates on the left side of each sheet?
Then, you can allow that column to be repeated on every page:

In *Excel 2013*:

⊕ **Click** ←

In *Excel 2013* and *2010*:

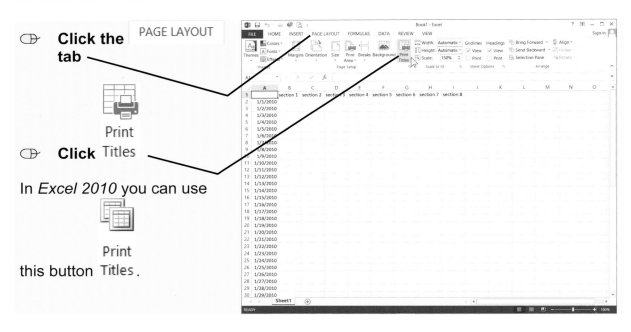

⊕ **Click the tab** PAGE LAYOUT

⊕ **Click** Titles (Print)

In *Excel 2010* you can use

this button Titles (Print).

You will see the *Page Setup* window again:

☞ **Click the box by**
 <u>C</u>olumns to repeat at l∣

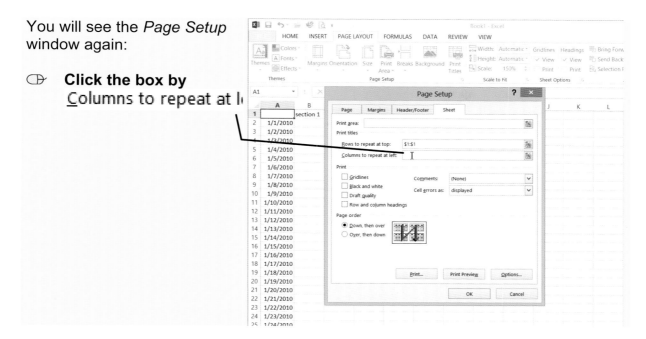

Next, you select the column:

☞ **Click a spot in column A**

Excel will copy the column to
<u>C</u>olumns to repeat at left: │ $A:$A∣

View the result in the print preview:

☞ **Click** Print Pre<u>v</u>iew

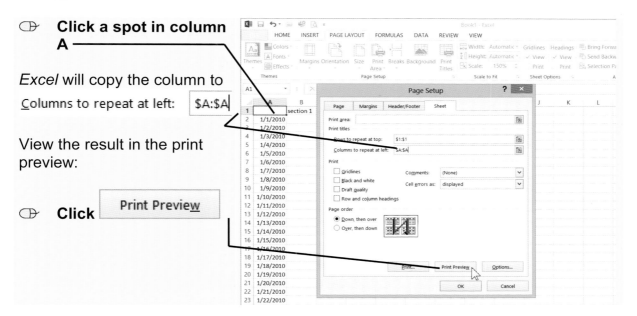

The sections will be shown above and the dates are shown on the left side of the page:

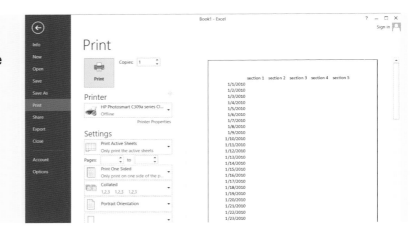

☞ **Go to page 2** ¹³

On page 2 the sections and dates are displayed as well.

☞ **Go to page 3** 🦶¹³

And on page 3 you will also see the sections and dates.

☞ **Go to page 4** 🦶¹³

Likewise, the same on page 4.

The titles will only be displayed in the print preview and on the printed paper, not in the actual worksheets. You can change these settings on the worksheet.

3.14 Freeze Titles on the Screen

At a certain point you will no longer be able to see the sections and dates on the screen. You can freeze these titles on the screen without changing the print output settings. As you scroll downwards on the worksheet, the titles will remain visible above the columns. First, take a look at what happens if you do not freeze the titles:

In *Excel 2013*:

👆 **Click** ⬅

In *Excel 2013* and *Excel 2010*:

👈 **Click the**

    PAGE LAYOUT **tab**

⌨ **Keep pressing until the titles (sections) have disappeared**

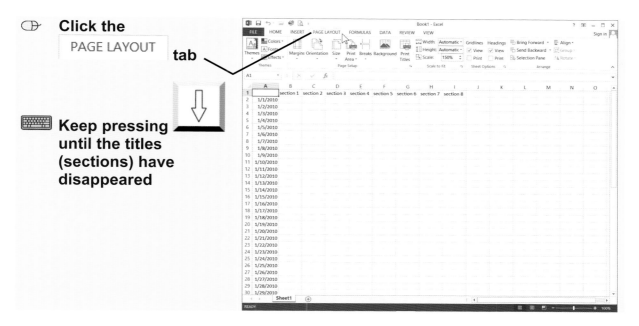

You can change this setting like this:

⌨ **Simultaneously press**

    Ctrl **and** **Home**

Cell A1 is selected again. You need to select a cell that is directly below the row with the title(s) you want to display:

⌨ **Press** ⬇

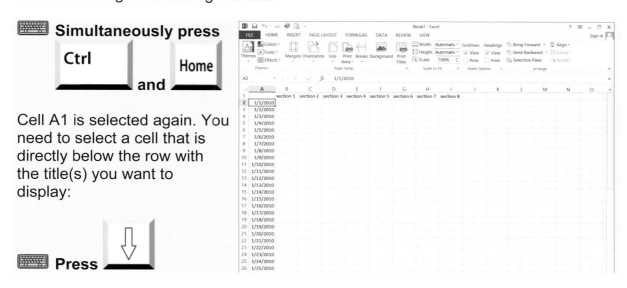

You can freeze the sections titles:

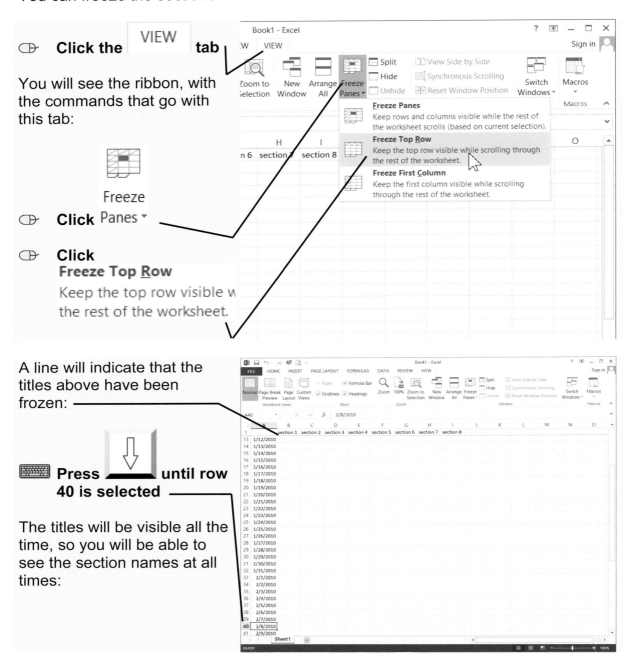

☞ **Click the** VIEW **tab**

You will see the ribbon, with the commands that go with this tab:

☞ **Click** Freeze Panes ▾

☞ **Click**
Freeze Top Row
Keep the top row visible w
the rest of the worksheet.

A line will indicate that the titles above have been frozen: ─────────

⌨ **Press** ⬇ **until row 40 is selected** ─────────

The titles will be visible all the time, so you will be able to see the section names at all times:

You can also disable the freezing of the title again. This is how you do it:

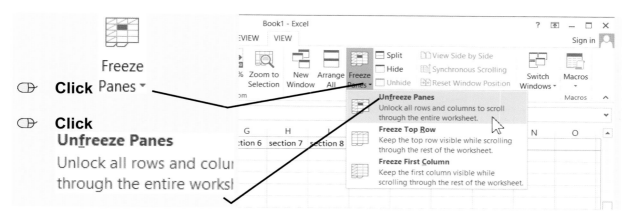

☞ **Click** Freeze Panes ▾

☞ **Click**
Unfreeze Panes

Unlock all rows and colur
through the entire worksł

You can freeze the left-hand column as well, in order to permanently display the dates when you scroll to the right-hand side of the worksheet. To do this, you need to place the cursor in the cell to the right of the column you want to freeze:

☞ **Click cell B1**

☞ **Click** Freeze Panes ▾

☞ **Click**
Freeze First Column

Keep the first column visib
scrolling through the rest c

A thin line indicates that the titles in the left-hand column have been frozen:

⌨ **Press** ➡ **until you see column P**

Now the titles in column A are always shown:

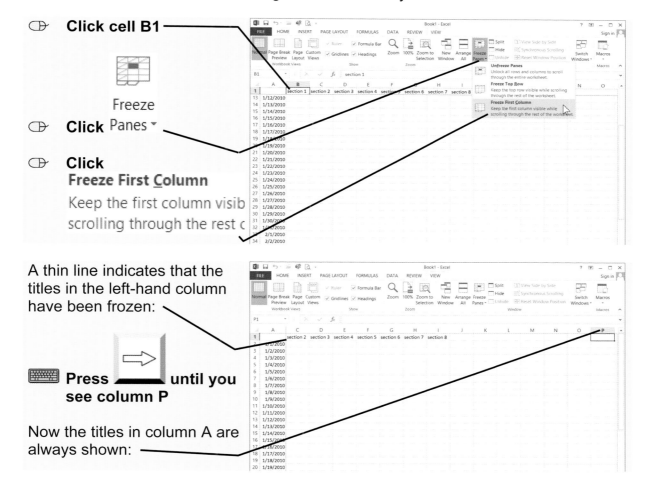

You are going to disable the freezing of the titles again:

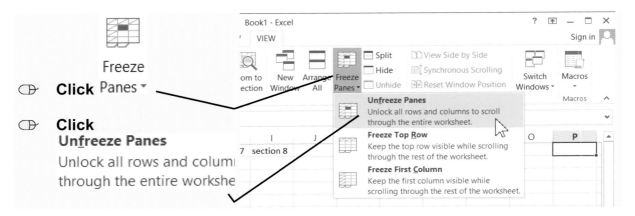

☞ **Click** Freeze Panes ▾

☞ **Click**
    Unfreeze Panes
    Unlock all rows and columr
    through the entire workshe

Until now you have frozen the titles on just one side, but you can also combine this action. You will need to select a cell to the right of the column with the dates, and below the row of which you want to view the titles. In this example it is cell B2:

☞ **Click cell B2**

Freeze both titles:

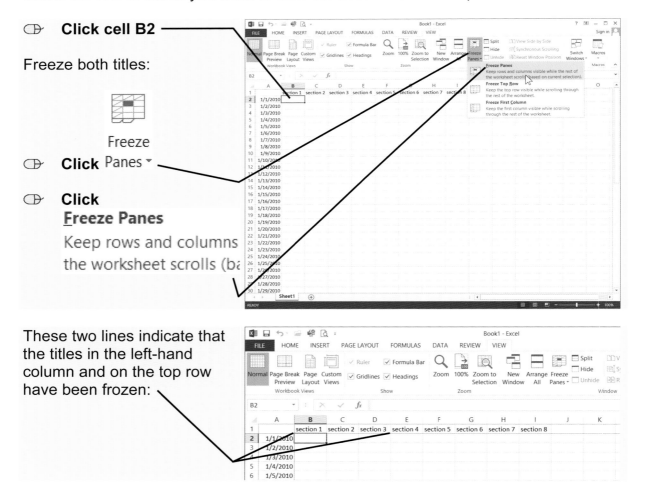

☞ **Click** Freeze Panes ▾

☞ **Click**
    Freeze Panes
    Keep rows and columns
    the worksheet scrolls (b

These two lines indicate that the titles in the left-hand column and on the top row have been frozen:

If you scroll downwards, you will keep seeing the titles in row 1. If you scroll to the right, you will keep seeing the dates in column 1. You are going to disable this function again:

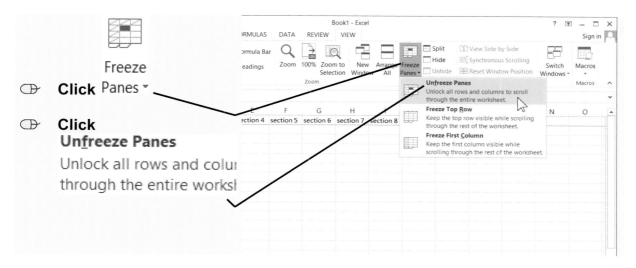

Freeze

☞ **Click** Panes ▾

☞ **Click**
Unfreeze Panes

Unlock all rows and colur

through the entire worksh

Freezing titles will only affect the view on the screen. Nothing will change in the print preview, or when you print the worksheet on paper.

☞ **Close the worksheet and do not save the changes** 👣**21**

In the next couple of exercises you can repeat the operations we have discussed in this chapter.

3.15 Exercises

Have you forgotten how to do something? Use the number beside the footsteps to look it up in appendix *B How Do I Do That Again?* at the end of this book.

 Let op!

In this exercise you will continue to work on the *members* workbook that you used in the exercises for *Chapter 2 Worksheets and Workbooks*. If you have not completed these exercises, you can use the file named *members - ch 3* from the folder with the practice files. If you have not copied this folder to your computer, you can read how to do that in *Appendix A Downloading the Practice Files*.

Exercise 1: Enlarge a Print

☞ Open the *members* workbook. $\mathscr{CC}^{22}$

☞ Go to sheet *2011*. $\mathscr{CC}^{19}$

☞ Open the print preview. $\mathscr{CC}^{28}$

☞ Enlarge the print to 150%. $\mathscr{CC}^{29}$

☞ Add gridlines to the model. $\mathscr{CC}^{30}$

☞ Close the print preview. $\mathscr{CC}^{31}$

☞ Print the worksheet. $\mathscr{CC}^{38}$

Exercise 2: Set the Print Area

☞ Select columns A and B. $\mathscr{CC}^{10}$

☞ Set the print area to columns A and B. $\mathscr{CC}^{32}$

☞ Open the print preview. 𖠿**28**

You will only see the descriptions in column A, and the male members.

☞ Close the print preview. 𖠿**31**

☞ Clear the print area. 𖠿**33**

Exercise 3: Hide Columns

☞ Select columns B and C. 𖠿**10**

☞ Hide these columns. 𖠿**34**

☞ Open the print preview. 𖠿**28**

Now you will only see the various groups of members in column A, and the totals of column D.

☞ Close the print preview. 𖠿**31**

☞ Unhide columns B and C again. 𖠿**35**

Exercise 4: Insert Columns

☞ Go to the *membership development* sheet. 𖠿**19**

☞ Insert a new column to the left of column B. 𖠿**36**

☞ Narrow the column and make it roughly the same size as column C. 𖠿**2**

☞ Enter the following data:

◢	A	B	C	D
1		2010	2011	2012
2	youngsters and juniors	78	72	66
3	seniors	58	60	55
4	veterans	42	37	29
5			169	150
6				

☞ Add up the total of column B with *Sum*. ✇⁵

☞ Close the workbook and save the changes. ✇¹⁷

☞ Close *Excel*. ✇¹¹

3.16 Background Information

Dictionary

Gridlines   The lines that indicate the borders of the cells. You can make the printed worksheet or workbook clearer by printing the gridlines around the cells too.

Freeze titles   A function in *Excel* with which you can select rows or columns that need to stay visible when you scroll through the worksheet. For example, you can freeze titles to keep row and column headings visible while you scroll.

Page Setup   A function in *Excel* that enables you to adjust the arrangement and formatting of the data in the worksheet before you print it.

Print area   The selected part of the worksheet that will be printed.

Print preview   An example of what the page will look like when printed on paper.

Source: Microsoft Excel Help

Paper
In spite of all the expectations regarding a paperless office, the use of paper has increased instead of diminished. Even with the very large screens available these days, most people still prefer to save and view their information on paper. Of course this is understandable if the information needs to be stored for longer periods of time, such as financial balance sheets or salary slips. Proofing a text, budget or report is often much easier on paper as well.

3.17 Tips

💡 Tip

Print the entire workbook

Until now you have only printed the worksheet on which you were working. If a workbook contains multiple worksheets, you can also print them all at once:

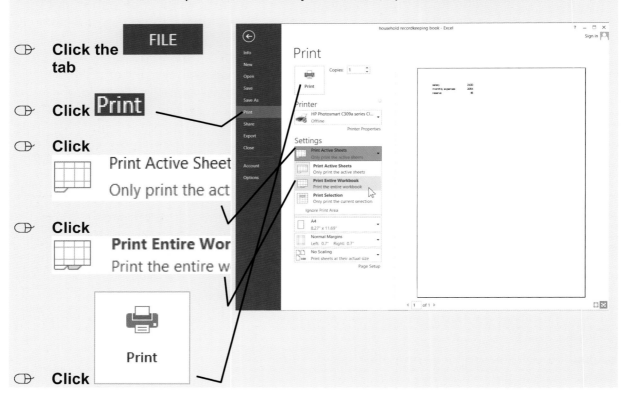

☞ **Click the** FILE **tab**

☞ **Click** Print

☞ **Click**
Print Active Sheet
Only print the act

☞ **Click**
Print Entire Wor
Print the entire w

☞ **Click** Print

4. Charts

The popular saying 'a picture is worth a thousand words' certainly applies to *Excel*. A worksheet can become an indistinct mass of text and numbers, which makes it difficult to understand and is less pleasing to the eye. You may be able to sort things out, but outsiders will have a hard time unravelling your worksheet. In these cases, a chart (also called diagram of graph) may be a good solution. At a glance, you can see ascending and descending curves, or highs and lows.

Excel lets you create a well-arranged chart with just a few mouse clicks. You can choose between various presentation styles (such as circles, columns and lines) and layout options (colors, backgrounds and labels). In this way, you can quickly and easily create an attractive chart for your report or presentation.

In this chapter you will learn how to create and assemble a chart. You will also get to know a few important types of charts. There are many types of charts to choose from, but not every chart will be suited to the data you use. If you prefer another format, you will see how easy it is to change the chart when needed.

In this chapter you will learn how to:

- select parts of the worksheet in order to create a chart;
- insert titles above charts;
- distinguish column, line, and pie charts;
- change the type of chart in retrospect;
- enter names for chart sheets;
- create a single chart with different areas on the worksheet;
- change the colors of a chart;
- use color effects;
- apply 3D effects;
- change the legend;
- add titles;
- change the scaling;
- change the measurement units.

4.1 The Numbers

In order to create a chart you will need to have a worksheet first. Here you are going to create a simple model that is only intended to show you the options for creating charts.

☞ **Open *Excel*** 😊⁹

☞ **If necessary, open a new worksheet** 😊¹²

⌨ **Type these data in the worksheet**

☞ **Widen column A** 😊²

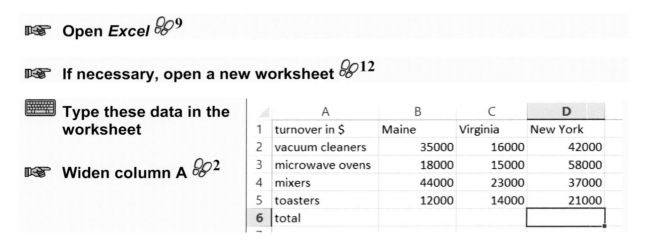

	A	B	C	D
1	turnover in $	Maine	Virginia	New York
2	vacuum cleaners	35000	16000	42000
3	microwave ovens	18000	15000	58000
4	mixers	44000	23000	37000
5	toasters	12000	14000	21000
6	total			

You can add up the amounts in the columns:

☞ **Select cells B2 up to D5** 😊¹⁰

Use the *Sum* function:

👆 **If necessary, click the**

HOME **tab**

👆 **Click Σ**

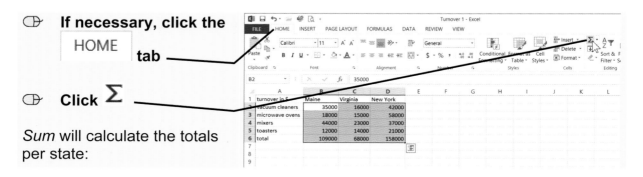

Sum will calculate the totals per state:

With a few simple formatting options you can make the worksheet look much nicer:

☞ **Select cells B1 up to D1** 😊¹⁰

The formatting options can be found on the HOME tab:

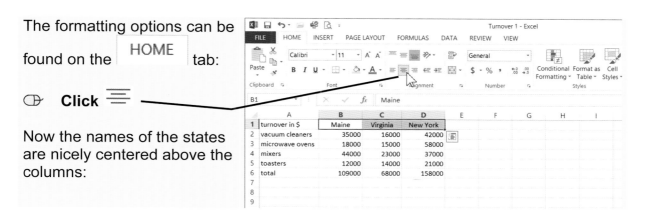

☞ **Click** ≡

Now the names of the states are nicely centered above the columns:

You can change the formatting of the totals, to make them stand out more:

☞ **Select row 6** ✎⁹⁰10

☞ **Click** **B**

☞ **Click** *I*

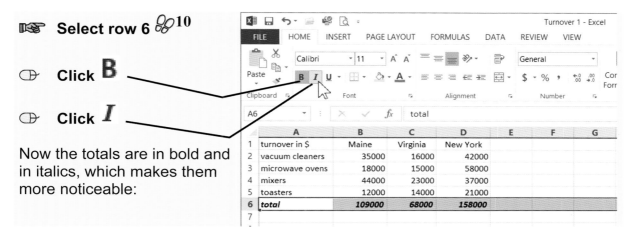

Now the totals are in bold and in italics, which makes them more noticeable:

In order to improve the legibility, you can insert commas and periods between the digits:

☞ **Select cells B2 up to D6** ✎⁹⁰10

☞ **Click** ⁹

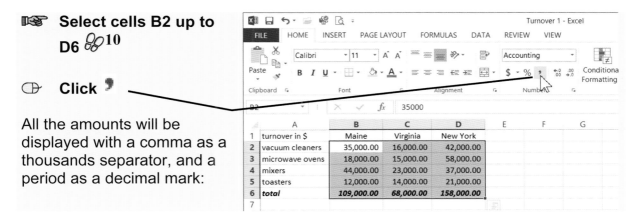

All the amounts will be displayed with a comma as a thousands separator, and a period as a decimal mark:

If you do not want to see two decimals, you can delete the decimal mark again:

 Click twice

Now all the amounts will be displayed with a comma as a thousands separator:

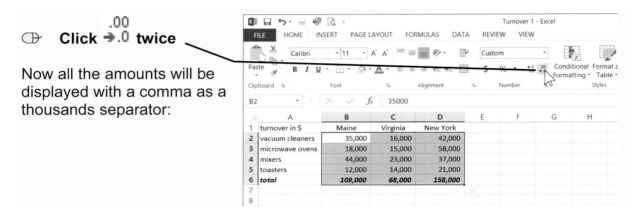

 HELP! I see strange symbols.

Have you clicked ? Then you may see these symbols #### in the worksheet. This is due to the amounts being too wide for the columns.

☞ **Widen the columns** ℓℓ²

☞ **Save the workbook and name it *Turnover 1*** ℓℓ⁶

4.2 Your First Chart

This model will allow you to create a number of different charts even though it is very simple. First, you are going to create a simple chart of the turnover per product in the state of Maine. You can always change the chart later on.

First, you need to select the data you want to use in the chart:

☞ **Select cells A1 up to B5** ℓℓ¹⁰

💡 **Tip**

Usually it is not very practical to include totals in a chart
If the amounts that need to be included in a chart are very far apart, it will be more difficult to present a clear chart. The smallest amount will be barely visible, and the largest amount will stand out too much. That is why it is a good idea not to include the totals in a chart.

Next, you need to select the type of chart, in this case a column chart. You can find the chart functions on the ribbon of the INSERT tab:

⟳ **Click the** INSERT **tab**

⟳ **Click**

Select one of the types of column charts:

⟳ **By** **2-D Column**, **click**

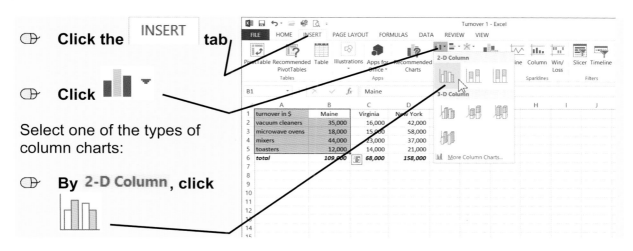

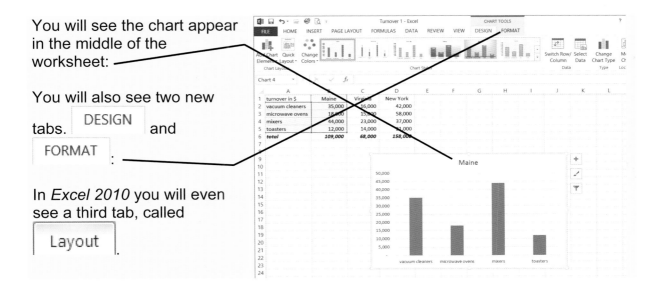

🔆 **Tip**

Description of chart type
If you place the pointer on the various types of column charts, you will notice a small window with a brief description of the characteristics of this type of column chart.

Such a description will be displayed for all the other chart types too.

Clustered Column

Use this chart type to:
• Compare values across a few categories.

Use it when:
• The order of categories is not important.

You will see the chart appear in the middle of the worksheet:

You will also see two new tabs. DESIGN and FORMAT :

In *Excel 2010* you will even see a third tab, called Layout .

Tip

The Design, Format and Layout tab
The *Design*, *Format* and *Layout* tab are only visible if a chart has been selected. If you click next to the chart, the tabs will be closed. When you click the chart again, the tabs will be opened once again.

In *Excel 2013* you will see three icons along the right side of the chart: , and

. You can use these icons to format the style, color, and captions of the chart. You can switch the functions on and off (toggle) by clicking them. In this example you will display the legend.
If you use *Excel 2010*, you will not see these icons, and the legend will already be displayed on the screen. In that case, you can skip the next step.

☞ **Click** ➕

☞ **Check the box ☑ by**
   Legend

■ **Maine** has appeared in
the chart area. This is the
legend:

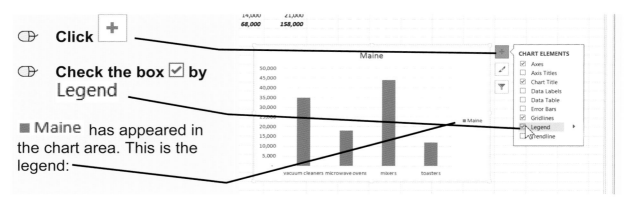

The data of the selected cells is neatly included in the chart. But the title does not provide a lot of information. You can change the title of the chart:

☞ **Click the title**

☞ **Double-click the title**

You will see a text box. The
title has already been
selected:

⌨ **Type:** Turnover in $

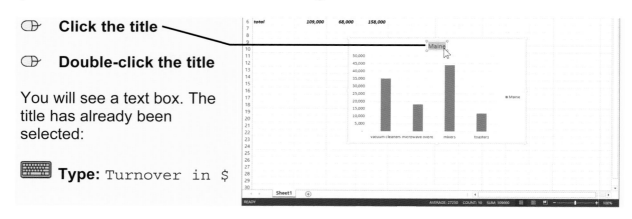

◯ **Click the chart area to the left of the text box**

The title is nicely displayed above the chart:

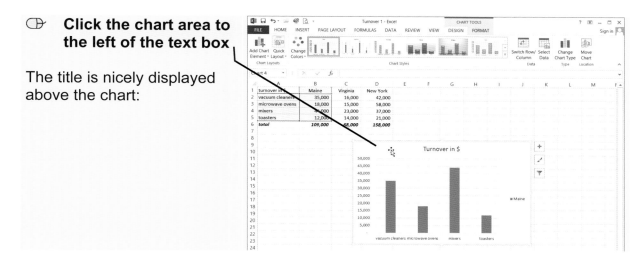

💡 **Tip**

Create the basic chart first
In a few steps you can quickly create a basic chart. When you have finished creating the chart you can adjust the arrangement or formatting. It is better to edit the chart after you have created the basic chart. This changes you make will then be more apparent.

You can leave the chart on the existing worksheet (where the data is), but generally it is better to move the chart to a separate worksheet:

◯ **If necessary, click the**

DESIGN **tab**

Move
◯ **Click** Chart

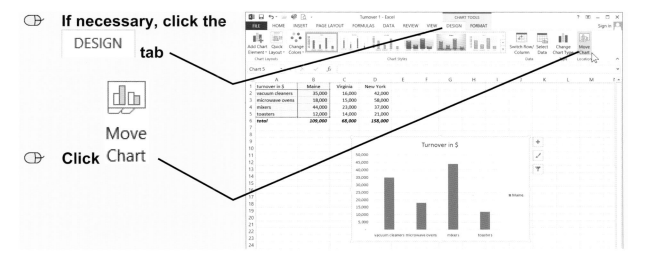

👆 **Click the radio button**
   by New sheet:

👆 **Click** OK

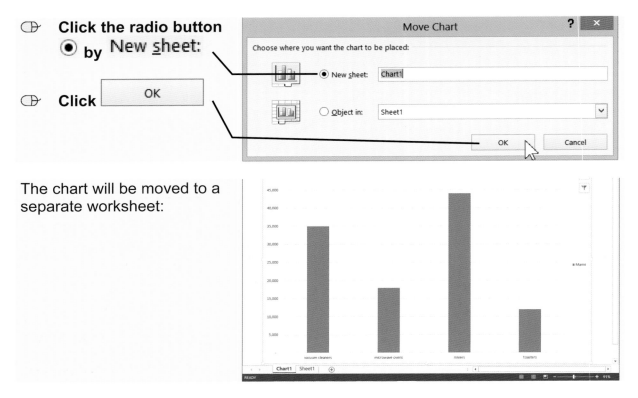

The chart will be moved to a separate worksheet:

With this action, the basic chart has been completed. The chart is linked to the numbers you have entered on the worksheet with the turnover data. If these numbers change, the chart will change as well:

👆 **Click** Sheet1

You will see the worksheet again, with all the turnover data. You can change the numbers a bit, by lowering the number of mixers from 44,000 to 32,000:

⌨ **In cell B4, type:**
   32000

⌨ **Press Enter**

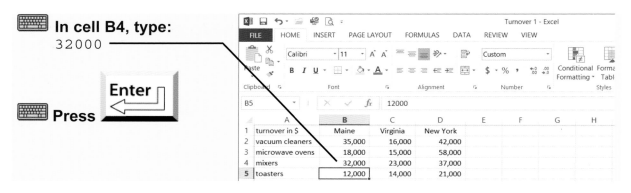

Take a look at the effect this change has on the chart:

Click Chart1

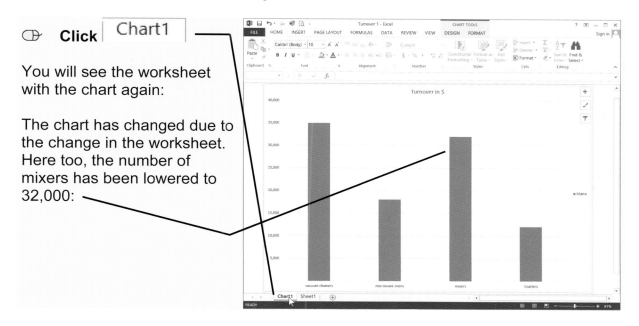

You will see the worksheet with the chart again:

The chart has changed due to the change in the worksheet. Here too, the number of mixers has been lowered to 32,000:

You have seen how you can create a simple chart. You can use this example later on to experiment with various other options.

☞ **Save the workbook** ✄⁷

4.3 Changing the Chart Type

The chart you just created is one of the most common models: a *column chart*. This type of chart is often used for comparing different data or periods with each other.

Another popular chart type is the *circle* or *pie chart*. These types of charts are handy when you want to clearly show the mutual relationships between different products. In other words: how important is a certain product with regard to the other products, or with regard to the total number of products. With just a few mouse clicks you can turn the chart you just made into a circle chart.

Click the DESIGN tab

Click Change Chart Type

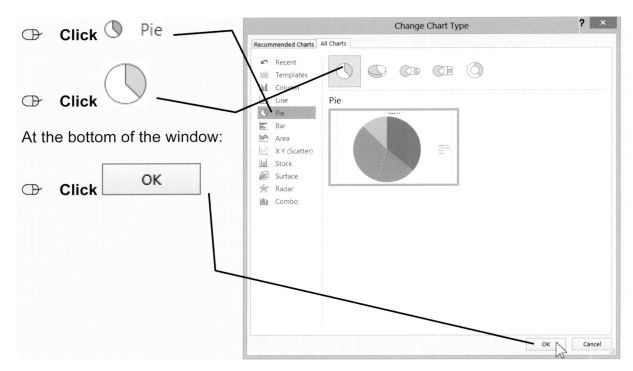

☞ **Click** ◔ Pie

☞ **Click** 🥧

At the bottom of the window:

☞ **Click** | OK |

Right away, you will see the portion that each product contributes to the total turnover:

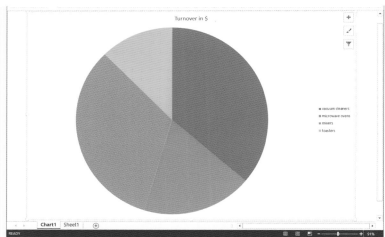

![bandaid icon] **HELP! I do not see the legend in Excel 2013.**
If you cannot see the legend, this is what you do:

☞ **Click** ➕

☞ **Check the box** ☑ **by** Legend

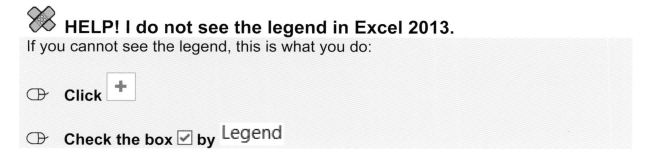

☞ **Save the workbook** ⦜⁷

4.4 Clustered Charts

You can link various charts to your data, and copy each chart to a separate worksheet. In this way you can create different types of charts, or create charts based on different data sets.

If you want compare the turnover of the products between different states, you can create a chart in which both the states and the products are displayed. This is called a *clustered chart*. First you select the data:

☞ **Click** | Sheet1 |

☞ **Select cells A1 up to D5** ⦜¹⁰

Next, you select the chart type:

☞ **Click the** INSERT **tab**

☞ **Click**

☞ **By 3-D Column, click**

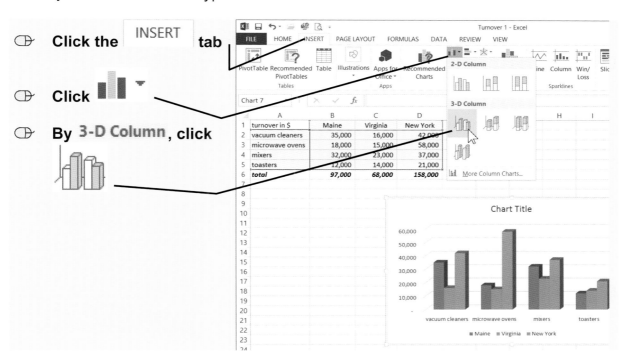

Once again, the chart will appear in the worksheet:

Since the chart is still selected, you will also see the extra tabs:

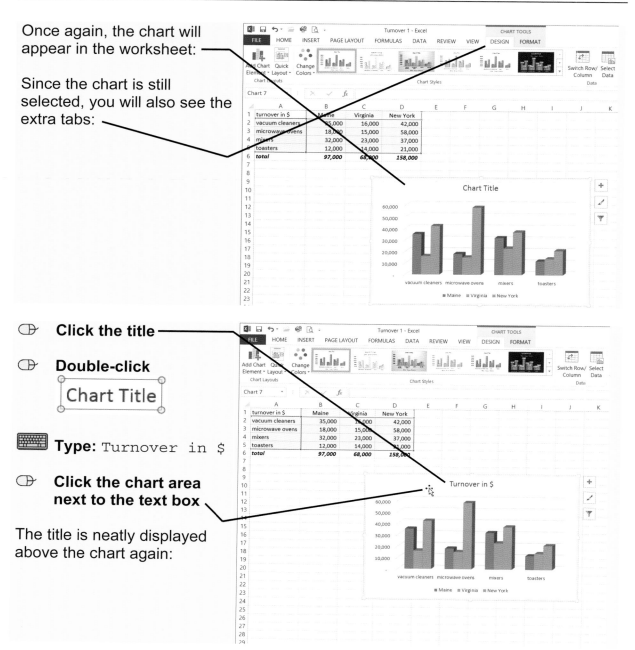

Click the title

Double-click

Chart Title

Type: Turnover in $

Click the chart area next to the text box

The title is neatly displayed above the chart again:

HELP! I do not see the title of the chart.

If you cannot see the chart title, you can do this in *Excel 2013*:

☞ **Click** +, Chart Title, ▶, Above Chart

In *Excel 2010*:

☞ **Click the** Layout **tab**

☞ **Click** Chart Title ▾,   **Above Chart**
                                   Display Title at top of
                                   chart area and resize chart

You are going to move this chart to a new sheet too:

☞ **Click the** DESIGN **tab**

☞ **Click** Move Chart

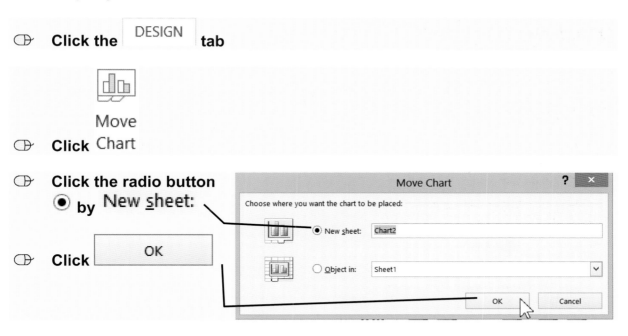

☞ **Click the radio button**
   ⊙ **by** New sheet:

☞ **Click** OK

You will see this chart:

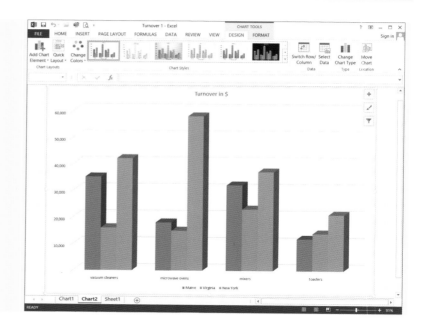

4.5 Choose the Right Chart

Here too, you can change the type of chart according to your own taste and preferences. On the basis of two charts we will demonstrate that a chart is not just about a nice design, but also about the type you choose. Using the same data in another chart type can lead to an unclear, incomplete, or even incorrect representation of the facts. Just see it for yourself:

The  tab is still open:

☞ **Click** Change Chart Type

You will see the *Change Chart Type* window:

☞ **Click** ◔ Pie , ◔ , [OK]

The chart displays the turnover distribution in Maine. The other states are not displayed:

This is because a pie chart can only display a single type of data.

⊕ **Click** Change Chart Type

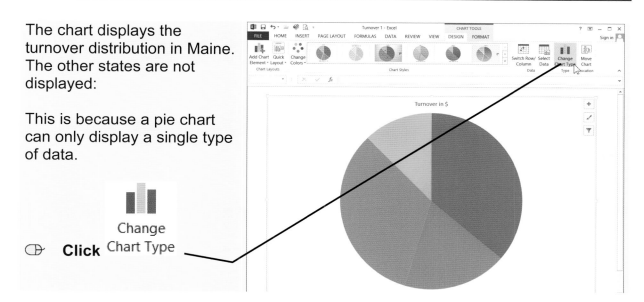

But a column chart can display multiple types of data alongside each other, in a single chart. Just try another type of chart, a so-called line chart:

⊕ **Click** ∠ Line

⊕ **Click**

⊕ **Click** OK

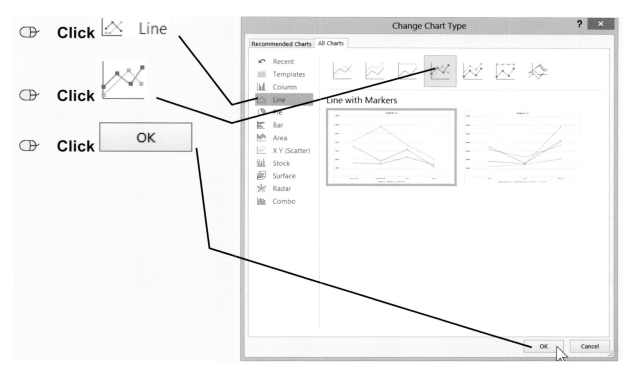

You will see a line chart that looks quite good, but it is not the best choice:

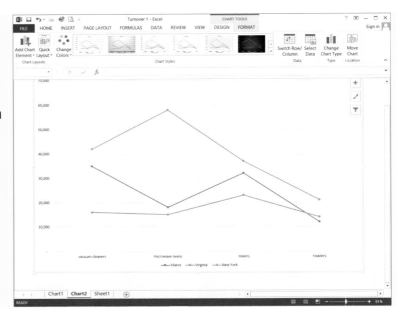

The lines for each state suggest a certain trend, but in this case this trend does not exist. Generally speaking, there is no connection whatsoever between the sale of *microwave ovens* and *mixers* in a country. This means there is no point in creating a line chart.

Take a look at the other chart types and try to decide which type you could or could not use in this case. The chart with a 3D effect is a special type of column chart:

Change
👆 **Click** Chart Type

You will see the *Change Chart Type* window:

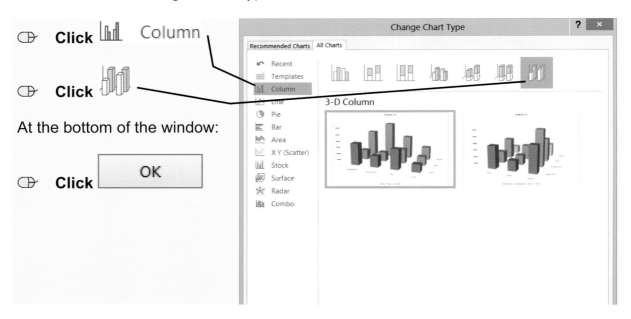

👆 **Click** 📊 Column

👆 **Click** 📊

At the bottom of the window:

👆 **Click** OK

The columns in this column chart have been placed behind each other, instead of next to each other:

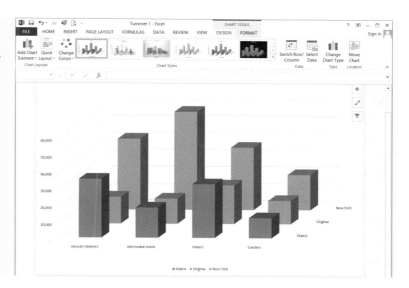

☞ **Save the workbook** ✂️ ⁷

4.6 Charts and Selections

Up till now, you have selected a single area and created a chart with the data from this area. But you may sometimes need to use worksheet data that are not in close proximity to each other. For instance, because there are other columns or rows in between these data. In this example, this problem occurs when you want to create a chart of the turnover distribution per state. This is how you create such a chart:

☞ **Click** Sheet1

The names of the states are in row 1, and the total turnover is in row 6:

You cannot drag from row 1 to row 6 and skip the rows in between.

But you can select both rows separately. This is how you do it:

☞ **Select cells B1 up to D1** ✂️ ¹⁰

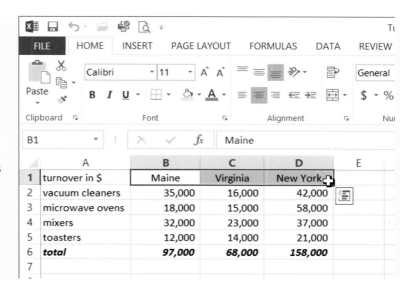

You can select a second row:

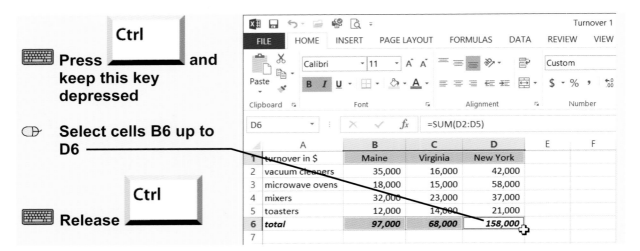

Both rows have been selected. Now you can create a chart of the data in these rows:

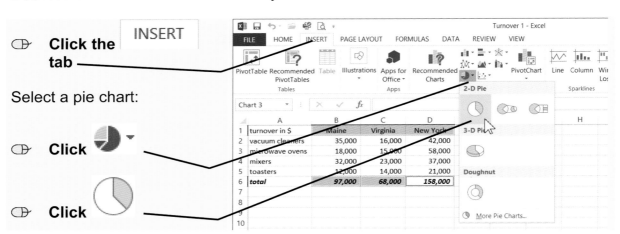

The pie chart will be created. If necessary, add a title:

In *Excel 2013*, beside the chart:

In *Excel 2010*:

👉 **Click** Title ▾,

Above Chart
Display Title at top of
chart area and resize chart

👉 **Double-click**

Chart Title

⌨ **Type:** Turnover per
state

👉 **Click the chart area
next to the text box**

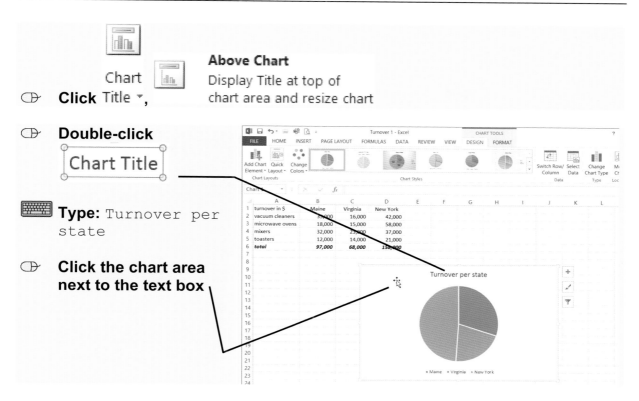

You are going to move this chart to a new worksheet as well:

👉 **Click the** DESIGN **tab**

👉 **Click** Move Chart

👉 **Click the radio button
    ● by** New sheet:

👉 **Click** OK

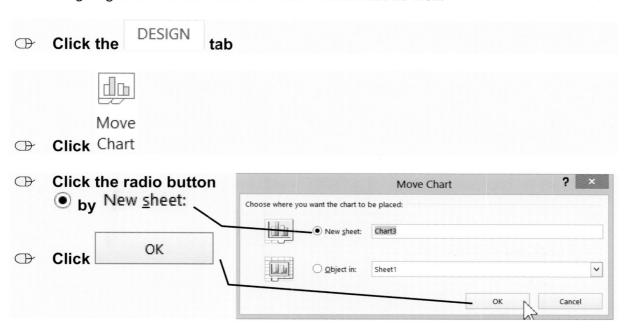

The chart is finished:

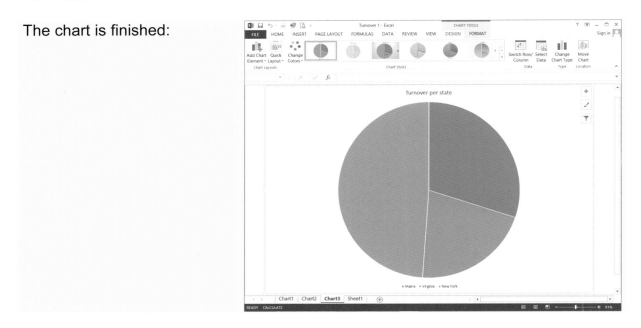

You can also select multiple columns. First, you can add a new column to the worksheet, containing the total turnover per product. That is, the combined turnover of all the states:

☞ **Click** Sheet1

⌨ **In cell E1, type:**
  Total

⌨ **Press** ⬇

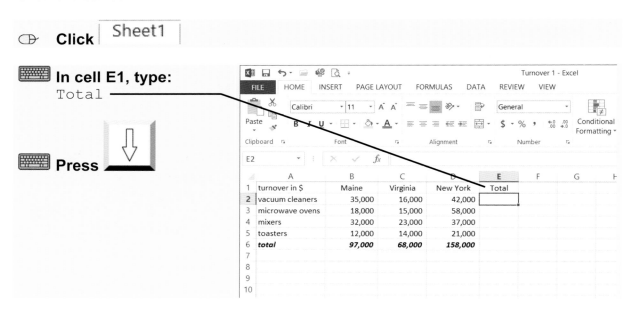

Now you can calculate the total number of vacuum cleaners sold in all three states:

The HOME tab is still open:

On the right-hand side of the ribbon:

☞ **Click Σ**

⌨ **Press Enter**

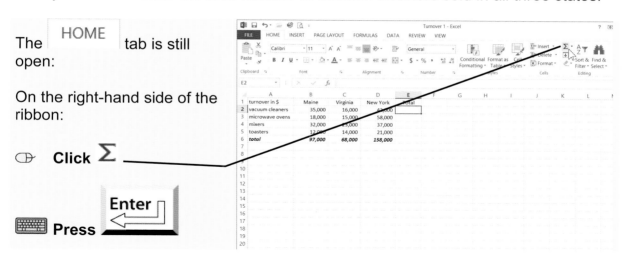

In cell E2 you will see the total turnover of vacuum cleaners: 93,000. You can apply the formula to other products too:

☞ **Click cell E2**

☞ **Drag the handle of cell E2 to cell E6**

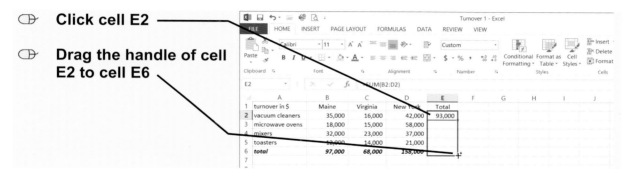

The formula of cell E2 has been copied to cells E3 up to E6. The results will be displayed in these cells. Now you can create a chart with this data. To do this, you will need to select a number of cells in columns A and E:

☞ **Select cells A2 up to A5** 🦶10

The data in column A have been selected. Now you need to select the data in column E:

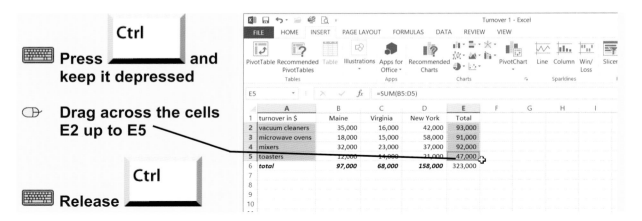

Press Ctrl **and keep it depressed**

☞ **Drag across the cells E2 up to E5**

Release Ctrl

Now the data in column E have been selected as well. You can create a chart with these data:

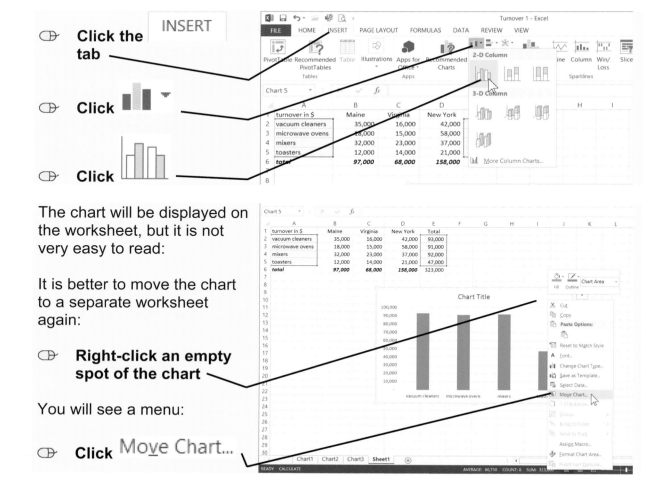

☞ **Click the** INSERT **tab**

☞ **Click** ▮▮▮ ▾

☞ **Click** ▮▮▮

The chart will be displayed on the worksheet, but it is not very easy to read:

It is better to move the chart to a separate worksheet again:

☞ **Right-click an empty spot of the chart**

You will see a menu:

☞ **Click** Move Chart...

You can move the chart to a new sheet:

- **Click the radio button** ⊙ **by** New sheet:

- **Click** OK

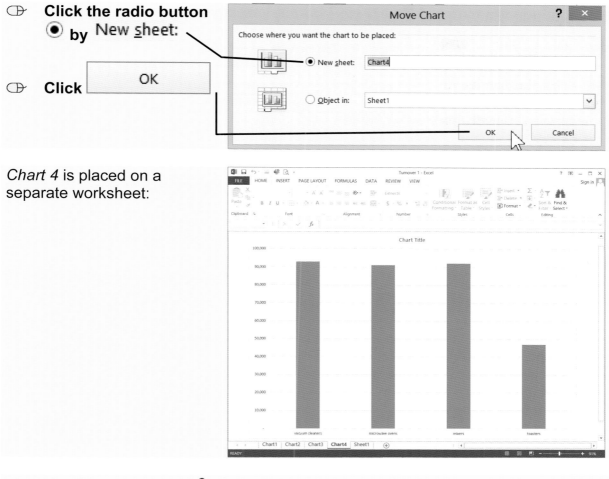

Chart 4 is placed on a separate worksheet:

☞ **Save the workbook** 🐾7

4.7 Naming Chart Sheets

If you use a lot of worksheets you can give each worksheet its own name. This is how you do it:

- **Double-click** Chart1

- ⌨ **Type:** Turnover Maine

You can change the name of the other charts in the same way:

☞ **Change the name of *Chart2* to *Products per state***

☞ **Change the name of *Chart3* to *Turnover per state***

☞ **Change the name of *Chart4* to *Turnover per product***

Now all the chart sheets have a name.

☞ **Save the workbook** ⸋⸋⁷

4.8 Changing the Chart Colors

You are going to change the colors of the chart. At the bottom of the window:

👆 **Click** | Turnover per product |

Sometimes, there is just little difference in color between the columns and their background. This can be a problem if you do not print the chart on a color printer. Or you might also want to print the chart in a very different color.

👆 **Click one of the columns**

All the columns will be framed by a border with circles on each corner. This tells you that the columns have been selected.

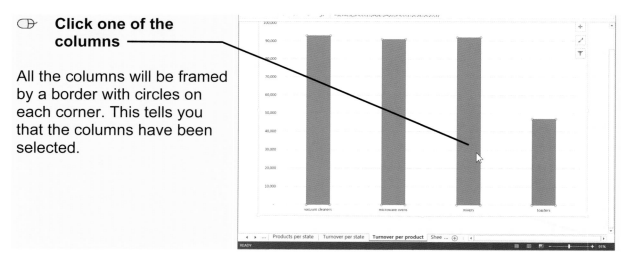

In *Excel 2013*:

☞ **Right-click a column**

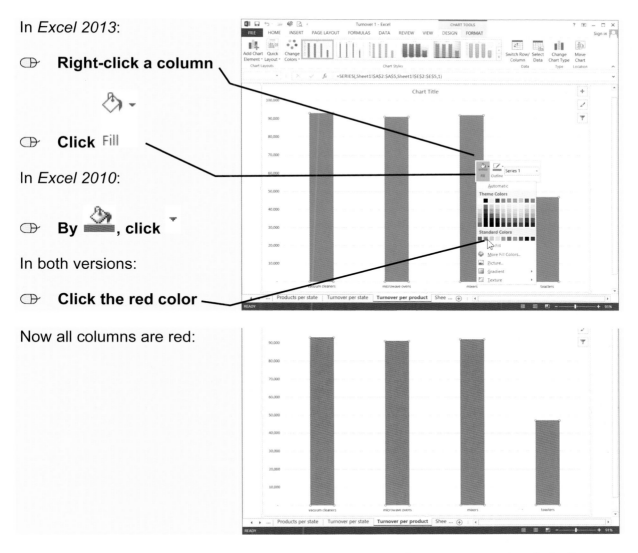

☞ **Click** Fill

In *Excel 2010*:

☞ **By** , **click**

In both versions:

☞ **Click the red color**

Now all columns are red:

Three of the columns are practically the same height. If you want to clearly indicate which column is highest (the most important), you can give this column a different color. In this chart, the *vacuum cleaners* column is slightly higher than the *mixers* column.

 Tip

Display column values
When you place the pointer on a column you will see a label with the column name and its value. In order to find out which column has the highest value, you need to place the pointer on each column and compare the values. You can do the same thing with other types of charts.

- Continue on the next page -

☞ **Place the pointer on the *vacuum cleaners* column** ——

You will see the label appear by the column:

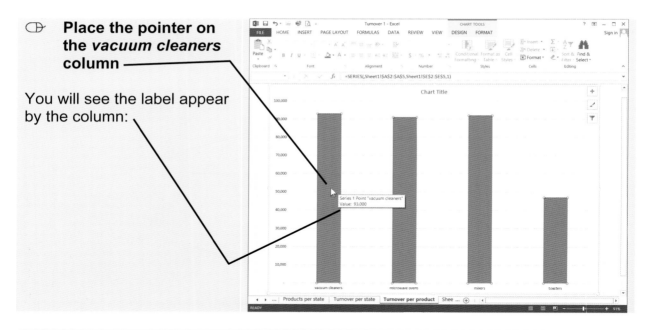

☞ **Click the *vacuum cleaners* column**

The selection frames around the other columns will disappear. Only the *vacuum cleaners* column still has a selection frame:

☞ **Right-click the column**

☞ **Click** Fill **(*Excel 2013*) or by** , **click** **(*Excel 2010*)**

☞ **Click the yellow color**

Now the *vacuum cleaners* column has turned yellow:

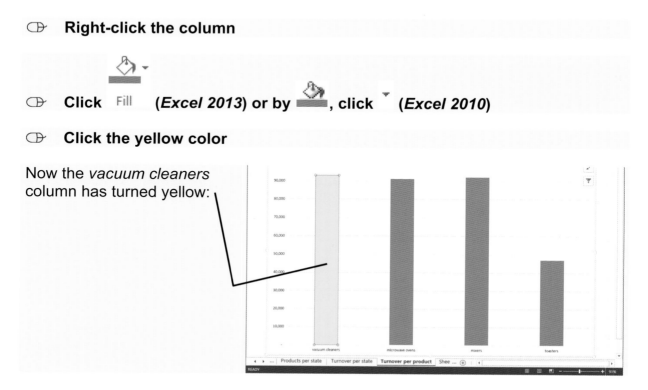

In the same way, you can give the other columns their own color. But be careful with adding colors. It is always useful to give the column or section that you discuss in a report or presentation a different color. This way, your audience will immediately see what the main subject is.

You can also change the colors in other chart types:

At the bottom of the window:

☞ **Click**

⟨ Turnover per state ⟩

☞ **Click the chart**

The whole chart will be framed within a selection frame:

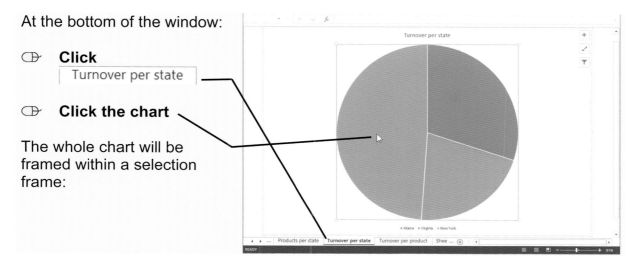

☞ **Click the *Virginia* section**

Now only this section is selected:

☞ **Right-click the *Virginia* section**

☞ **Click** Fill **or**

☞ **Click yellow**

Since you have used the yellow color the last time, this has become the temporary default color of this button. The *Virginia* section will turn yellow right away.

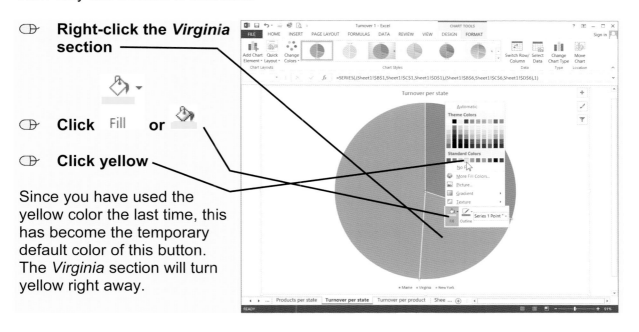

Please note:

The color of the *Virginia* section has also changed to yellow in the legend at the side or bottom of the chart. These data will automatically change, along with the chart.

4.9 Color Effects

You do not need to limit yourself to plain colors. *Excel* also offers some special color effects. You can select gradient colors that gradually change from dark yellow to light yellow, for example. At the bottom of the window:

☞ **Click** | Turnover per product |

You can use gradient colors for the *vacuum cleaners* column. First, you select this column:

☞ **Click the *vacuum cleaners* column**

The selection frame appears all around this column. Select the color:

In *Excel 2013*:

☞ **Click the** FORMAT **tab**

In both versions:

☞ **Click** Shape Fill

☞ **Click** Gradient

☞ **Click a color variation**

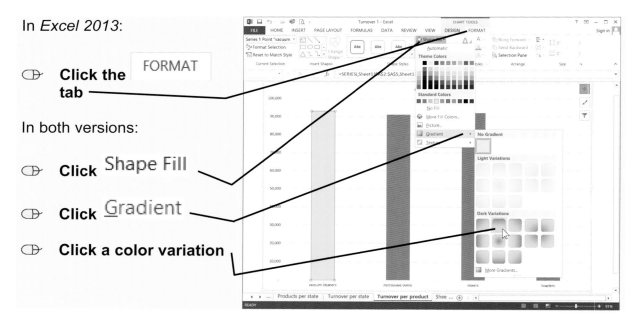

You will see a gradual change in the color of the *vacuum cleaners* column, from dark yellow to lighter yellow:

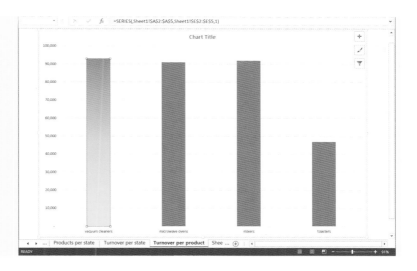

4.10 Background Color

Now that the columns have a color, the background looks a bit dull. It may also be too dark or pronounced when you print the chart. This will spoil the effect of the actual data. The background actually consists of two parts:

- the white background of the chart behind the columns;
- the white background all around this area. The part where the data are displayed.

You can change both these parts, independently of each other:

☞ **Click the white background by a column**

Now there is a selection frame around the section behind the columns:

☞ **Click** Shape Fill

☞ **Click Orange (Accent 2, lighter 80%)**

Please note: in *Excel 2010* you select dark orange (Accent 6, lighter 80%).

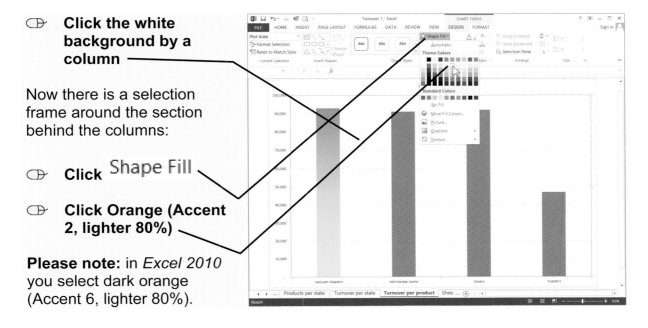

You can select the background beside the chart and color it:

 Click the white area next to the chart

The selection frame around the columns section of the chart will disappear. Now you will only see the frame around the whole chart.

 Click Shape Fill

 Click Orange (Accent 2, lighter 60%)

Please note: in *Excel 2010* you select dark orange (Accent 6, lighter 60%).

Now your chart is colored:

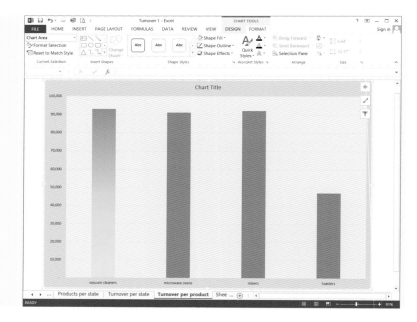

💡 **Tip**

Uniformity in formatting

If you use multiple charts in a presentation, it will look more professional if all the charts have been formatted in the same way. Do not use different colors for each chart.

4.11 3D Effects

The chart on this worksheet is two-dimensional. There is no 'depth' in this chart. With a few clicks you can change this and add a 3D effect to the chart.

 Please note:
The right mouse button is often used when formatting charts.

☞ **Right-click a spot in the chart** ——

You will see a menu:

☞ **Click**
  Change Chart Type...

 HELP! I do not see Change Chart Type... **.**
If you have clicked a gridline, or one of the texts, you will not see the
Change Chart Type... option.
☞ **Right-click a different spot in the chart**

You can change the chart type:

☞ **Click**

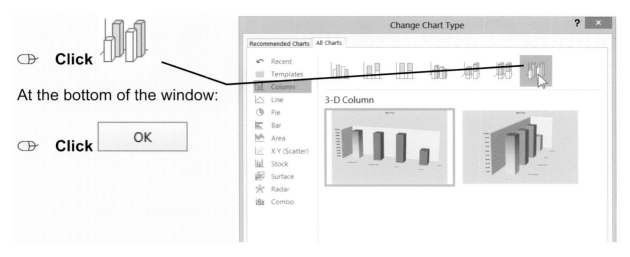

At the bottom of the window:

☞ **Click** OK

The chart has acquired a 3D effect. The columns have become three-dimensional. You can increase or diminish this effect, if you wish.

Right-click a spot in the background

Click 3-D Rotation...

In *Excel 2013* you will see *Format Chart Area* pane:

You can rotate the chart to the left or to the right with

X Rotation   20°

You can tilt the chart forwards or backwards with

Y Rotation   15°

☞ **Use ▲▼ to select the settings you like**

If you are satisfied with the result you can close the pane:

Click ✕

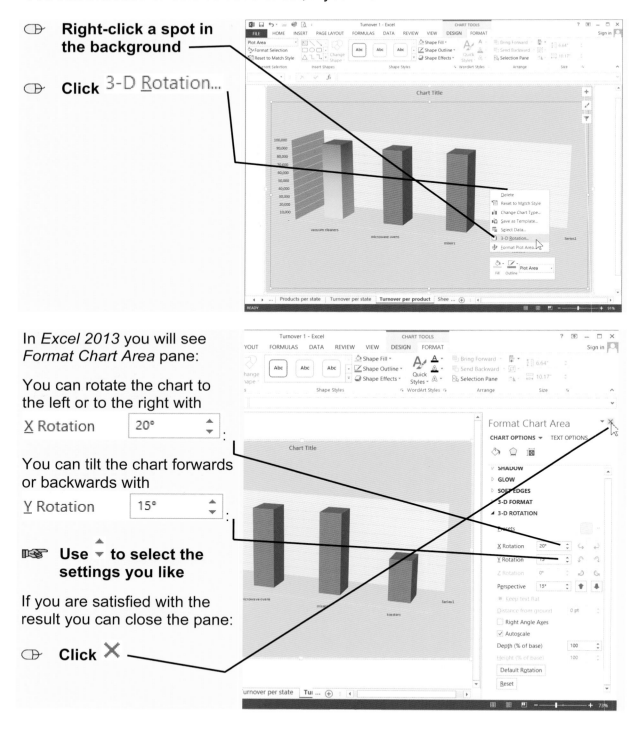

In *Excel 2010*:

You can rotate the chart to the left or to the right with

X: 20° :

You can tilt the chart forwards or backwards with

Y: 15° :

☞ **Use to select the settings you like**

If you are satisfied with the result:

☞ **Click** Close

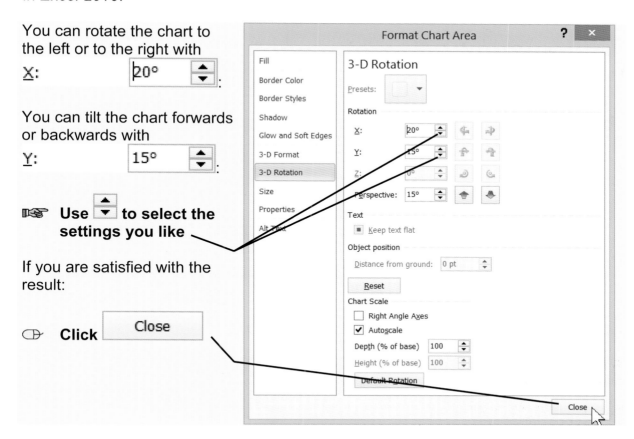

🖎 **Please note:**

You will immediately see the effect of your settings in the chart. If necessary, you can move the *Format Chart Area* pane to the edge of the screen, in order to get a clear view of the chart. You can move the pane by placing the pointer on the upper border of the pane, depressing the left mouse button, and dragging the pane to another spot.

This is the result if you select these settings

X̲ Rotation   0°

Y̲ Rotation   0°:

Please note: your own chart may look different.

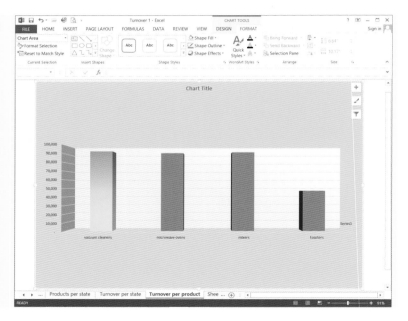

💡 **Tip**

Too much change?

With the Default Ro̲tation button in the *Format Chart Area* pane you can reset the chart settings to their default values.

4.12 Changing the Legend

The legend consists of the comments that go with the chart. You can display them, hide them, or format them in a different way.

This is what you do to display the legend in *Excel 2013*:

👉 **Click** ➕

👉 **Check the box** ☑ **by** Legend

In *Excel 2010* the legend is already shown.

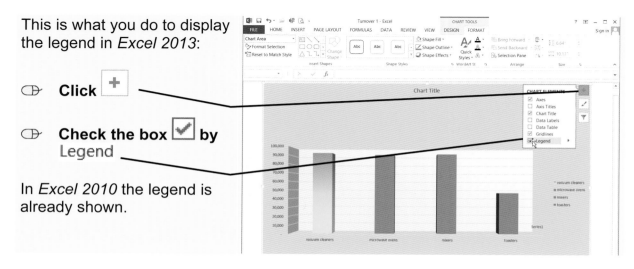

The legend on the right-hand side of this chart is not really essential, as it is also displayed below the columns. You can delete the legend again:

☞ **Click the legend**

You will see a selection frame:

⌨ **Press** Delete

The legend has disappeared and the chart will take up more space. You can also change the font, font size, and font color of the text below the columns:

☞ **Right-click** vacuum cleaners

☞ **Click** Font...

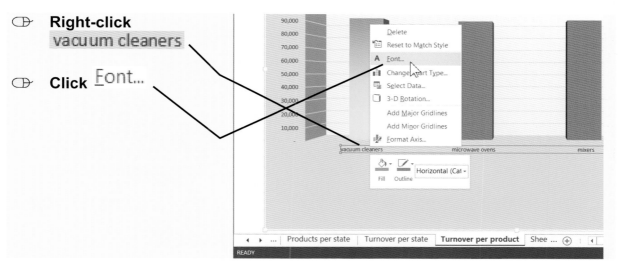

You will see the *Font* window:

☞ **By** Font style: **, click** ⌄

☞ **Click** Bold Italic

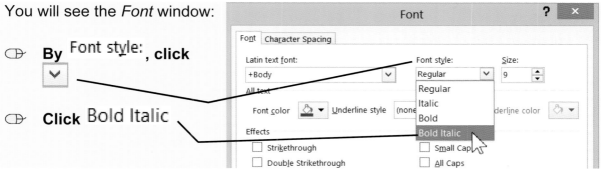

By Font color, click

Click Orange, Accent 2

Click OK

In *Excel 2010*, choose
Orange, Accent 6.

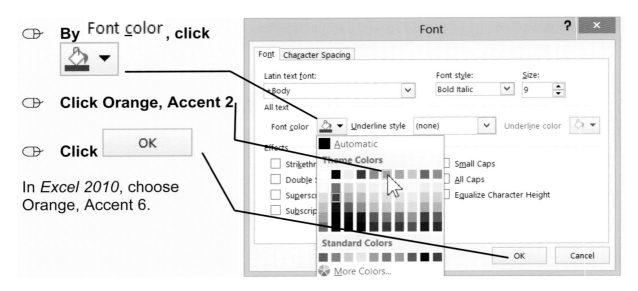

You can do the same thing with the values on the left-hand side of the chart.
Sometimes you can even do this directly:

Right-click one of the
values

Click Font...

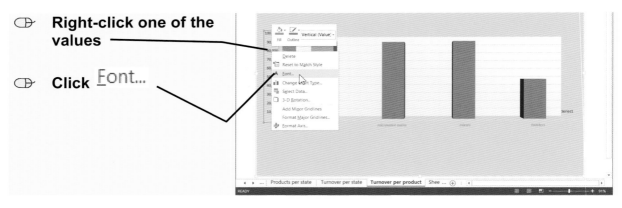

Double-click the box
by Size:

Type: 14

Click OK

The values will be displayed
in a larger font.

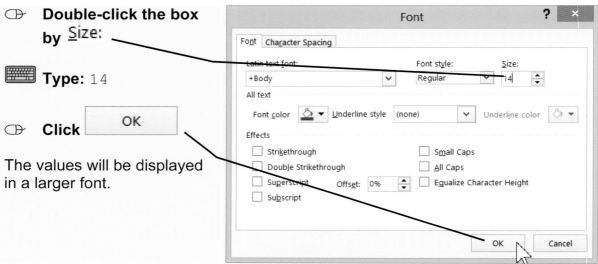

You can also change the formatting of the title above the chart in this way.

4.13 Adding a Chart Title

If the chart does not yet have a title, you can add a title too:

☞ **Click the** FORMAT **tab**

In *Excel 2013*, in the top left-hand corner of the window:

☞ **Click** ▼

☞ **Click** Chart Title

In *Excel 2010*:

☞ **Click** Layout **,** Title ▼**,** **Above Chart**
Display Title at top of chart area and resiz

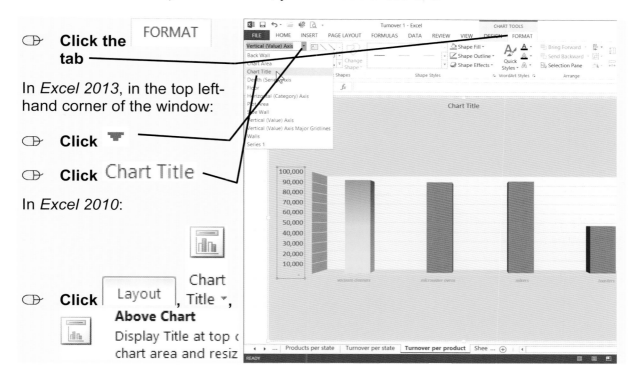

Now you can type the title:

☞ **Double-click the text box**

⌨ **Type:** Turnover per product

☞ **Click beside the text box**

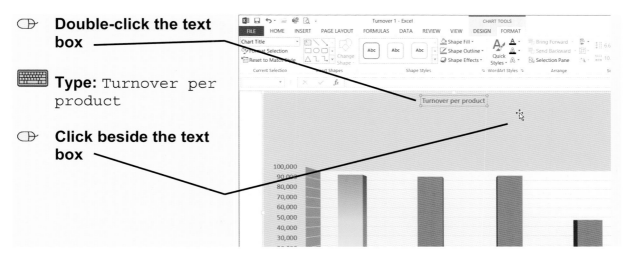

4.14 Changing the Graduation Rules

In the standard chart, basic maximum and minimum values are set, and a certain scale is used. Sometimes, this graduation is not very practical, or too crowded. In such a case you can set your own scale.

In the sample chart you will see lines for every 10,000 units. But you would like to see lines for every 20,000 units. You can change the scale like this:

- ☞ **Right-click one of the values**

- ☞ **Click** Format Axis...

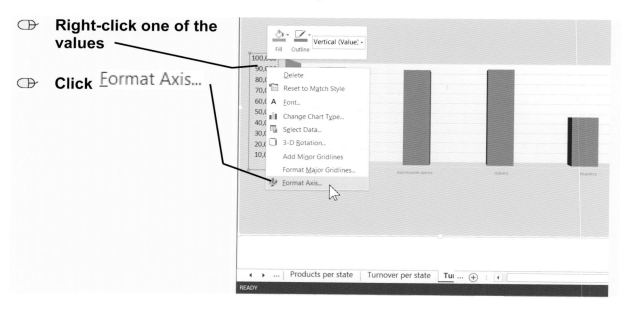

In *Excel 2013*:

- ☞ **If necessary, click** AXIS OPTIONS ▼

- ☞ **Double-click the box by** Major

- ⌨ **Type:** 20000

- ☞ **Click** ✕

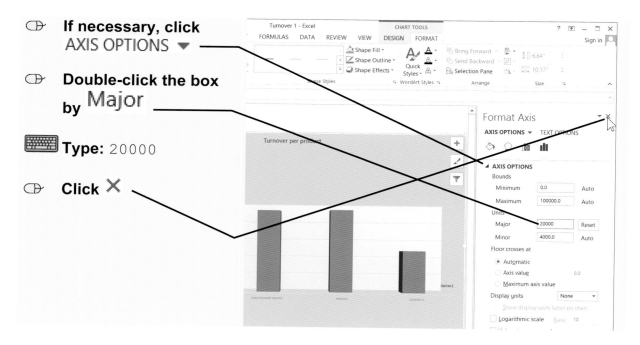

In *Excel 2010*:

☞ **If necessary, click** Axis Options

By Major unit:.

☞ **Click the radio button ◉ by** Fixed

☞ **Double-click the box by** Fixed

⌨ **Type:** 20000

☞ **Click** Close

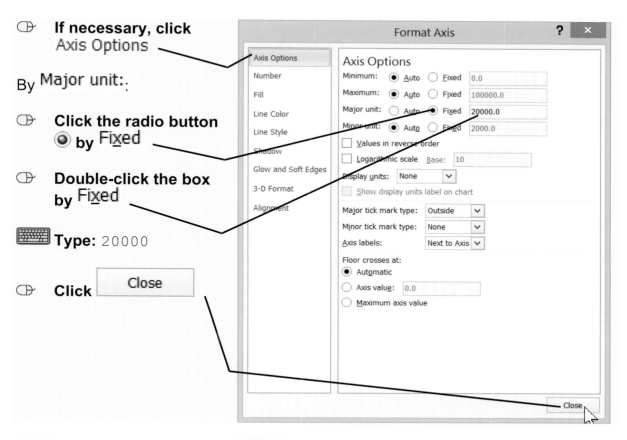

Now the lines in the chart will be displayed for every 20,000 units:

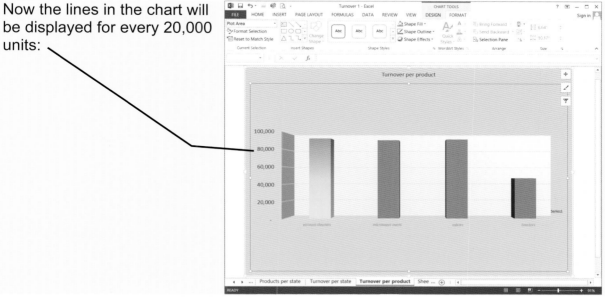

If all the amounts are large, for instance, thousands or millions, you can automatically leave out the zeroes. This will make the chart easier to read:

☞ **Right-click one of the values**

☞ **Click** Format Axis...

In the screenshot below you will see the window in *Excel 2013*. In *Excel 2010* you will see a window that looks slightly different, which is the same as the one on the previous page. In that window you can select the same options as in *Excel 2013*.

☞ **If necessary, click**
AXIS OPTIONS ▼

☞ **By** Display units **,**
click ▼

☞ **Click** Thousands

☞ **Click** ✕

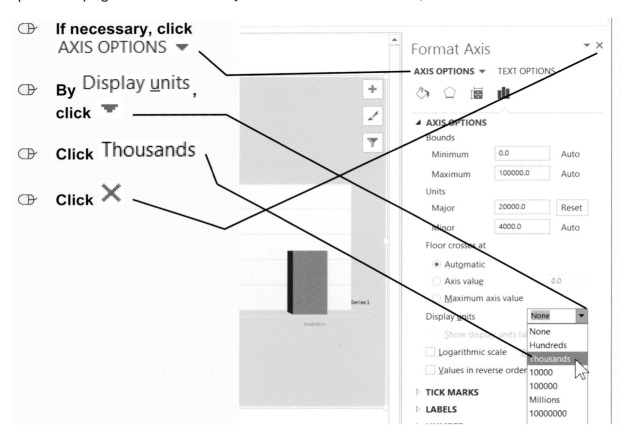

🖐 **Please note:**
The *Format Axis* window may be a bit too narrow, in which case you will not be able to view all the options. If this happens, click the vertical line to the left of the window. The cursor will turn into ◀┼▶ and you can widen the window. If you do this, the part of the window containing the chart will become less wide.

Now you will see
Thousands next to the
vertical axis, and the last
three zeroes have
disappeared in all the
amounts: ──────

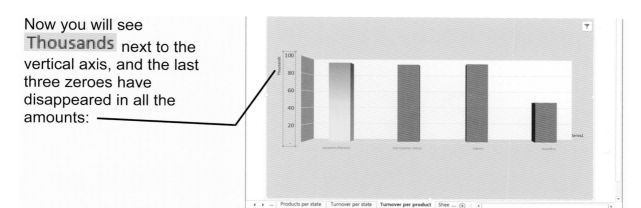

If you right-click a section of the chart, you will find even more formatting options.

 Tip

Right-click to change
When working with charts and if you want to change anything, right-click the item and view the options in the menu that appears on the screen. You will find lots of useful and interesting options.

☞ **Close the workbook and save the changes** 🔗17

In the next couple of exercises you can repeat the operations we have discussed in this chapter.

Formatting functions
Formatting functions can be very useful, especially with charts. You can make the really important figures stand out, make trends more clearly visible and make other data less noticeable. You have seen a few examples of the formatting options in this chapter.

You may notice that formatting takes up a lot of your time, sometimes more than the time it took to create the chart itself. When you create a sheet for a presentation, it will only be visible on the screen for a few seconds. In this case it is wise to limit the formatting for this sheet. But if your chart is going to be included in an annual balance sheet or another type of comprehensive report, it will be worth it to spend some time to make the charts look just right.

4.15 Exercises

Have you forgotten how to do something? Use the number beside the footsteps to look it up in appendix *B How Do I Do That Again?* at the end of this book.

Please note:

In this exercise you will continue to work on the *members* workbook that you used in the exercises for *Chapter 3 Printing*. If you have not completed these exercises, you can use the file named *members - ch 4* from the folder with the practice files. If you have not copied this folder to your computer, you can read how to do that in *Appendix A Downloading the Practice Files*.

Exercise 1: Creating a Chart (1)

☞ Open the *members* workbook. ⚹**22**

☞ Go to sheet *2011*. ⚹**19**

☞ Select cells A1 up to D4. ⚹**10**

☞ Create a clustered column chart on a separate worksheet, on the basis of these data. The result should look like this, more or less:

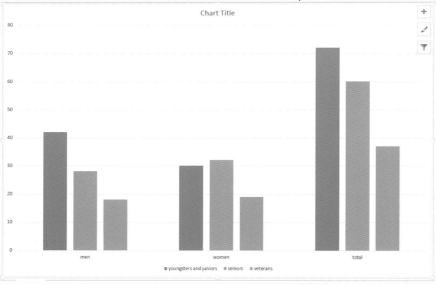

⚹**71**, ⚹**64**

☞ Select the *youngsters and juniors* columns. ⚹**43**

☞ Color these columns red. ✂**42**

☞ Select the seniors columns. ✂**43**

☞ Color these columns blue. ✂**42**

☞ Select the white background of the chart. ✂**44**

☞ Give this background a yellow color. ✂**42**

Exercise 2: Pie Chart

☞ Go to sheet *2011*. ✂**19**

☞ Select cells A2 up to A4. ✂**10**

☞ Select cells D2 up to D4 as well. ✂**10**

☞ Create a pie chart on a separate worksheet. The result should look like this:

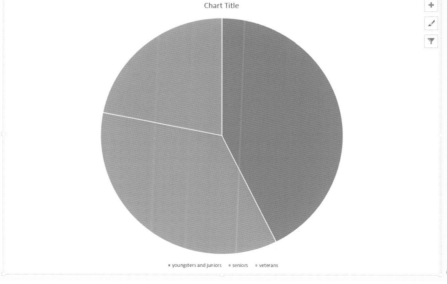

✂**71**, ✂**64**

Exercise 3: Creating a Chart (2)

If you want to see the actual development in the various age categories, you should create another type of chart.

☞ Go to the *membership development* worksheet. 🦶¹⁹

☞ Select cells A1 up to D4. 🦶¹⁰

☞ Create a clustered column chart on a separate worksheet, on the basis of these data. 🦶⁷¹, 🦶⁶⁴
The result should look like this:

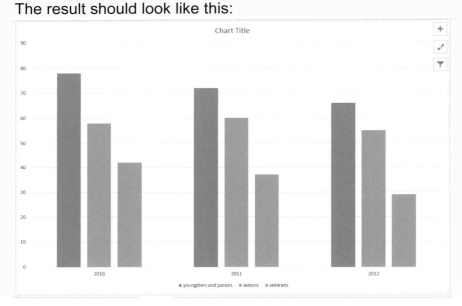

Exercise 4: Clustering a Chart in a Different Way

You see the membership development per year, but now you would like to see the development per category.

☞ Go to the *membership development* worksheet. 🦶¹⁹

☞ Make sure that cells A1 up to D4 are still selected.

☞ Create a clustered column chart. 🦶⁷¹

☞ Click the DESIGN tab.

Switch Row/
☞ Click   Column   .

☞ Move the chart to a separate worksheet again. ☙☙**64**

The chart will look like this:

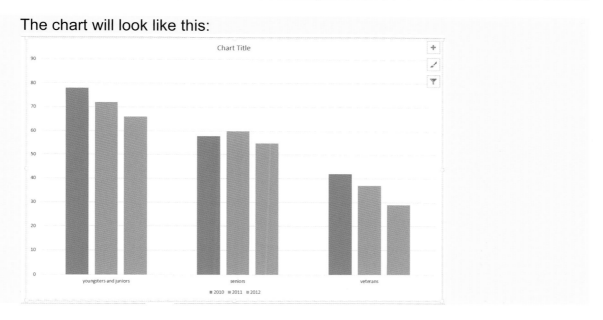

☞ Add the chart title *Membership development.* ☙☙**15**

☞ Increase the font size to 24. ☙☙**14**

☞ Close the worksheet and save the changes. ☙☙**17**

☞ Close *Excel*. ☙☙**11**

4.16 Background Information

Dictionary

3D effect	3D stands for three-dimensional. Display a chart with information regarding the height, width, and depth of the chart.
Chart	A chart or a diagram (or a graph) is a graphic rendering (a drawn image) of a series of data.
Clustered chart	In a clustered chart, values of various categories are compared to each other, by using vertical rectangles.
Column chart	Displays columns of a size that corresponds to the individual data.
Diagram	See chart.
Graduation	The values used in a diagram or chart; they are evenly distributed between a minimum and a maximum value.
Legend	A list with an explanation of the symbols used in a chart or diagram.
Line chart	Used to display trends over a certain period of time.
Maximum/ minimum value	The highest or lowest possible value in the graduation of a chart.
Pie chart	A pie chart is a chart type in which the contribution of each single value to the total is displayed.
Sparkline	With sparklines you can create mini-charts within a single cell. In this way you can show a trend in a simple way.

Source: Microsoft Excel Help

4.17 Tips

 Tip

Move components
You can move the legend (the block with the comments at the side of the chart) and many other parts of the chart by dragging them.

 Click the legend

A selection frame all around the legend indicates that it has been selected:

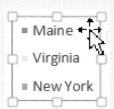

 Drag the legend to another location

 Tip

Mini-charts with sparklines
You can use sparklines to create mini-charts within a single cell. This is a simple way of demonstrating a trend.

In order to create sparklines of the turnover per product in this worksheet:

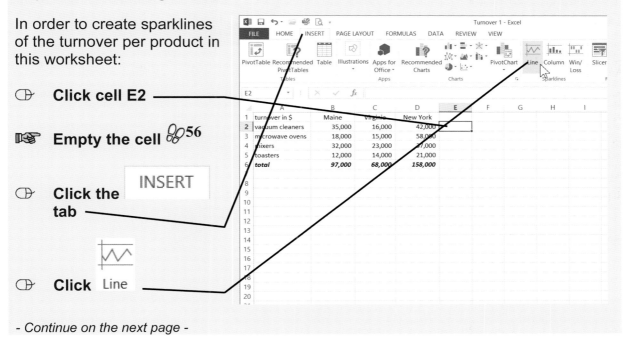

 Click cell E2

☞ **Empty the cell** *⁊⁊56*

 Click the | INSERT | **tab**

 Click Line

- Continue on the next page -

You will see the *Create Sparklines* window:

⊕ **Drag across cells B2 to D2**

⊕ **Click** OK

You will see the chart:

Here you can select a different type or style:

⊕ **Drag the handle of cell E2 to cell E6**

Now you will see sparklines for all the products:

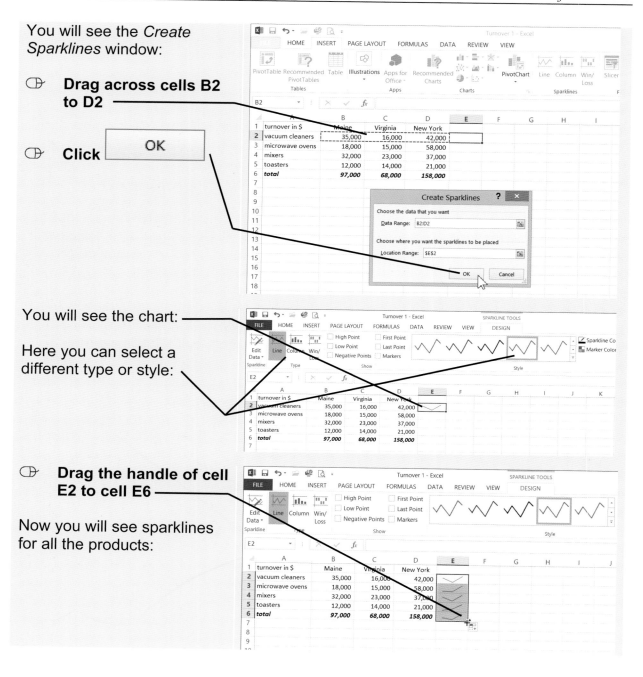

5. Using Excel as a Database

You can use the tables in *Excel* in lots of different ways. They are very useful if you want to keep track of things, such as lists with various data. For example, merchandise lists, personnel lists, or membership information. The data regarding a DVD, stamp or other type of collection can also be recorded in *Excel*.

When you collect and organize your data in this way you are actually using *Excel* as a *database*. A worksheet allows you to start working right away arranging the data in your list. You will not be performing calculations with this data, but the simple yet powerful sorting function in *Excel* will let you make excellent use of this program.

Moreover, you will have many options for selecting specific data from these long lists (in *Excel* this is called *filtering*). With this function you can very quickly find the persons or articles you are looking for in the list you have selected, no matter if the list is sorted or unsorted.

In this chapter you will learn how to:

- create an address list;
- sort the data in ascending and descending order;
- sort data on multiple levels;
- filter data from a list;
- use custom filters;
- create mailings in *Word* with data from *Excel*;
- link an *Excel* list to a *Word* document;
- insert data from *Excel* into a *Word* document.

5.1 Creating Your Own Address List

In order to explore the options for using *Excel* as a database, you will need to have a list available. In this chapter we will use a short address list of the members of a club. But such a list could also contain customer or vendor information, names of employees, or even titles of the DVDs in your DVD collection.

☞ **Open *Excel* $\mathscr{G}^9$**

☞ **If necessary, open a new workbook $\mathscr{G}^{12}$**

➥ **Please note:**

In this chapter you will be using a club's membership list. If you do not want to type this list yourself, you can use the *club* worksheet from the practice files folder.
If you have not copied this folder to your computer, you can read how to do that in *Appendix A Downloading the Practice Files*.

 Enter the following data in the worksheet

	A	B	C	D	E	F	G	H	I
1	number	first name	last name	address	zip code	city	state	team	
2	162	Hank	Dune	44 Porter Street	98108	Seattle	WA	B1	
3	163	John	Bergman	119 Starlight Avenue	98108	Seattle	WA	A1	
4	164	Marion	Zane	3 Columbus Street	98102	Bellevue	WA	B2	
5	165	Petra	Aronson	16 Porter Street	98108	Seattle	WA	B2	
6	166	Simone	Bergman	119 Starlight Avenue	98108	Seattle	WA	B1	
7	167	John William	Koban	45 Roundabout Lane	98102	Bellevue	WA	A1	
8	168	Andy	Zucconi	101 Kings Road	98108	Seattle	WA	B1	
9	169	John	Aronson	16 Porter Street	98108	Seattle	WA	A1	
10	170	Harry	Ackerley	7 Postal Square	98108	Seattle	WA	B2	
11	171	Edith	Bergman	119 Starlight Avenue	98108	Seattle	WA	B2	
12	172	Paul	Zane	3 Columbus Street	98102	Bellevue	WA	A1	
13	173	Kyle	Sikorski	231 Ventura Road	98108	Seattle	WA	B1	
14									

☞ **Make row 1 bold $\mathscr{G}^{63}$**

☞ **Align the text in column H to the right $\mathscr{G}^{62}$**

☞ **Make the columns wider or narrower $\mathscr{G}^2$**

☞ **Use the *fill handle* to fill in the range of numbers $\mathscr{G}^{25}$**

After all this typing it is a good idea to save your membership list, before you continue.

☞ **Save the workbook and call it *club* ✂⁶**

5.2 Sorting

The members have been entered according to their membership number, which is fine, but finding a member would be easier if the list had been sorted by last name, in alphabetical order. This is how you sort a list in alphabetical order:

👉 **Click a last name**

You will find the sort & filter function on the ribbon of the HOME tab:

👉 **Click Filter ▾**

👉 **Click Sort A to Z**

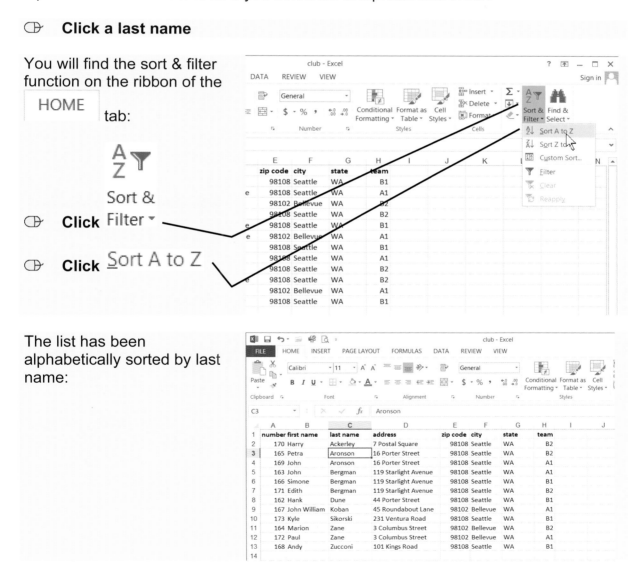

The list has been alphabetically sorted by last name:

Please note:

The list has not just been sorted by last name, but the data on the rows that go with these names, have been sorted too. Each last name still matches the correct address, team, etc.

Please note: this will not work if there are any blank columns inserted between the data columns of this list.

Click a city

Sort &

Click Filter ▾

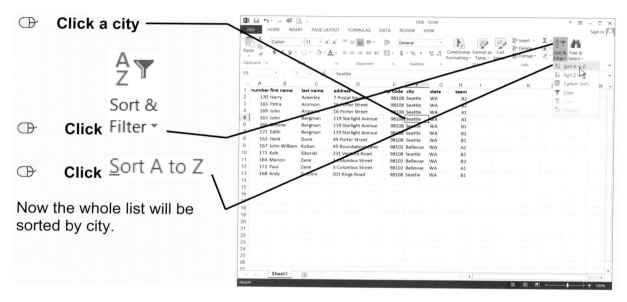

Click Sort A to Z

Now the whole list will be sorted by city.

In this way you can quickly sort your list according to the order you need.

 Please note:

In order to correctly sort the data, you need to select a single cell in the column you want to use. If you have selected multiple cells, only these cells will be sorted. And the corresponding data, such as first names, addresses and numbers, will not be included. The list will no longer be correct.

HELP! The sorting operation went wrong.

If the sorting operation went wrong, you can click the *Undo* button ↶ on the *Quick Access* toolbar.

Tip

Sorting in reverse order

Up till now you have sorted the data in ascending order. That is to say, from low (at the top of the column) to high (at the bottom of the column). This is the most frequently used method of sorting.

By clicking Filter ▾, S̲ort Z to A on the ribbon of the HOME tab, you can also sort the data in descending order. From high (at the top of the column) to low (at the bottom of the column. You can use this option to keep track of scores (the person with the most points wins the game), or lists of turnovers (the customer with the largest turnover will be at the top of the list).

5.3 Multiple Level Sorting

If there are multiple persons with the same last name, it is practical to sort these persons by their first name too. This way, *John Aronson* will come first, before *Petra Aronson*. You can achieve this by sorting the list twice. You start with the least important sorting order, that is, the first name:

☞ **Sort the list by first name** 🦶⁴⁶

Andy is at the top:

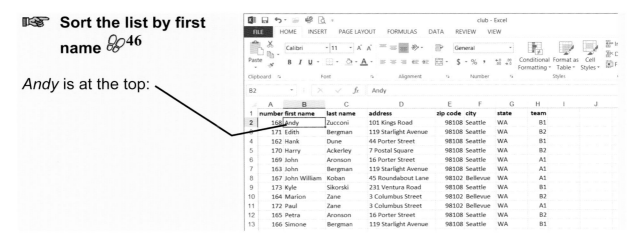

☞ **Sort the list by last name** ✍️46

Now the list has been sorted by last name:

In the second instance, persons who have the same last name have been sorted by their first name:

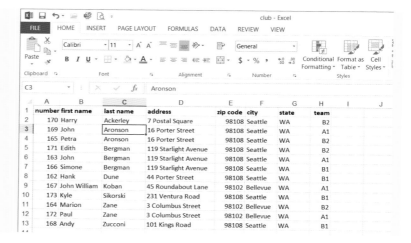

Just to be on the safe side, you are going to save the changes in the *club* workbook:

☞ **Save the workbook** ✍️7

It is wise to save your work at regular intervals, even if you are just working in *Excel* for a short while. After you have saved the file you can continue working.

5.4 Filtering

If you do not want to see all the data, but only a specific category, you can *filter* (select) the data you want to see. This function is called the *Filter*. This is particularly helpful if you have very long lists, as unnecessary information will not be displayed.

⌖ **Click the members' list**

⌖ **Click** Filter ▾

⌖ **Click** Filter

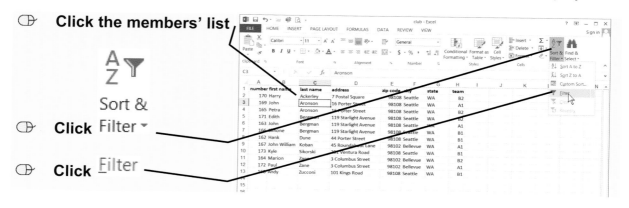

You will see drop-down menus appear next to the titles in row 1 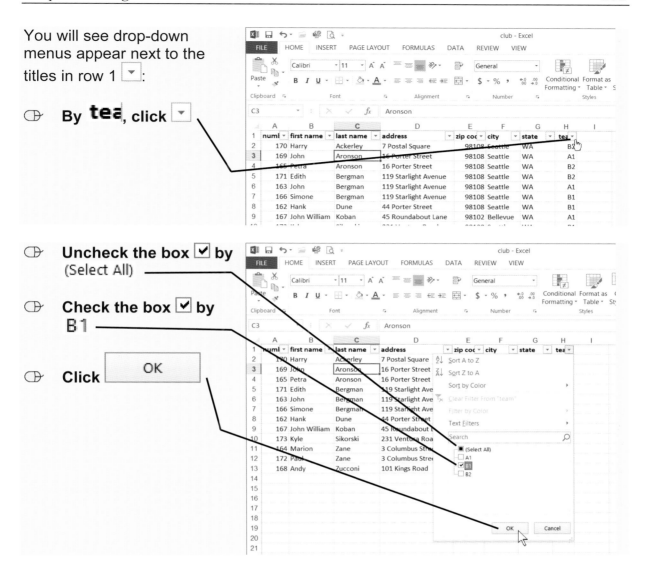:

By **tea**, click

Uncheck the box ☑ by
(Select All)

Check the box ☑ by
B1

Click **OK**

Now only the members of team B1 will be visible:

The row numbers for the filtered members have turned blue:

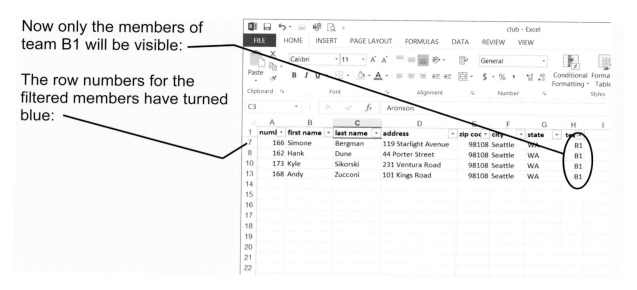

The blue row numbers indicate that you are no longer looking at the whole list, but just a part of it. And the symbol on the button by **tea** has changed as well. This indicates that the filter is set on this title.

You can display the whole file again with (Select All):

☞ **By tea, click** ▾

☞ **Check the box** ☑ **by** (Select All)

☞ **Click** OK

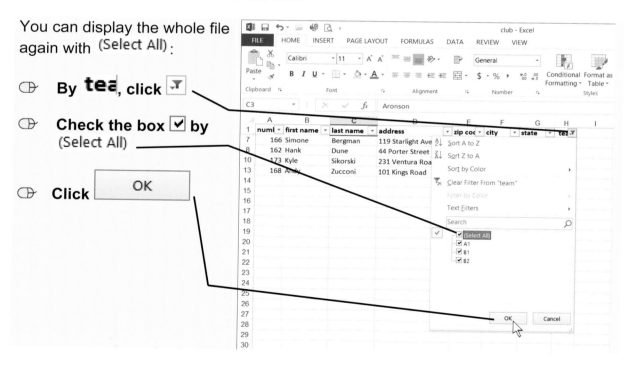

Tip

Searching

You can also use the search box to filter specific data. This is how you do it:

In the search box, type: `B1`

Click OK

You will only see the members of team B1.

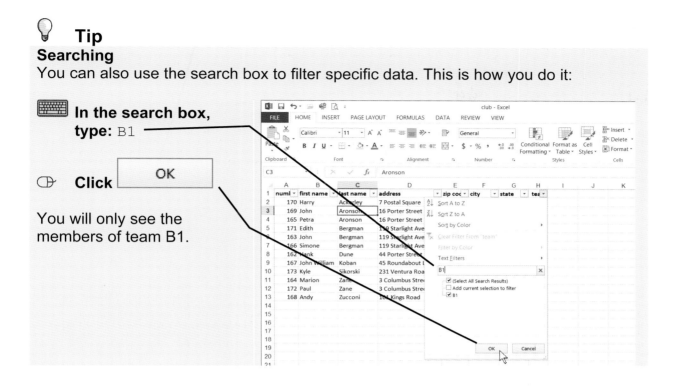

5.5 Custom Filters

You can also enter other conditions to set the filter. For example, you can filter all the new members with a membership number higher than 168:

By numl, click ▼

Click Number Filters

Click Greater Than...

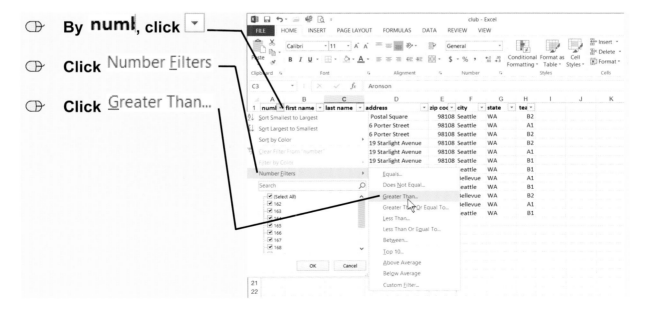

Enter the number:

⌨ **Type:** 168

⊕ **Click** OK

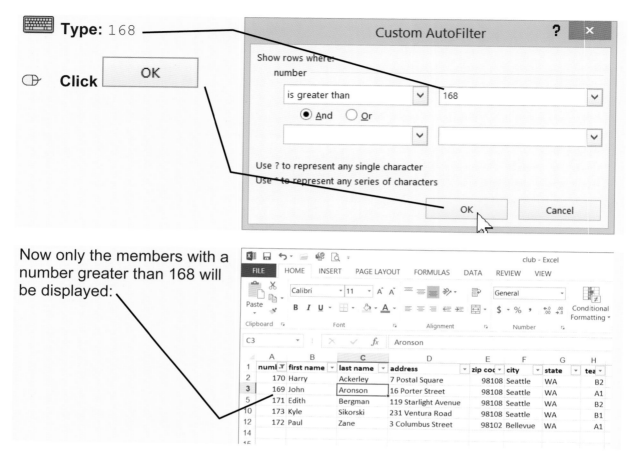

Now only the members with a number greater than 168 will be displayed:

Of course, you can sort these members by their numbers again:

⊕ **Click column A**

⊕ **Click** Sort & Filter ▾ , Sort Smallest to Largest

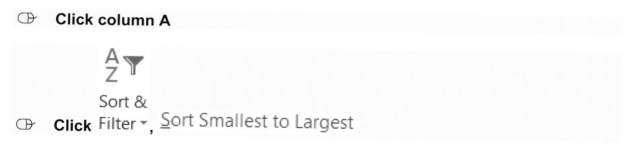

This way, it is easier to check if all the members actually have a number greater than 168:

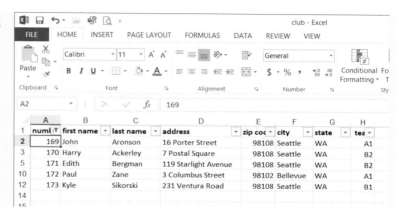

Now you can remove the filter:

👉 **By numr, click** 🔽

👉 **Check the box** ☑ **by** (Select All)

👉 **Click** ⬚ OK ⬚

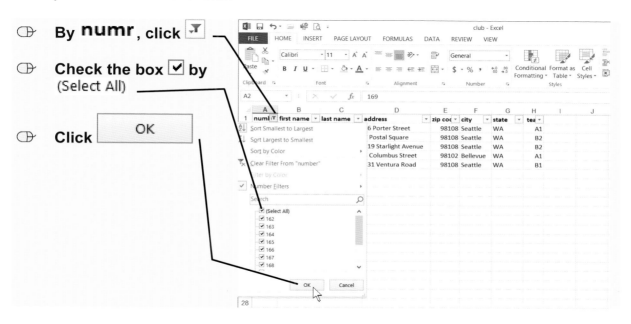

Now the members' list is complete again. You can remove the filter buttons:

👉 **Click** Sort & Filter ▾, Filter

5.6 Mailing with Word

You can use the members' list you have just created in *Excel* to make a *mailing*. A mailing is a personalized letter that you send to all of the members. You cannot do this in *Excel*, but you can use the data from *Excel* to create a mailing in the text editing program *Word 2013* or *Word 2010*.

 HELP! I do not have Word.
If you do not have *Word 2013* or *Word 2010* installed on your computer, you can just read through this section.

In *Windows 8* you open *Word* from the Start screen:

⊕ **Click**   **or**

In *Windows 7* or *Vista* you can open the *Word 2013* or *Word 2010* using the Start button:

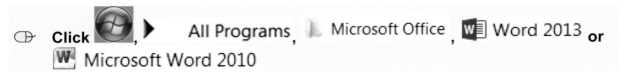

⊕ **Click** ⬤ , ▶ **All Programs** , Microsoft Office , W Word 2013 **or** W Microsoft Word 2010

☞ **If necessary, open a new document** ∂∂72

You will see the *Word 2013* or *2010* window. All the commands needed to create a mailing are grouped on the ribbon on the MAILINGS tab. You are going to start on the left-hand side of the tab, and end on the far right-hand side. The first operations are about selecting address information.

Click the MAILINGS **tab**

Click Start Mail Merge ▾

Click Directory

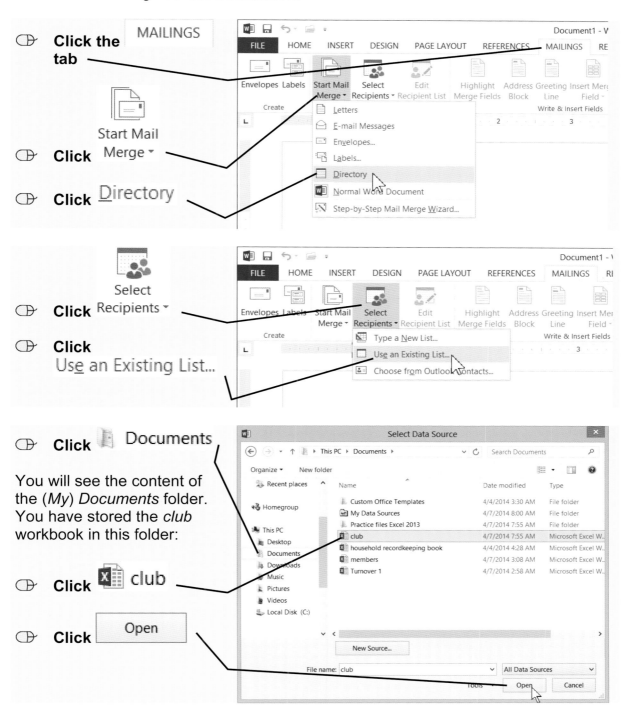

Click Select Recipients ▾

Click Use an Existing List...

Click Documents

You will see the content of the (*My*) *Documents* folder. You have stored the *club* workbook in this folder:

Click club

Click Open

You do not need to change anything in this window. This is because the members' list has been entered on *Sheet1* of the workbook:

 **Click** [OK]

Now the *club* workbook has been linked to the *Word* document. You will not see anything on your screen. You are going to check whether you want to use all the addresses in the workbook for your mailing:

 **Click** Recipient List

In the next window you will see your club's member list. Each checkmark ☑ in the row indicates that this address will be included in the mailing. By unchecking the box ☑ you can remove an address from the *Mail Merge Recipients* list. In this example you will be using all the addresses, so you do not need to change anything:

 **Click** [OK]

In this document you can indicate where you want to place the address information. This is done by inserting merge fields:

 **By** Insert Merge Field ▼ **, click** ⊞

In this window you will see a list of the fields present in your *club* workbook. These are identical to the column headings in your club's member list. You can indicate which fields need to be used in the mailing. You can start with the first name:

☞ **Click** first name

At the bottom of the window:

☞ **Click**

> Insert

☞ **Click**

> Close

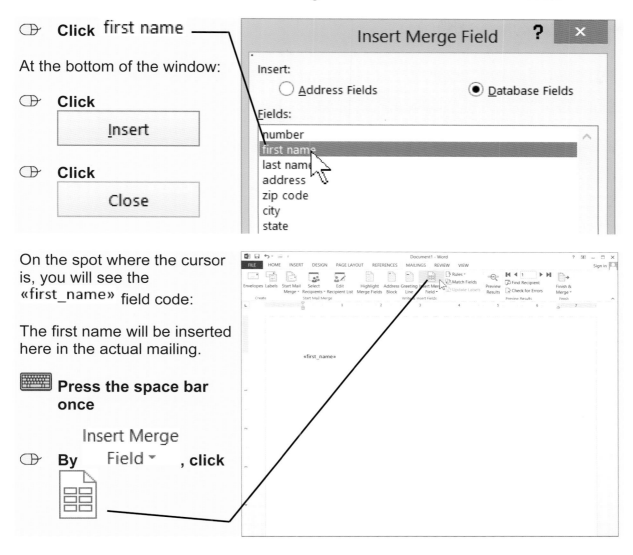

On the spot where the cursor is, you will see the «first_name» field code:

The first name will be inserted here in the actual mailing.

⌨ **Press the space bar once**

☞ **By** Insert Merge Field ▾ **, click**

Now you can insert the *last name* field:

☞ **Insert the *last name* field** 👀[52]

The address should go on the next line:

⌨ **Press** Enter

☞ **By** Insert Merge Field ▾ , **click**

You can insert the *address* field:

☞ **Insert the *address* field** 🦶52

On the next line you can insert the *city*, *state* and *zip code* field codes.

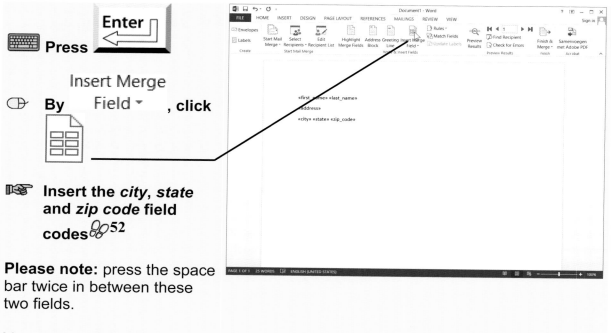

⌨ **Press** Enter ⏎

☞ **By** Insert Merge Field ▾ , **click**

☞ **Insert the *city*, *state* and *zip code* field codes** 🦶52

Please note: press the space bar twice in between these two fields.

Your letter will look like this:

💡 **Tip**

Insert the merge fields all at once

Instead of typing a blank space, or pressing Enter ⏎ and opening the *Insert Merge Field* window after every field you have inserted, you can also insert all the fields at once. All the fields will be put on a single line. Then you can type the necessary blank spaces between the fields or move a field to the next line.

You can type your letter below the fields you have inserted. After the beginning of the letter (Dear) you add the «first_name» merge field again. After the word 'team' in the text, you insert the «team» merge field.

Type the text of the letter and insert the merge fields 🦶52

Simultaneously press

Ctrl and Enter ↵

«first_name» «last_name»

«address»

«city» «state» «zip_code»

Dear «first_name»,

For the upcoming playing season you have been assigned to team «team».

Kind regards,

The Team Committee

You can take a look at the results:

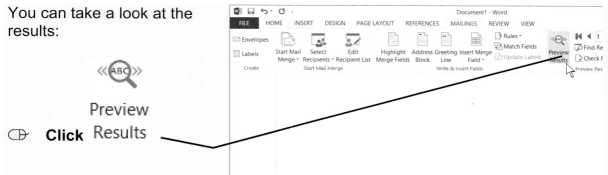

«ABC»

Preview
☞ **Click** Results

☞ **If necessary, drag the scroll bar upwards**

You will see an example of the letter, where the data from the *club* workbook has already been entered:

You can also look at a preview of the letters for the other recipients:

☞ **Click** ▶

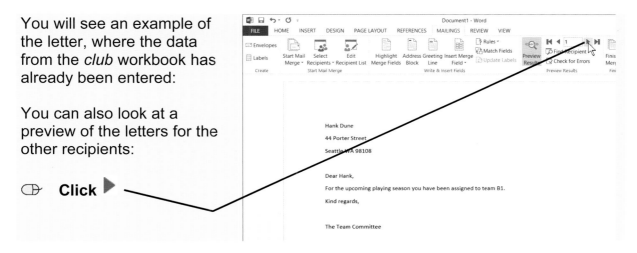

Hank Dune

44 Porter Street

Seattle WA 98108

Dear Hank,

For the upcoming playing season you have been assigned to team B1.

Kind regards,

The Team Committee

Tip

Errors

Did you notice any small errors in your letter? Something misspelled, for instance, or perhaps you have forgotten to insert a blank space in one of the address fields? You can still go back to the previous step:

 **Click** Preview Results

Now you can edit the text and correct the mistakes.

If you are satisfied with the results, you can go on with the last step. In this step you will actually be merging this document with the addresses from the *Excel* file.

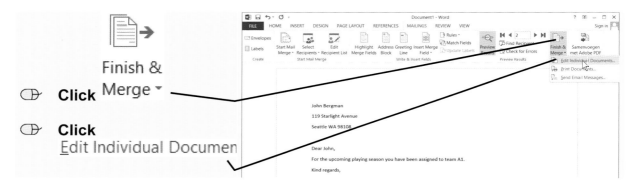

Click Finish & Merge ▾

Click Edit Individual Documen

In the *Merge to New Document* window:

Click [OK]

All the merged letters will be displayed in a single document. Each letter is placed on a separate page:

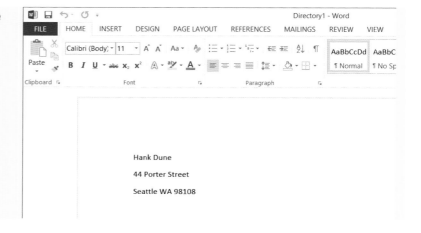

Afterwards, you can edit the merged document, print it, or save it, just like you always do in *Word*. With this step we have finished our little detour to the *Word* program, and now you will continue in *Excel* again.

☞ **Close *Word* without saving the documents** ${\wp}$59

Now you are back in *Excel* again.

☞ **Close the workbook and save the changes** ${\wp}$17

In this chapter you have learned how to create an address list, and how to sort and filter the data. You have also linked this address list to a *Word* document. To help retain the information that was discussed, you can repeat some of these tasks in the following exercises.

5.7 Exercises

Have you forgotten how to do something? Use the number beside the footsteps to look it up in appendix *B How Do I Do That Again?* at the end of this book.

 Please note:

In these exercises you are going to work with a worksheet that contains various data about automobiles. If you do not want to enter all the data yourself, you can use the *car* workbook from the practice files folder. If you have not copied this folder to your computer, you can read how to do that in *Appendix A Downloading the Practice Files*.

Exercise 1: Sorting

☞ Open a new workbook. $\wp\wp 12$

☞ Enter the following data in the worksheet:

	A	B	C	D	E
1	license plate	make	build date	driver	mileage
2	ACG8095	Ford	2002	Hank	3100
3	GAS8368	Chevrolet	1996	John	131000
4	CKL7689	Chevrolet	2000	Ingrid	36500
5	HGF4381	Nissan	2002	Peter	7500
6	BDH9034	Chevrolet	2000	Marion	101000
7	ZGH6127	Nissan	2001	Kyle	58200
8	DZV6439	Ford	1995	Harry	166000
9					

☞ Save the list and call it *car*. $\wp\wp 6$

☞ Sort the list in alphabetical order by the drivers' names. $\wp\wp 46$

☞ Sort the list by the license plate number. $\wp\wp 46$

☞ Undo the last sorting operation. $\wp\wp 16$

☞ Sort the list in descending order by the build date (this means the newest car will appear at the top of the list). $\wp\wp 47$

Exercise 2: Filtering

☞ Enable the *Filter* function. ↝**48**

☞ Set the filter to display only the Chevrolets. ↝**49**

☞ Display the full list again. ↝**50**

☞ Use a custom filter to only display the cars with a build date older than 2000. ↝**51**

☞ Display the full list again. ↝**50**

Exercise 3: Top 10

Among the filter buttons you will also find a *Top 10* option. With this option you can filter the highest or lowest values from the list. You can select the number of values that is displayed and make a list of ten, three, or even fifteen values, or any other number you would like to display.

☞ Make sure the *Filter* function is enabled. ↝**48**

☞ Click the filter button by *mileage*.

☞ Click Number Filters , Top 10...

You will see the window called *Top 10 AutoFilter*:

☞ Click ▼ until you see number 3.

☞ Click | OK |

In this way, you can see the top three cars with the highest mileage.

☞ Display the full list again. ↝**50**

☞ Close *Excel* without saving the worksheet. ↝**8**

5.8 Background Information

Dictionary

Database	A database is a digitized archive. Its main feature is that the data is stored in such a way that it is optimized for being searched.
Field	A box in which a number or a word is inserted.
Field code	A temporary marker within a document, indicating the spot where information from your data source will be displayed.
Filter	A function in *Excel* with which you can display selected data. When you remove the filter, the full list of data is displayed again.
Mailing	Merging data from a data source with a document, in order to print a series of documents that each have their own characteristics. A mailing is used to publish documents that are custom-made for several persons, or for automatically adding addresses to envelopes, labels, postcards, leaflets, newsletters, and other types of documents.
Query	A command to get the database to start a specific search, which will result in a series of records (data).
Sort	Arranging data according to a certain order. Sorting in ascending order results in a low-to-high values list, sorting in descending order results in a high-to-low values list.

Source: Microsoft Excel Help

Other programs
In this chapter you have seen a first example of how *Excel* and *Word* can work together. Both programs have some overlap regarding their functions and options, but each program has its own specific features.

You can also decide to keep a members' list in *Word*, but the sorting and filtering options are mainly focused on printing documents. And you will notice that *Word* will become slower when processing long lists, although this also depends on the speed and capacity of your computer.

On the other hand, *Word* is just the right program for creating mailing documents. Also, the filtering or sorting options will work better if they are used through the query function in *Word*.

If you need to use extremely long lists, usually called databases, then the *Access* program is the best choice within the *Office* family. Databases with thousands of records can be sorted or filtered within seconds. *Access* can be used together with the mailing options in *Word* as well.

Sorting by date
Excel sorts data by numerical or alphanumerical order, and checks the cells that contain the data to determine whether the data are (alpha)numerical. Normally, this would cause when sorting dates. If you just look at the numbers, this would be a correct ascending order:
01/30/2015
06/21/2016
12/01/2015

But when you realize these are dates, you would rather like to sort the list in this ascending order:
01/30/2015
12/01/2015
06/21/2016

Excel can display the list of dates as in the second example only if you enter the data in the correct numeric format. You can specify the correct numeric format when you enter a date in a cell. You do this by first clicking the cell, then clicking the *Number Format* group by the *Home* tab. Then you click *Date* and select the type of date format you want to use.

5.9 Tips

 Tip

Select cells to sort
Take good care not to select multiple cells, rows, or columns when you want to sort data. If you have done this by accident, only the selected area will be sorted, and the sorted data will only move along within this selection. As a result, the name may no longer match the address.

 Tip

Apply multiple filters
You can apply other filters after you have already applied a certain filter to view part of a list. For example, first you can filter all the members in your members' list who live in Seattle, and then you can filter those who play in team A1. Both the filter button of the *city* city ⧨ and that of the *team* tea ⧨ will get a different symbol. It can be very useful to filter on multiple levels, especially with large databases.

6. Estimates and Budgets

Preparing an estimate and allocating budgets for a new year, a new product, or a new department is always a somewhat uncertain activity. *Excel* can help you gain some insight into the uncertain factors that play a role when preparing an estimate.

Based on figures from past experiences and expectations, you can try to appraise the figures for your new estimate in the best possible way. This is also the case when you need to allocate budgets for company departments or activities.

In this chapter, for demonstration purposes, you will be creating a simple estimate for a club. You do not need to create your own estimates in exactly the same way. Each estimate will be different, depending on the goal or the organization for which it is created. By working through this chapter you will learn some useful calculations that may come in handy when you need to prepare your own estimates and budgets.

In this chapter you will learn how to:

- create a budget model;
- compare annual figures;
- delete cells;
- calculate increases in percentage;
- use absolute cell references;
- set the notation for thousands;
- adapt forecasts;
- use the budget as a policy model;
- use *Conditional formatting*;
- copy formatting characteristics;
- present the budget in the form of a chart;
- use the *Goal seek* function.

6.1 Creating a Budget Model

You are going to create a worksheet with a budget model.

☞ **Open *Excel* ⅋⁹**

☞ **If necessary, open a new workbook ⅋¹²**

➥ **Please note:**

In this chapter you are going to use a worksheet with a budget. If you do not want to enter all the data yourself, you can use the *Budget* worksheet from the practice files folder. In *Appendix A Downloading the Practice Files* you can read how to copy the practice files to your computer's hard disk.

⌨ **Enter the following data in the worksheet**

	A	B	C	D	E
1		actual	estimate	%	budg.2013
2		2011	2012	increase	5%
3	Rent	2400	2500		
4	Maintenance	850	800		
5	Energy	1300	1450		
6	Coaches	2000	2300		
7	Contribution to Federation	3200	3500		
8	Club magazine	400	420		
9	Additional expenses	200	225		
10	*Expenses*				
11					
12	Fees	8000	8400		
13	Activities	1500	1600		
14	Sponsors	2800	3000		
15	*Revenue*				
16					
17	Surplus/deficit				

☞ **Save the worksheet and call it *Budget* ⅋⁶**

Now the fixed data have been entered, and you can let *Excel* execute the calculations. First, you are going to compute the total expenses and total revenue:

☞ **Select cells B3 up to B9** 🐾**10**

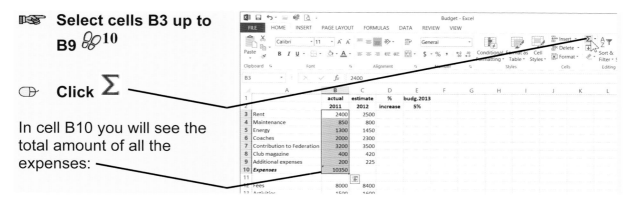

☞ **Click Σ**

In cell B10 you will see the total amount of all the expenses:

The formula in cell B10 also applies to column C10. So, you can copy this formula to cell C10 (expenses in the 2012 estimate).

☞ **Click cell B10**

☞ **Drag the handle to cell C10**

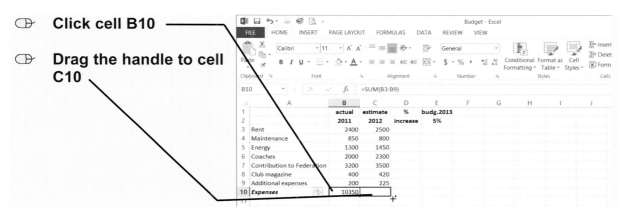

The total expenses for the 2012 estimate will be calculated. Calculating the total revenue is done in the same way:

☞ **Use *Sum* to calculate the total of cells B12 up to B14** 🐾**5**

The total amount in revenues is calculated. You can use the same calculation for the 2012 estimate, in cell C15:

☞ **Click cell B15**

☞ **Copy the formula to cell C15** 🐾**4**

The revenues for 2012 will be calculated and displayed in cell C15 (13000). You can calculate the surplus or deficit with a mathematical formula:

In cell B17, type:
=B15-B10

Press

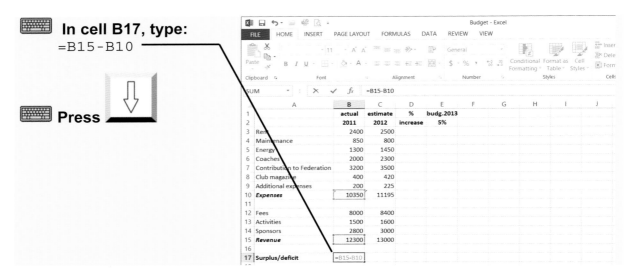

You can copy this formula to cell C17, and also use it for the 2012 estimate:

☞ **Click cell B17**

☞ **Copy the formula to cell C17** &&4

6.2 Comparing Annual Figures

Usually, the estimate is partly based on past trends. That is why it is useful to compare the 2011 figures to the 2012 estimate. As soon as the final figures for 2011 are available, you can base your calculations on these figures.

In cell D3, type:
=C3/B3

Press

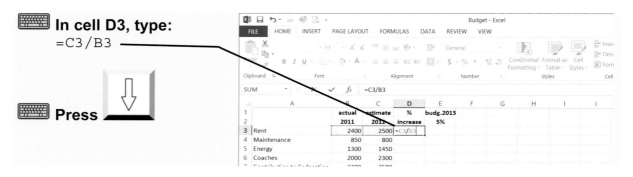

The answer is 1.041667, which reflects the relationship between both figures. In itself, this is correct, but it is easier if the increase is directly displayed as a percentage:

☞ **Click cell D3**

You can find the percentage calculation on the ribbon of the ⬚ HOME ⬚ tab:

☞ **Click** %

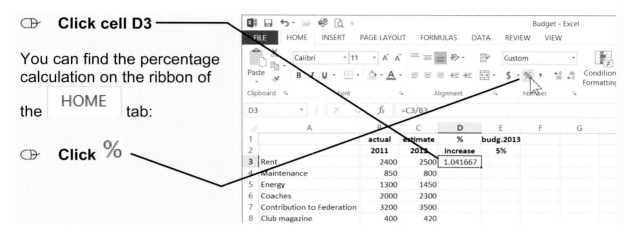

Now you have a percentage, but this is not yet the percentage in increase. To obtain this percentage you will need to subtract 100% of the result:

☞ **Click the *Formula Bar*, beside** =C3/B3

⌨ **Type:** -100%

In the *Formula Bar* you see =C3/B3-100%.

⌨ **Press** ⏎ **Enter**

In cell D3 you will see: 4%:

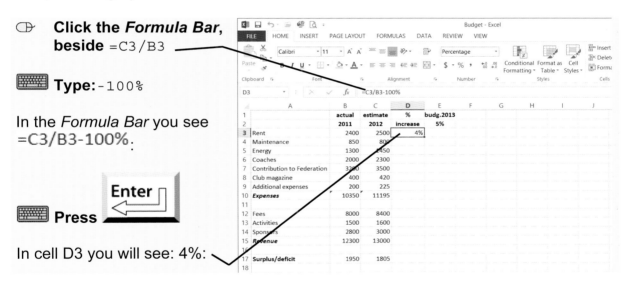

You can copy this formula for the whole column:

☞ **Copy the formula to cells D4 through D17** ✂️**4**

The rate of increase has been calculated for the entire column:

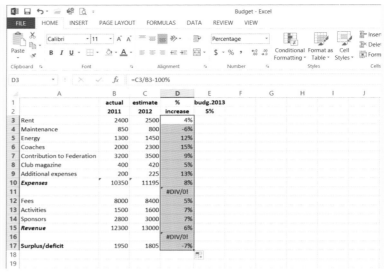

6.3 Deleting Cells

Cells D11 and D16 cannot be calculated. *Excel* will indicate this by displaying a warning: #DIV/0! . It is better to delete these cells:

Click cell D11

Press Delete

Delete cell D16 ✂️ 56

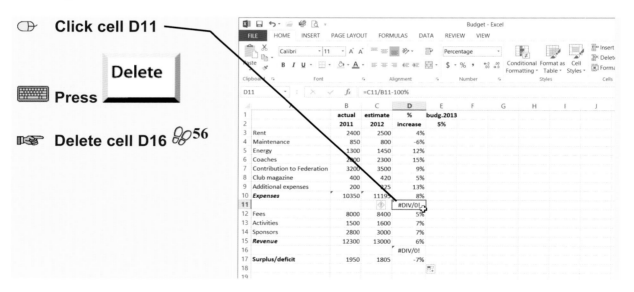

 HELP! I have deleted the wrong cells.

If you have deleted the wrong cells, just click ↶ on the *Quick Access* toolbar.

Delete the right cells ✂️ 56

6.4 Rise and Fall of Percentages

For the 2013 estimate you are going to take the 2012 estimate as a starting point, with a 5% increase of all the figures:

This percentage is displayed at the top of the column, in cell E2:

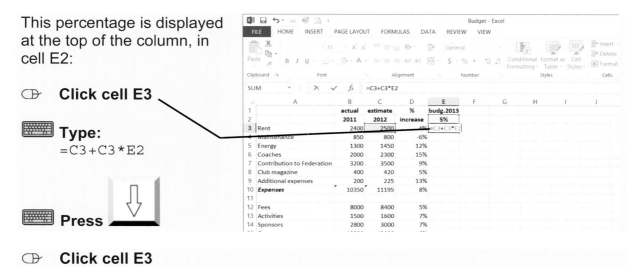

☞ **Click cell E3**

⌨ **Type:**
=C3+C3*E2

⌨ **Press** ⬇

☞ **Click cell E3**

☞ **Copy the formula to cells E4 through E17** ✂️⁴

✖ HELP! I see strange numbers.

After you have copied the formula, column E may contain some strange numbers or characters ### (instead of long numbers). This occurs because *Excel* has adapted the copied formula. In this example the adjustment of the formula should not have been applied to all the cells. You can read how to change this a bit further on in this chapter.

6.5 Absolute cells

When a formula is copied, it will be automatically adapted. If you copy a formula to the next row below the selected cell, *Excel* will automatically increase the row number with one. If you copy the formula =A1+B1 (on row 1) to a lower row, the formula on row 2 will be changed to: =A2+B2, on row 3: =A3+B3, etcetera.

This is correct in most cases, but not if you are working with a fixed value placed in a cell. In that case, the cell that contains the constant should not be changed when the formula is copied. In this estimate, the constant is placed in cell E2 (5%). This percentage needs to be used for each row.

If you want to make sure that the reference to the percentage 5% in cell E2 does not change when you copy this cell, you will need to make an absolute reference to this cell. An absolute cell reference will not change when you copy the cells or formulas.

 Click cell E3 ――――

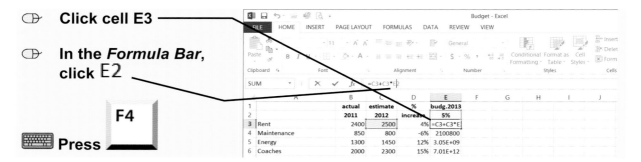

 In the *Formula Bar*, click E2 ――

F4

Press ▬▬

💡 Tip

Colored cells
If you click a formula in the *Formula Bar*, the cells will be colored. In this way it is easier to see which cell is indicated by the formula.

In the *Formula Bar*, E2 changes to E2. This means that *Excel* considers this cell to be an absolute cell:

Enter ⏎

Press ▬▬

$E means that column E is blocked, and $2 indicates that row 2 is blocked during the copy operation. In specific cases, it may be necessary to block only the column or only the row. You can do this by pressing F4 multiple times, instead of just once:

- pressing F4 once results in E2
- pressing F4 twice results in E$2
- pressing F4 three times results in $E2
- pressing F4 four times will disable the absolute function, and will result in E2 again

✖ HELP! The F4 key does not work.
Some keyboards require you to activate the row of F-keys first, by pressing an F-lock button, for example. Afterwards, the F-keys will work.

☞ **Read the manual that came with your keyboard**

☞ **Click cell E3**

🖝 **Copy the formula to cells E4 through E17** 👣⁴

Now you will see regular numbers in the *Excel* worksheet.

6.6 Thousands Notation

By using the decimal buttons ◄.0/.00 and .00/►.0 on the ribbon of the HOME tab, you can display numbers with two decimals, and you can use a comma as a thousands separator. Just try this with the columns that is selected:

☞ **Click** ⌐

Now the numbers on your screen will have a comma as a thousands separator, and two decimals.

If you do not want two decimals, you can delete them.

☞ **Click** .00/►.0 **twice**

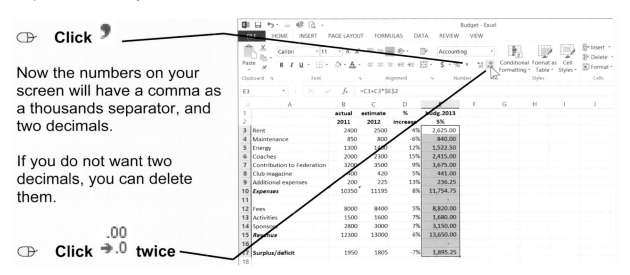

Columns B and C will also become easier to read if you insert a comma between the thousands:

🖝 **Select cells B3 through C17** 👣¹⁰

☞ **Click** ⌐

☞ **Click** .00/►.0 **twice**

Cells E11 and E16 still need to be cleared. They do not need any calculations. These cells have only been inserted to enhance the legibility. You can delete them:

☞ **Delete the content of cells E11 and E16** ℰℰ⁵⁶

6.7 Adjusting the Forecast

You want to adjust the forecast, based on the figures for 2011 compared to the estimate for 2012. For 2013 you are expecting an increase of 8%.

In cell E2, type: 8%

Press Enter

You will immediately see the consequences of this change for the surplus/deficit:

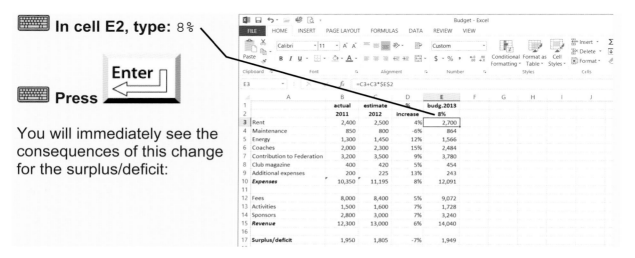

Some figures may be fixed. For instance, the fees have been estimated at a fixed amount, that is to say, 8,900:

In cell E12, type: 8900

Press ⬇

Does the surplus/deficit change?

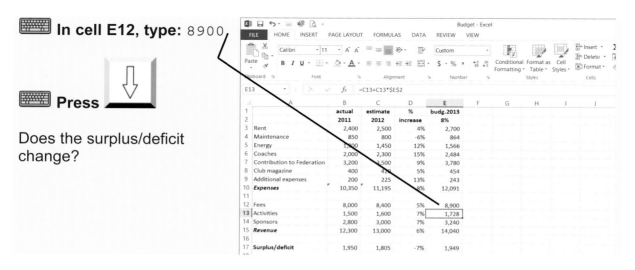

HELP! The surplus/deficit does not change.

Because you have increased all the amounts by a percentage, the intermediate calculations will use a percentage too. This will not be correct if you start changing some amounts manually. In that case the subtotals will need to be calculated again, based on the actual figures.

☞ **Delete the content of cell E10** ✂56

☞ **Select cells E3 through E9** ✂10

☞ **Click Σ**

In cell E10 you will see the new total amount that has been recalculated.

☞ **Delete the content of cell E15** ✂56

☞ **Use *Sum* to calculate the subtotal of cells E12 through E14** ✂5

Now cell E15 contains the new total. Finally, you need to calculate the surplus/deficit in cell E17 once again:

☞ **Click cell E17**

⌨ **Type:** =E15-E10

⌨ **Press** ⬇

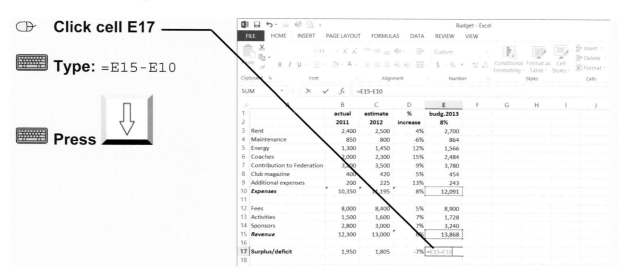

Now cell E17 contains the newly calculated surplus/deficit. The calculation model for the budget has been completed. This model will help you see the consequences of certain altered conditions in the future.

☞ **Save the worksheet before you continue** ✂7

6.8 Base Your Policy on the Budget

Since prospects are bound to change, you will need to alter the budget on a regular basis. In the previous section you have completed the budget and made sure that simple changes will automatically be applied in the correct way. For example, changes such as the percentage of increase, or changes in individual figures. Every time you change a figure, the budget will immediately show what the consequences are for the surplus or deficit. In this way, the budget becomes an instrument of economic policy for the club management or board. The board thinks an 8% increase is too much, and wants to limit the increase to 7%. Just try to change this:

In cell E2, type: 7

Press ⬇

All the amounts in the 2013 estimate will be calculated again, and the surplus will amount to 1,843:

If the number of members decreases, the fees will diminish as well. Try this change:

In cell E12, type: 8000

Press ⬇

Now the surplus will only be 943:

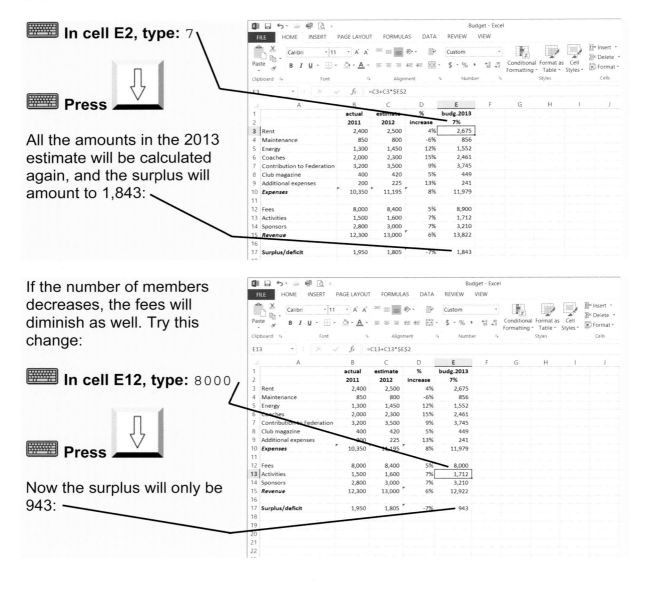

The energy costs appear to have risen a lot in 2012, so for 2013 the estimate is increased to 2000.

 In cell C5, type: 2000

Press ⬇

The surplus in 2012 will become 1,255, and for 2013 355:

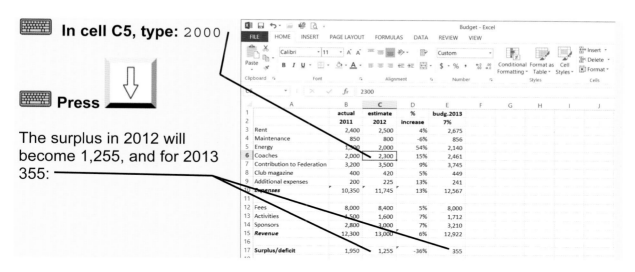

	A	B	C	D	E
1		actual	estimate	%	budg.2013
2		2011	2012	increase	7%
3	Rent	2,400	2,500	4%	2,675
4	Maintenance	850	800	-6%	856
5	Energy	1,300	2,000	54%	2,140
6	Coaches	2,000	2,300	15%	2,461
7	Contribution to Federation	3,200	3,500	9%	3,745
8	Club magazine	400	420	5%	449
9	Additional expenses	200	225	13%	241
10	Expenses	10,350	11,745	13%	12,567
11					
12	Fees	8,000	8,400	5%	8,000
13	Activities	1,500	1,600	7%	1,712
14	Sponsors	2,800	3,000	7%	3,210
15	Revenue	12,300	13,000	6%	12,922
16					
17	Surplus/deficit	1,950	1,255	-36%	355

You can see that the adjustments for 2012 will immediately be passed on to the 2013 estimate as well.

This will not always be intended, since it may concern lucky breaks or misfortunes that occur one time only. If that happens, you will need to correct the amount in the 2013 estimate manually.

➡ Please note:

If you have overwritten a figure in the 2012 estimate, the formula in this cell will have disappeared. New changes in the budget, or changes in the percentage of increase will no longer influence these figures. If you wish, you can copy the formula to the relevant cells again.

♀ Tip
Save the original budget
If you change any figures or percentages, it is recommended to save these budgets separately. If you want to revert to a previous state of affairs later on, you will still have these figures available in the budgets saved on your computer. If you want to save a workbook as a separate file with a different name, you can use *Save as*:

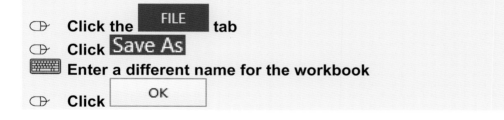

☞ **Click the** FILE **tab**

☞ **Click** Save As

 Enter a different name for the workbook

☞ **Click** OK

6.9 Conditional Formatting

The surplus is starting to approach the red figures. If a deficit should occur, it is important to be alerted right away. *Excel* can help you with this, by immediately coloring a deficit red, which makes it stand out more. You can do this with the *Conditional formatting* function on the ribbon of the HOME tab:

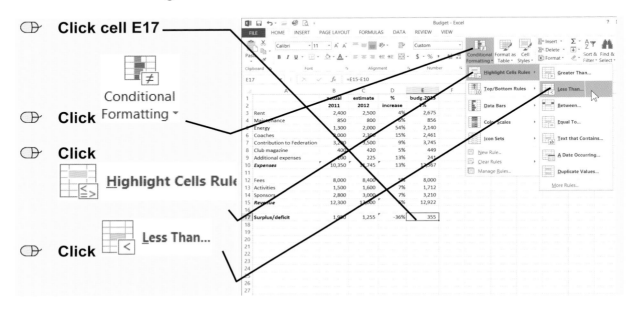

☞ **Click cell E17**

☞ **Click** Conditional Formatting ▾

☞ **Click** Highlight Cells Rule

☞ **Click** Less Than...

In the window that appears, you can enter the condition(s) for the formatting of the cell. In this example, you want to change the color of the amount as soon as a deficit occurs. This means that any number lower than zero will be displayed in red.

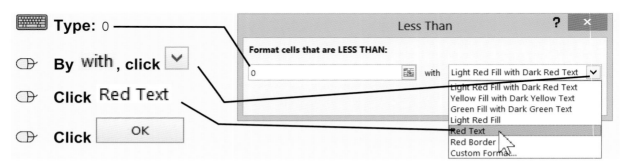

⌨ **Type:** 0

☞ **By** with **, click** ∨

☞ **Click** Red Text

☞ **Click** OK

From now on the amount will be colored red, as soon as a deficit occurs in the 2013 estimate:

If some sponsors withdraw their support, the amount for 2013 will be diminished. Let's say it is only 2600:

 in cell E14, type: 2600

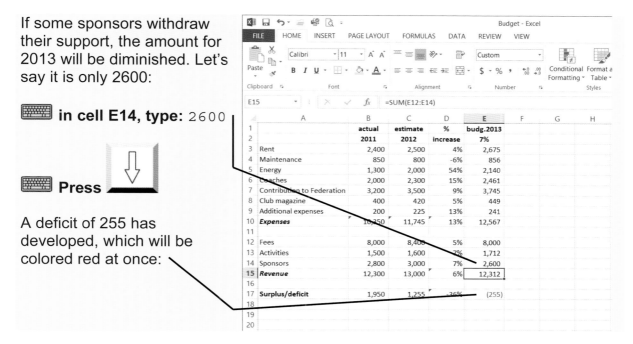

Press ⬇

A deficit of 255 has developed, which will be colored red at once:

	A	B	C	D	E	F	G	H
		actual	estimate	%	budg.2013			
1		2011	2012	increase	7%			
2								
3	Rent	2,400	2,500	4%	2,675			
4	Maintenance	850	800	-6%	856			
5	Energy	1,300	2,000	54%	2,140			
6	Coaches	2,000	2,300	15%	2,461			
7	Contribution to Federation	3,200	3,500	9%	3,745			
8	Club magazine	400	420	5%	449			
9	Additional expenses	200	225	13%	241			
10	*Expenses*	10,250	11,745	13%	12,567			
11								
12	Fees	8,000	8,400	5%	8,000			
13	Activities	1,500	1,600	7%	1,712			
14	Sponsors	2,800	3,000	7%	2,600			
15	*Revenue*	12,300	13,000	6%	12,312			
16								
17	Surplus/deficit	1,950	1,255	-36%	(255)			
18								
19								
20								

🖐 **Please note:**

The negative number 255 may still be displayed with two decimals. You can delete these decimals by pressing 🔘 twice.

6.10 Copying Formatting

The conditional formatting you have set for 2013 would also be useful for 2012 and 2011. To accomplish this, you can copy the formatting from the year 2013.

☞ **Click cell E17**

The button for copying the formatting can be found on the ribbon of the HOME tab:

☞ **Click**

The pointer turns into :

☞ **Click cell C17**

Now the conditional formatting has been set for this cell too.

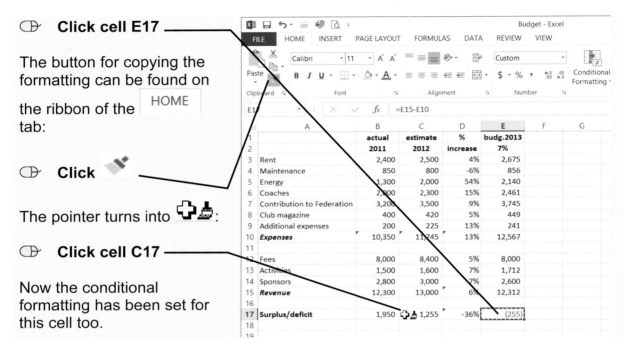

You can check this by changing the amount of the fees, for example:

⌨ **In cell C12, type:** 5000

⌨ **Press** ⬇

At once, the deficit will turn red:

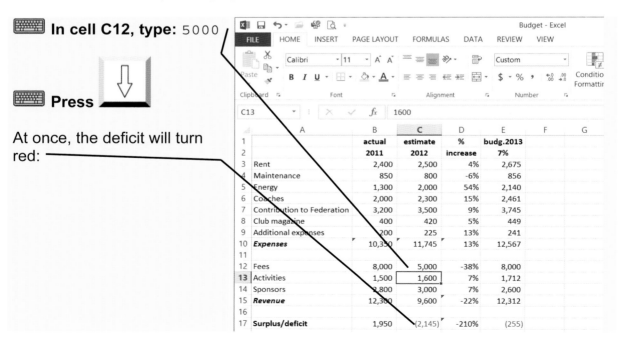

In the *Quick Access* toolbar:

☞ **Click**

The amount of the fees will return to 8400. You can do the same thing for the figures of 2011:

☞ **Click cell E17,** **, cell B17**

Now the conditional formatting has been set for this cell as well.

💡 **Tip**

Multiple conditions for Conditional formatting

Up till now you have set a single condition while using the *Conditional formatting* option. But this function allows you to set up to three conditions. After you have set the first condition:

☞ **Click the** HOME **tab**

☞ **Click** Conditional Formatting ▾ , **Highlight Cells Rules**

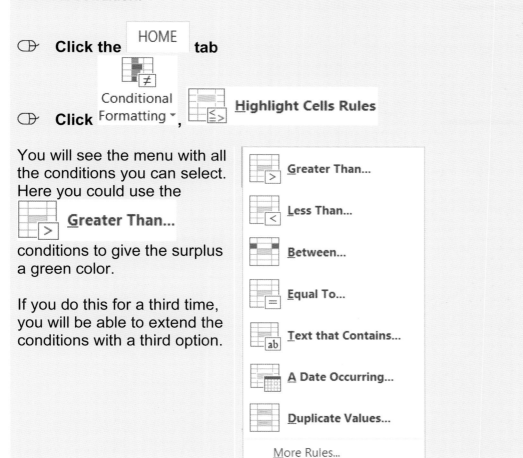

You will see the menu with all the conditions you can select. Here you could use the **Greater Than...** conditions to give the surplus a green color.

If you do this for a third time, you will be able to extend the conditions with a third option.

Greater Than...

Less Than...

Between...

Equal To...

Text that Contains...

A Date Occurring...

Duplicate Values...

More Rules...

You can save your work before continuing:

☞ **Save the workbook** ⚇⁷

6.11 View the Budget in a Chart

A budget that consists of numbers only, is not very suitable for presenting to a members' meeting. A diagram will make things easier to explain. In this case you are going to create a pie chart of the expenses, by using the numbers of the 2013 estimate.

☞ **Select cells A3 through A9** ⚇¹⁰

⌨ **Press** ⬛ **Ctrl** ⬛ **and keep it depressed**

☞ **Select cells E3 through E9** ⚇¹⁰

⌨ **Release** ⬛ **Ctrl** ⬛

You can insert a chart. First, you need to open the ⬚ INSERT ⬚ tab:

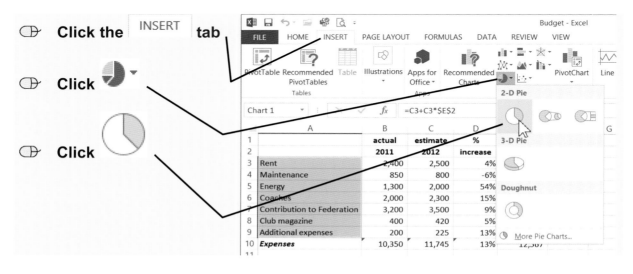

You will see a pie chart with the legend at the bottom:

Please note: In *Excel 2010*, the default setting shows the legend on the right-hand side of the pie chart.

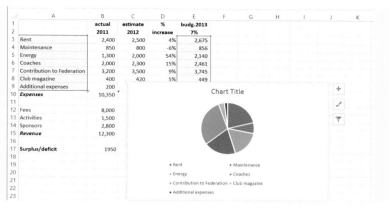

In *Excel 2013* you are going to place the legend at the right-hand side of the chart too:

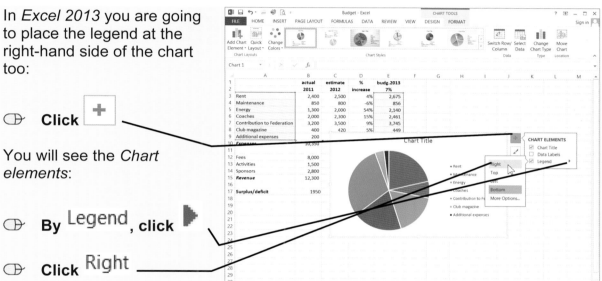

⊕ **Click** [+]

You will see the *Chart elements*:

⊕ **By** Legend **, click** ▶

⊕ **Click** Right

Now the legend is displayed at the right-hand side of the chart in *Excel 2013*.

 HELP! The chart has only one color.

If the chart has only a single color, the rows and columns may have been switched around. This will also affect a pie chart.

⊕ **Click the** DESIGN **tab**

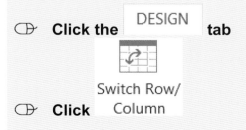

⊕ **Click** Switch Row/ Column

Now the pie chart will be correctly displayed.

By way of information you can display the amounts by the chart. In *Excel 2013*:

👆 **Click** ➕

👆 **By** Data Labels, **click** ▶️

👆 **Click** Outside End

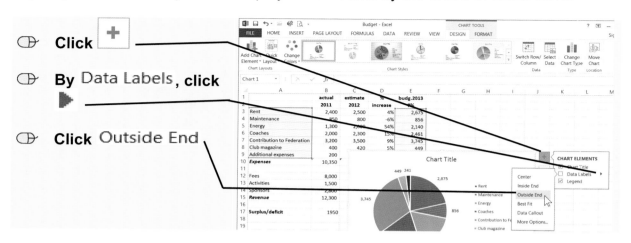

In *Excel 2010*:

👆 **Click the** Layout **tab**

👆 **Click** Data Labels ▾

👆 **Click**

Outside End
Display Data Labels outside the end of c

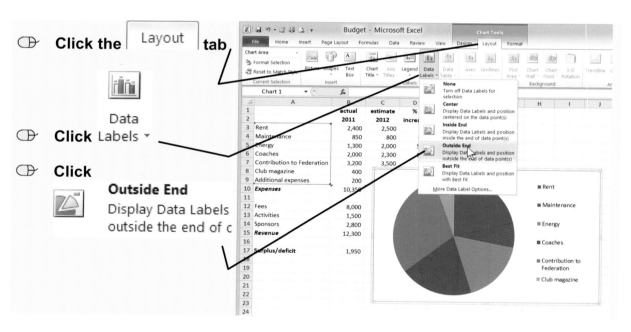

Now you can place the chart on a separate worksheet:

👉 **Move the chart to a separate sheet** ✂️**64**

The chart will be created:

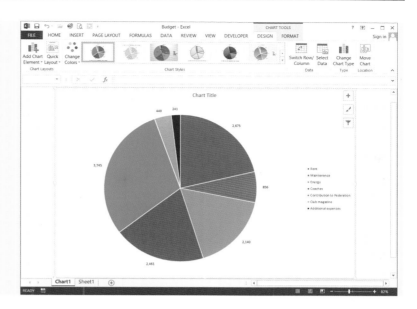

☞ **Close the workbook and save the changes** ✂ 17

In order to help you retain the information you have learned in this chapter, you can do the following exercises.

6.12 Exercises

Have you forgotten how to do something? Use the number beside the footsteps to look it up in appendix *B How Do I Do That Again?* at the end of this book.

Exercise 1: Absolute Cells

In this exercise you will be creating a small budget with one absolute value: the basic fee.

☞ If necessary, open a new workbook. ℘**12**

☞ Enter the following data in the worksheet:

	A	B	C	D	E
1	basic fee	100			
2					
3		number	% of fee	fee	total
4	junior members	60	60%		
5	seniors	95	100%		
6	veterans	30	80%		

☞ Enable the thousands separator for the *basic fee*. ℘**54**

☞ Calculate the fee for the *junior members* in cell D4 (*basic fee* multiplied by % of fee). ℘**3**

☞ Copy the formula from cell D4 to cells D5 and D6. ℘**4**

Why are the amounts for the fees wrong? Take a good look at the formulas.

☞ Undo the last operation. ℘**16**

☞ In the formula in cell D4, create an absolute reference to cell B1. ℘**53**

☞ Copy the formula from cell D4 to cells D5 and D6 once again. ℘**4**

Now the amounts should be correct.

☞ Calculate the total of the *junior members' fees* in cell E4 (number of *junior members* multiplied by the fee for the *junior members*). 🐾**3**

☞ Copy the formula from cell E4 to cells E5 and E6. 🐾**4**

☞ Check the amounts.

☞ Calculate the total amount of fees in cell E7, use *Sum*. 🐾**5**

☞ If necessary, widen column E. 🐾**2**

Exercise 2: Goal Seek

 Please note:

In order to be able to do this exercise you will need to have completed *Exercise 1: Absolute cells*.

In this exercise you will be learning how to use the *Goal Seek* function, which will help you achieve a specific result. The total amount of the fees in the worksheet of the previous exercise is 15500. Let's say that this amount needs to be at least 18000, in order to be able to pay for all the expenses. How high should the fee be for the various member categories? Just try to calculate this:

☞ Click cell E7.

☞ On the ribbon of the *Data* tab, click ⊞? What-If Analysis ▾ and in the menu that appears, click Goal Seek... .

The *Goal Seek* window appears:

☞ By To value:, type: 18000.

☞ By By changing cell:, type: B1.

☞ Click [OK] twice.

☞ You will see that the basic fee has been increased to 116.13, and that the amounts for each category have been adjusted:

	A	B	C	D	E	F
1	basic fee	116.13				
2						
3		number	% of fee	fee	total	
4	junior members	60	60%	69.68	4,180.65	
5	seniors	95	100%	116.13	11,032.26	
6	veterans	30	80%	92.90	2,787.10	
7					18,000.00	

☞ If necessary, set the thousands separator for the amounts. ⅍⅋54

☞ Save the workbook and call it *fees*. ⅍⅋6

☞ Close *Excel*. ⅍⅋11

6.13 Background Information

Dictionary

Absolute cell reference	Absolute cell references do not change when a formula is copied. A cell reference can be made absolute by inserting dollar signs before the column number and/or the row number. For example: A4. The two dollar signs indicate that both the row and the column are absolute.
Budget/estimate	A budget reflects the financial effects of decisions made or a strategy taken. Budgets and estimates help organizations that need to manage a certain cash flow, such as companies, governments and even clubs. The budget is a step-by-step balancing of wishes and possibilities. Estimates paint a picture of the financial expectations of an organization for the future.
Cell reference	A cell reference in a certain cell refers to another cell in a worksheet. *Excel* uses this to let you know where you can find the values or data that you want to use in a formula.
Conditional formatting	*Conditional formatting* will change the appearance of a cell, if a certain condition is met. If the condition is true, the cell will be formatted according to your settings. If the condition is false, the cell formatting will remain unchanged.
Forecast	A forecast is a prediction of the expected course of financial developments.
Goal seek	If you know which result you want to achieve with a formula, but if you do not know which cell values the formula needs to achieve this result, you can use the *Goal Seek* function.
Thousands separator/ decimal button	This function is used to display numbers in general. You can determine how many decimals are displayed, whether you want to use a thousands separator, and how you want to display negative numbers. When it concerns amounts, you can also display a currency symbol.

Source: Microsoft Excel Help

What-If-Analysis

After you have created a budget or some other type of calculation model, you can use this model to view various options. By changing specific values you can get an insight into what the consequences would be. Take a look at the following scenarios:

- The contribution to the federation increases by 5%: will the club be able to afford this or do the fees need to be raised?
- What will happen when the fees are raised by 20%, which has prompted twenty members to cancel their membership? With fewer members, the expenses of the coaches may decrease a bit but the revenues from various activities may diminish as well.

A spreadsheet is especially suited to provide answers in these 'what-if' situations. By changing a few figures you will immediately see the consequences. This way, the model can be an important tool for helping you make decisions.

Be sure to save your original model, before you start using it for this type of what-if analysis.

6.14 Tips

 Tip

Colored cells

In *section 6.9 Conditional Formatting* you have use the *Conditional Formatting* function to color an amount red, as soon as it became negative. *Excel* has many more options for coloring cells. For example, you can change the background color from white to another hue:

☞ **Click the**  **tab**

☞ **Click** Cell Styles ▾

You will see this menu, from which you can select a style:

There is another way of doing this:

☞ **Click the** HOME **tab**

☞ **Click** 🖃 Format ▾ , Format Cells…

You will see this window:

On the  tab you can select a background color for the cell:

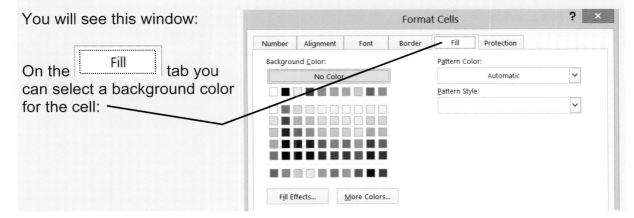

Tip

Enter numbers with decimals more quickly

If the figures in your spreadsheet are usually entered with decimals, you can set up *Excel* to automatically format all the numbers you enter as decimals. Then you can directly type 15 if you want to enter 15 cents, instead of 0.15. And for 1.25 you can type 125. The period will be automatically be inserted in the right place. This is how you set it up:

☞ **Open the *Excel Options* window** ✎**61**

⊕ **Click** Advanced

⊕ **Check the box** ☑ **by**
Automatically insert a dec

At the bottom of the window:

⊕ **Click** OK

⌨ **Type:** 25

⌨ **Press** Enter

⌨ **Type:** 1875

⌨ **Press** Enter

You will see 0.25 and 18.75:

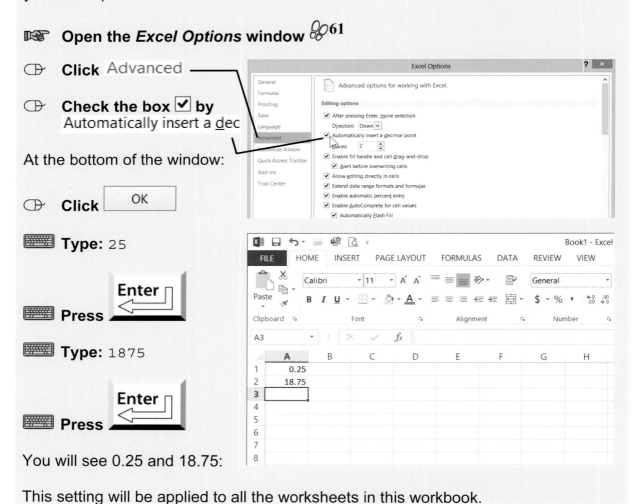

This setting will be applied to all the worksheets in this workbook.

7. Calculating with Time and the Search Function

Microsoft Excel has a large number of functions that can help you enter standard data a lot faster. A search function will save you time and energy, especially with data that has a relationship. For example: if you type a product number in an invoice, *Excel* can search for the description and the price of this product.

In this chapter you will learn how to use the search function. You will look for personnel data by entering a name. This not only saves time, but it can also prevent you from making typing errors. A search function may seem a bit complicated at first, but after you use it a few of times you will start to understand the terminology.

Furthermore, in this chapter you will learn how to calculate with hours and minutes. Since time notations are not displayed with decimals, calculating with time units is a bit different from standard calculations.

In this chapter you will learn how to:

- enter hours and minutes;
- calculate with time;
- name cells;
- create formulas with cell names;
- search for data within a table.

 Please note:

In order to execute the operations in this chapter, you will need to have copied the practice files to your computer. In *Appendix A Downloading the Practice Files* you can read how to download the practice files from the website accompanying this book and copy them to the (*My*) *Documents* folder.

7.1 Working with Time Units

You can use more than simple numbers in *Excel*, you can also work with time units. *Excel* can calculate in seconds, minutes, and hours. You can keep track of weekly working hours for example.

☞ **Open** *Excel* 𝄞⁹

☞ **Open the** *Time chart* **workbook** 𝄞²²

⊕ **If necessary, click** ┃ Enable Editing ┃

You will see this worksheet:

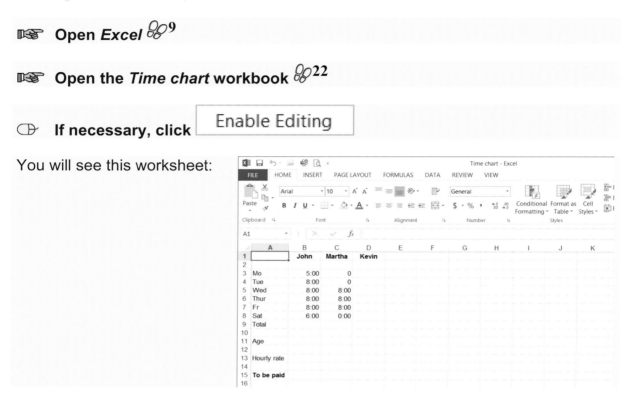

On this worksheet, a record is kept of all the working hours of the employees. The hours worked per worker have been entered in hours and minutes. The hours and minutes are separated by a colon ':'.

⊕ **Click cell D3**

⌨ **Type:** 4 : 3 0

This means 4 hours and 30 minutes, so 4½ hours.

⌨ **Press** [Enter]

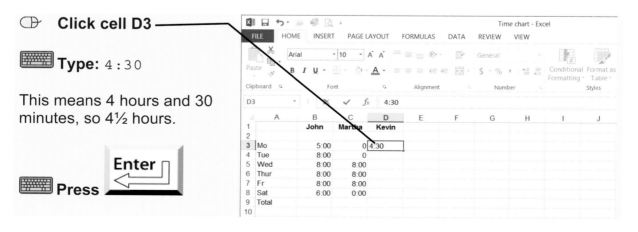

Since an hour only has 60 minutes, you cannot enter a number higher than 59, following the colon:

⌨ **In cell D4, type:** 2 : 80

Press Enter

You will see a number instead of the time format:

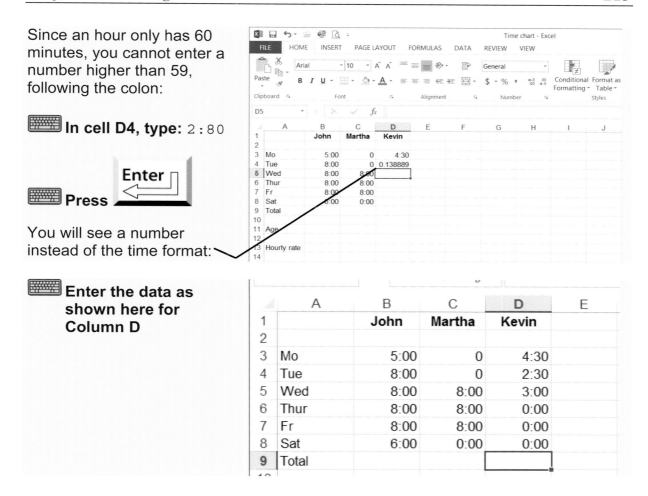

⌨ **Enter the data as shown here for Column D**

	A	B	C	D	E
1		**John**	**Martha**	**Kevin**	
2					
3	Mo	5:00	0	4:30	
4	Tue	8:00	0	2:30	
5	Wed	8:00	8:00	3:00	
6	Thur	8:00	8:00	0:00	
7	Fr	8:00	8:00	0:00	
8	Sat	6:00	0:00	0:00	
9	Total				

7.2 Calculating with Time

You can add up time units with the *Sum* function:

☞ **Calculate the total amount of time in cell D9 with *Sum* 🐾5**

The time units have been added up.

Copy this formula to columns B and C as well:

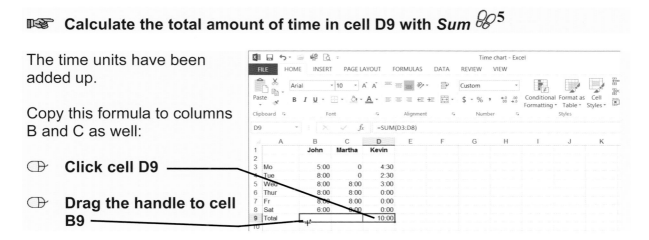

🖱 **Click cell D9**

🖱 **Drag the handle to cell B9**

The hours will be added up.
But the results appear to be
wrong.

Because *Excel* calculates
with time, 24 hours will be
counted as a single day, and
days are not displayed in
these cells.

You can see this in column C:

Column B would have to add
up to 43 hours. That is 1 day
of 24 hours plus 19 hours.

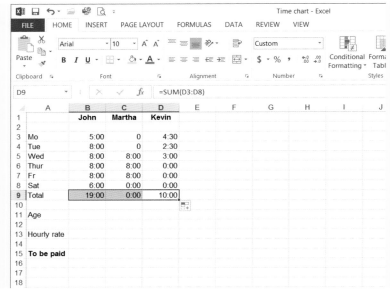

To display the actual number
of hours:

By
Custom ▼ ,
click ▼

Click
More Number Formats.

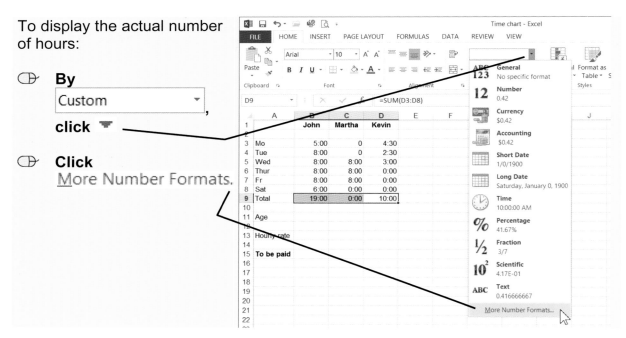

By **Type:** you will see the time format in hours and minutes **h:mm** :

⊖ **Click just before** h

⌨ **Type:** [

⌨ **Press** ⟹

⌨ **Type:**]

Now it says **[h]:mm** and the actual number of hours will be displayed.

⊖ **Click** OK

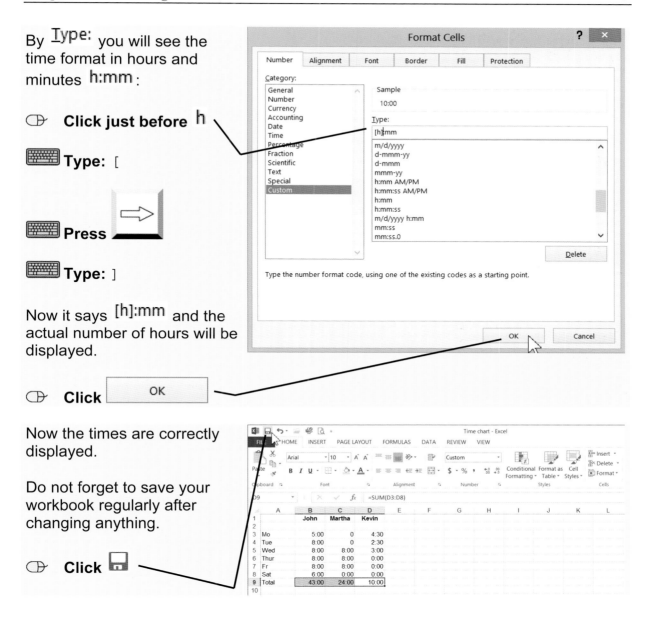

Now the times are correctly displayed.

Do not forget to save your workbook regularly after changing anything.

⊖ **Click** 💾

7.3 Cell Names

Formulas that contain the default cell labels are very difficult to read. This can be awkward when you want to trace errors in a formula, or if you want to change a formula. You can also use cell names in a formula, instead of cell labels. You can set the cell names for a single cell or for a selected group of cells:

Cells B9 up to D9 have been selected:

 Click the *Name Box*

⌨ **Type:** worked

⌨ **Press** Enter

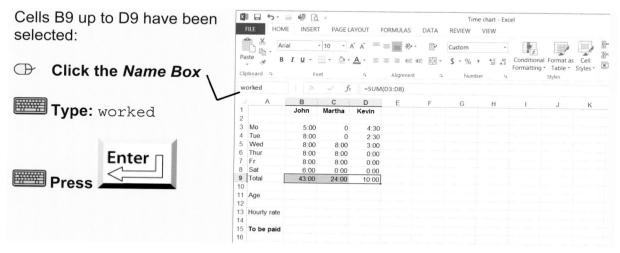

🔖 Please note:

You will see the name of a cell after you have selected this cell. If you have named a group of cells you will only see its name if you select the whole group.

☞ **Select cells B13 up to D13** 👣[10]

⌨ **In the *Name Box*, type:** wages

⌨ **Press** Enter

⌨ **In cell B13, type:** 6

⌨ **In cell C13, type:** 8

⌨ **In cell D13, type:** 5

⌨ **Press** Enter

You can use the names in the formula to calculate the amount that has to be paid:

In cell B15, type:
=worked*wages

Press **Enter**

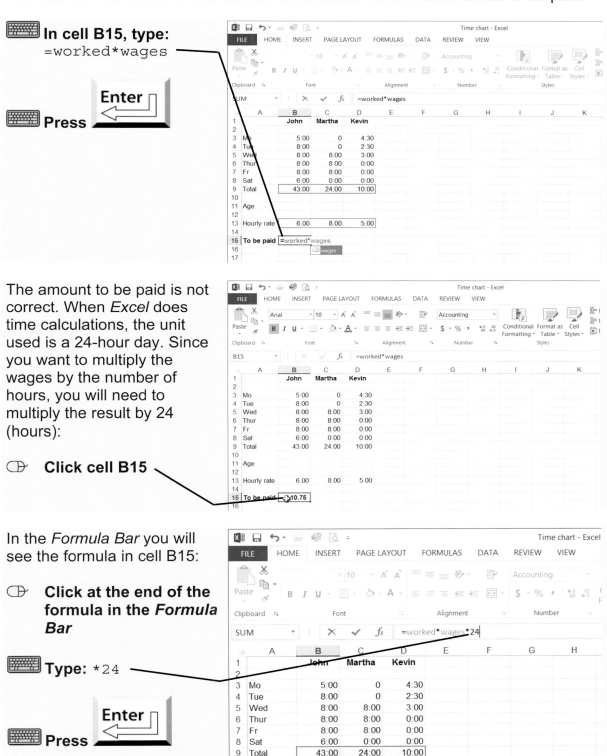

The amount to be paid is not correct. When *Excel* does time calculations, the unit used is a 24-hour day. Since you want to multiply the wages by the number of hours, you will need to multiply the result by 24 (hours):

Click cell B15

In the *Formula Bar* you will see the formula in cell B15:

Click at the end of the formula in the *Formula Bar*

Type: *24

Press **Enter**

The wages have been correctly calculated; 43 * 6 = 258:

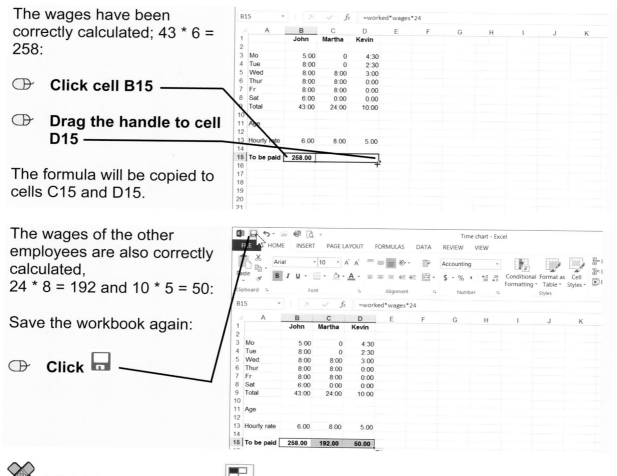

☞ **Click cell B15** ———

☞ **Drag the handle to cell D15** ———

The formula will be copied to cells C15 and D15.

The wages of the other employees are also correctly calculated,
24 * 8 = 192 and 10 * 5 = 50:

Save the workbook again:

☞ **Click** 🖫 ———

HELP! Why do I see ▣ next to the copied cells?

When you copy a cell, you can copy the content along with its formatting, copy only the formatting, or copy only the content of the cell. To access these options:

☞ **Place the pointer on**
▣

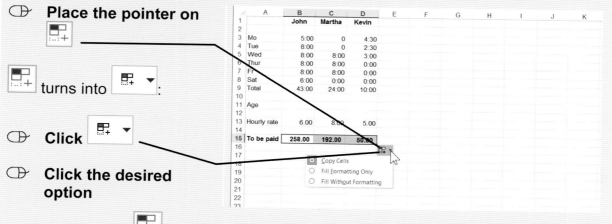

▣ turns into ▣ ▾:

☞ **Click** ▣ ▾

☞ **Click the desired option**

If you do not click ▣, it will disappear by itself after a while. If you continue working, it will also disappear.

7.4 Searching for Values in a Table

You have decided to show the employees' ages on this worksheet. You can search for these ages among the employees' data. The data has been entered in a separate sheet of the workbook:

☞ **Open the *Employees* worksheet**

You will see the information concerning the employees. You can look up the ages with one of the search functions in *Excel*. In order to do this, it is best to name the table (group of cells) with employee data first:

☞ **Select cells A1 up to C10** 🦶 10

This way you can also take any new employees into account.

👉 **Click the *Name Box***

⌨ **Type:** employees

⌨ **Press** Enter

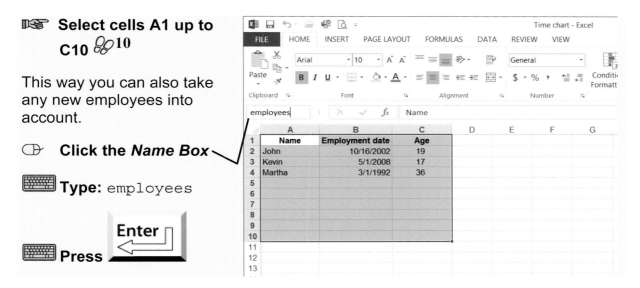

☞ **Open the *Hours* worksheet** 🦶 19

👉 **Click cell B11**

👉 **Click** *fx*

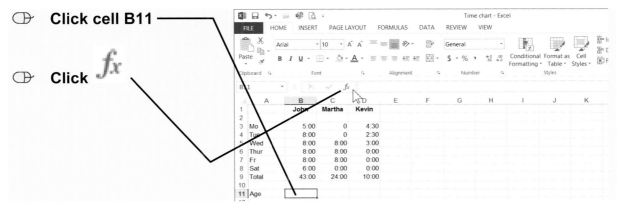

By
Or select a <u>c</u>ategory:,
click

Click
Lookup & Reference

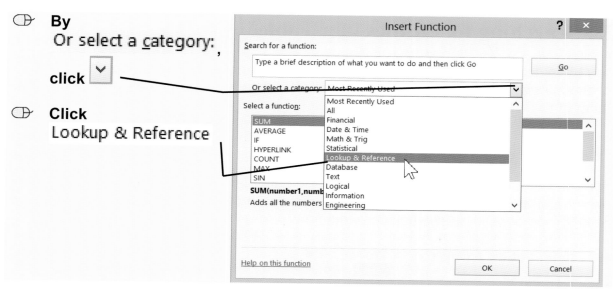

Drag the scroll bar down

Click VLOOKUP

Click OK

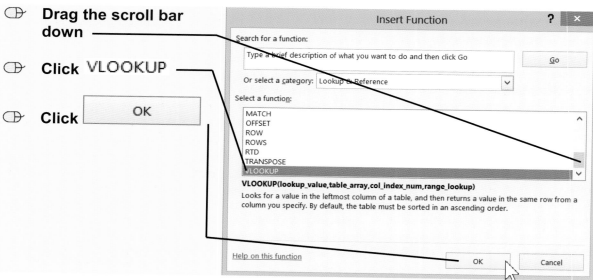

By **Lookup_value** you need to enter the cell that contains the name of the person whose age you want to look up:

👉 **Click cell B1**

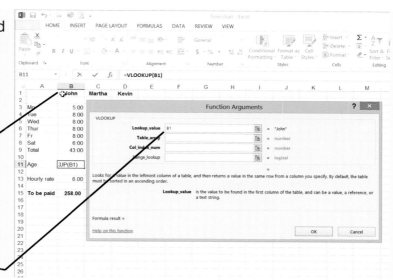

If necessary, you can move the window to enable you to click cell B1.

B1 will be entered into the field by **Lookup_value**.

👉 **Click the field by Table_array**

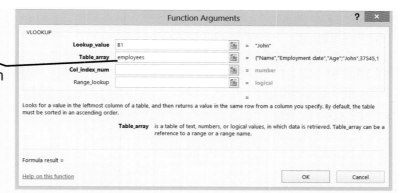

Here you indicate the location of the data you want to look up. You can select the cells, or refer to a table name. In this case, the data has been entered in the *employees* table:

**Type:** employees

👉 **Click the field by Col_index_num**

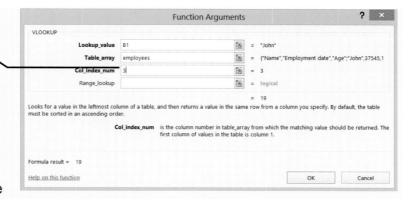

Here you enter the column number of the column in the table that contains the age:

Type: 3

The first column contains the name, and the second column contains the date of employment.

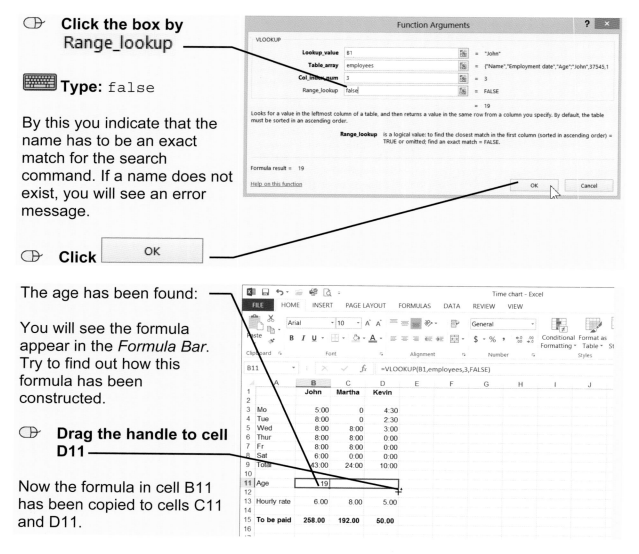

☞ **Click the box by Range_lookup**

⌨ **Type:** `false`

By this you indicate that the name has to be an exact match for the search command. If a name does not exist, you will see an error message.

☞ **Click** [OK]

The age has been found:

You will see the formula appear in the *Formula Bar*. Try to find out how this formula has been constructed.

☞ **Drag the handle to cell D11**

Now the formula in cell B11 has been copied to cells C11 and D11.

All the ages have been found. Many *Excel* users find it difficult to use functions such as the search function. It is a good idea to practice using this function a bit more. You can do this in the next step by looking up the hourly rates. First, to make things easier, you can name the table that contains the hourly rates:

☞ **Open the *Hourly rates* worksheet** 🦶🦶**19**

You will see the hourly rates per age:

☞ **Select cells A1 up to B9** 👣 10

☞ **Click the *Name Box***

⌨ **Type:** rates

⌨ **Press** Enter

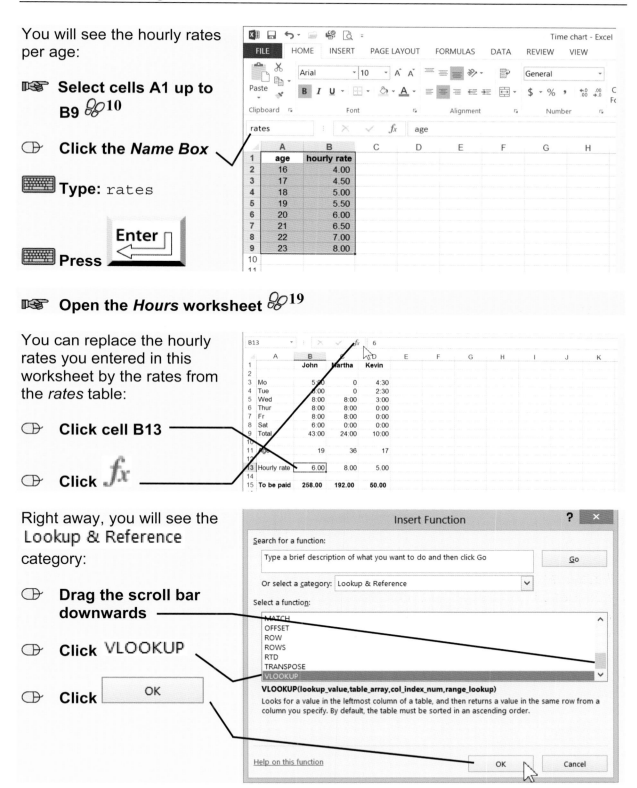

☞ **Open the *Hours* worksheet** 👣 19

You can replace the hourly rates you entered in this worksheet by the rates from the *rates* table:

☞ **Click cell B13**

☞ **Click** *fx*

Right away, you will see the Lookup & Reference category:

☞ **Drag the scroll bar downwards**

☞ **Click** VLOOKUP

☞ **Click** OK

By **Lookup_value** you need to enter the cell that contains the age for which you want to look up the hourly rate:

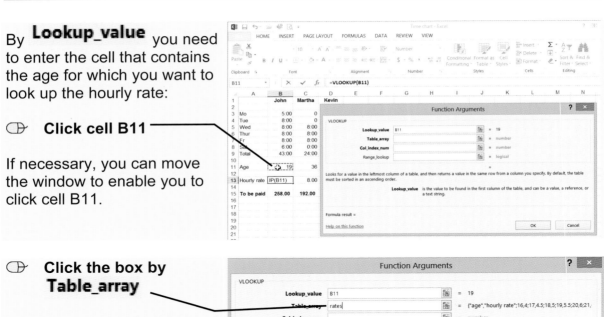

☞ **Click cell B11**

If necessary, you can move the window to enable you to click cell B11.

☞ **Click the box by Table_array**

The hourly rates have been entered in the *rates* table:

⌨ **Type:** rates

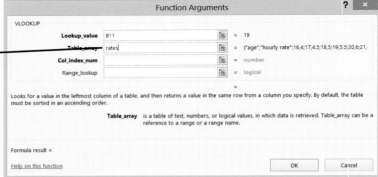

☞ **Click the box by Col_index_num**

Here you can enter the column number of the column in the *rates* table that contains the age:

⌨ **Type:** 2

The first column contains the age, the second column contains the hourly rate.

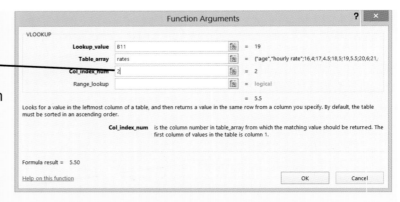

⏚ **Click the box by** Range_lookup

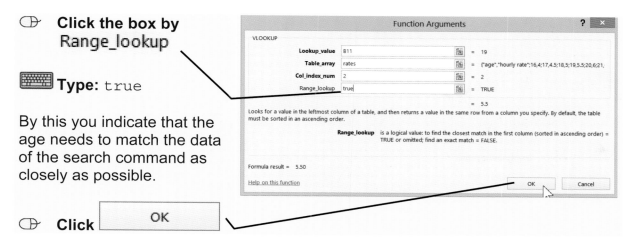

⌨ **Type:** `true`

By this you indicate that the age needs to match the data of the search command as closely as possible.

⏚ **Click** OK

 HELP! Why do I need to use 'true' instead of 'false' by Range_lookup **?**

The table with the ages only contains the ages of 16 up to and including 23. In this example, employees older than 23 years of age all need to receive the wages of a 23-year old. If you would type *false* you would get an error message for all the employees older than 23, because their age is not mentioned in the table. If you use *true*, *Excel* will select the value that is nearest to the age of the employee, which will be 23 for anyone over 23 years old.

⏚ **Drag the handle to cell D13**

You will see the hourly rates that go with the age of the employee:

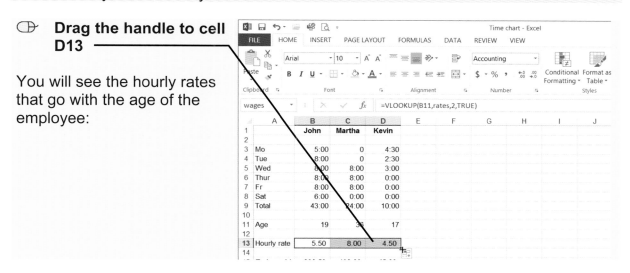

If the hourly rate on the *Hourly rates* worksheet changes, the rate and the amount to be paid will also be adjusted on the *Hours* worksheet:

☞ **Open the *Hourly rate* worksheet** ✂ **19**

You will see the rates per age:

⌨ **In cell B9, type:** `10`

⌨ **Press** Enter

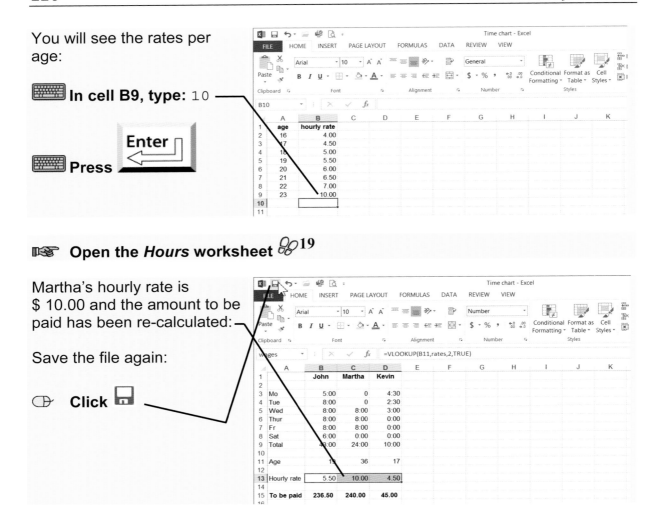

☞ **Open the *Hours* worksheet** ✔**19**

Martha's hourly rate is $ 10.00 and the amount to be paid has been re-calculated:

Save the file again:

🖰 **Click** 💾

The *Vertical lookup* function is the most frequently used search function.

☞ **Close *Excel*** ✔**11**

7.5 Exercises

Have you forgotten how to do something? Use the number beside the footsteps to look it up in appendix *B How Do I Do That Again?* at the end of this book.

Exercise 1: Calculations with Time (1)

☞ Open *Excel.* 🦶**9**

☞ If necessary, open a new workbook. 🦶**12**

☞ Enter these data in the worksheet:

	A	B	C	D	E
1	**Rent bill**				
2					
3	End time				
4	Start time				
5	Hours				
6					
7	Hourly rate				
8					
9	Amount due				

☞ In cell B3, type: `16:30`

☞ In cell B4, type: `9:30`

☞ Calculate the number of hours in cell B5: `=B3-B4`

☞ In cell B7, type: `5`

☞ Set the currency format for cell B7. 🦶**23**

☞ Change the name of cell B5 to *hours.* 🦶**24**

☞ Change the name of cell B7 to *rate.* 🦶**24**

☞ Calculate the amount due in cell B9: `=hours*rate`

☞ Set the currency format for cell B9. 🐾²³

Because *Excel* calculates time in days, the answer needs to be multiplied by 24 hours:

☞ Change the formula in B9 like this: `=hours*rate*24` 🐾²⁶

☞ Save the worksheet and call it *rent bill*. 🐾⁶

Exercise 2: Calculating with Time (2)

The model will not function correctly if the rental period extends beyond a single day. Look what happens if the rented item is not returned until the next day at 11:00 am:

☞ In cell B3, type: `11:00`

☞ You will see:

	A	B	C	D	E
1	**Rent bill**				
2					
3	End time	11:00			
4	Start time	9:30			
5	Hours	1:30			
6					
7	Hourly rate	$5.00			
8					
9	Amount due	$7.50			

In order to correct this, you are going to enter the date too, along with the time:

☞ In cell B3, type: `7/2/2013 11:00`

☞ Widen column B, to make sure the date and time are clearly visible. 🐾²

☞ In cell B4, type: `7/1/2013 9:30`

The number of hours and the amount due has not changed yet.

☞ Go to the cell format in cell B5 and set the format to [h]:mm. 🐾²⁷

☞ You will see:

	A	B	C	D	E
1	**Rent bill**				
2					
3	End time	7/2/2013 11:00			
4	Start time	7/1/2013 9:30			
5	Hours	25:30			
6					
7	Hourly rate	$5.00			
8					
9	Amount due	$127.50			

☞ Save the worksheet. ✂⁷

☞ Close *Excel*. ✂¹¹

7.6 Background Information

Dictionary

Cell format	Rules or conditions that will affect how the data in a cell is seen, for instance, as text, number, date or time units, etc. Currency symbols, commas or other separators can also be used. Other formatting options, including font, background and alignment, can be accessed by using the buttons on the *Format Toolbar*.
Cell name	A name that has been given to a cell or a selected group of cells. Cell names can be used for calculations, just like cell labels.
Function	Functions are pre-defined formulas that do calculations by using specific values, called arguments, in a specific order or structure.
Name box	The box located on the left-hand side of the *Formula Bar* that is used for entering cell names.

Source: Microsoft Excel Help

7.7 Tips

 Tip

Searching for cells with names

You will only see the cell names if you select all the cells that have the same name. If you want to see which cells have a certain name, you can type this name in the *Name Box*. The cells with this name will be marked at once:

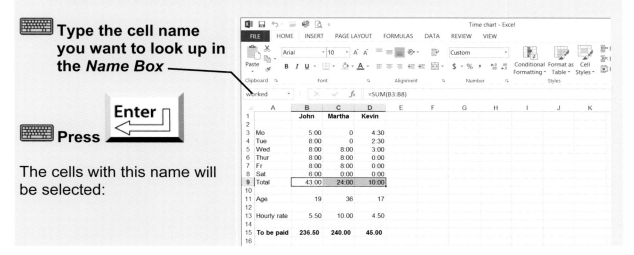

⌨ **Type the cell name you want to look up in the *Name Box* ——**

Enter

⌨ **Press**

The cells with this name will be selected:

 Tip

Display all the commands

On the tabs, you will see the ⛶ icon in the bottom right-hand corner of most groups. This means that not all the commands are displayed on the tab. This is how you display all the commands of a specific group:

For example, the Number group:

☞ **Click** ⛶

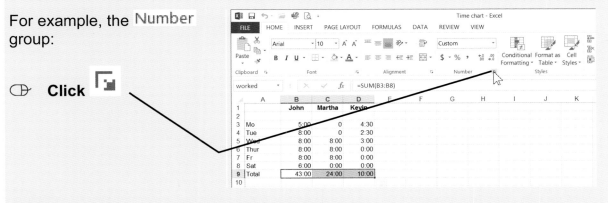

The window with all the other options will be displayed.

Notes

Write your notes down here.

8. Car Expenses

Do you know how much your car or truck costs you per mile? Whether it's for personal affairs or business purposes, it will not hurt to let *Microsoft Excel* help you calculate these expense every now and then. This chapter will show you how to build a worksheet to do just that. You will be taking into account variable expenses, such as gasoline and maintenance, as well as fixed expenses, such as depreciation, insurance and taxes.

As you build the worksheet you will be exploring other features in *Excel* that allow you to create dropdown lists for items that you use repeatedly. This saves time as you will not need to type them over and over again. You will also learn how to build complex formulas by *nesting* them. *Excel* can perform logical tests and calculate values based on different criteria.

It is also important that you strive to keep your workbooks neatly organized. You can do this for example, by moving some calculations to separate worksheets. Results produced by these calculations will not be affected as calculations can be done across multiple worksheets.

In this chapter you will learn how to:

- type your own data validation list;
- turn a table into a data validation list;
- nest formulas;
- use the *IF* formula;
- set *Conditional formatting*;
- create a new worksheet;
- add up entire columns with *Sum*;
- insert absolute references in formulas.

 Please note:

In order to perform all the tasks in this chapter, you will need to have copied the practice files to your computer. In *Appendix A Downloading the Practice Files* you can read how to download the practice files from the website accompanying this book.

8.1 Validation Lists

Many worksheets use the same description over and over again. If you create a validation list (dropdown list) for these items, you will not need to type them separately each time. This not only saves time but minimizes the chance of making typing errors.

☞ **Open *Excel*** 🦶⁹

☞ **Open the *Car expenses* workbook** 🦶²²

⊕ **If necessary, click** | Enable Editing |

You will see a worksheet. You can enter your car expenses in this worksheet, one below the other. Because some of these expenses occur on a regular basis, you can create a validation list for these items:

⊕ **If necessary, click the** | Car expenses | **sheet**

⊕ **Click cell B2**

⊕ **Click the** DATA **tab**

⊕ **Click** ☑ Data Validation

⊕ **By** Allow: **, click** ☑

⊕ **Click** List

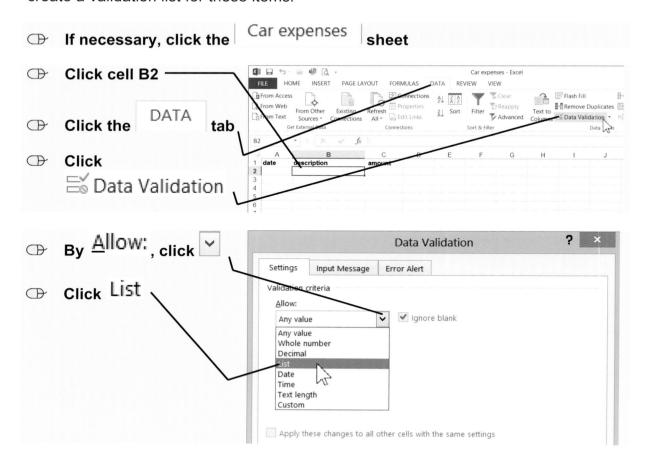

👆 **Click the field by**
Source:

⌨ **Type:** `gasoline,`
`maintenance,`
`taxes,`
`insurance`

Please note: type a comma and a blank space between the words.

👆 **Click** OK

By cell B2 you will see ▼:

Copy the cell to the next few rows:

👆 **Drag the handle to cell B10**

👆 **Click cell A2**

⌨ **Type:** 6/22

⌨ **Press** ⇒

The year will be inserted automatically and the date format will be used.

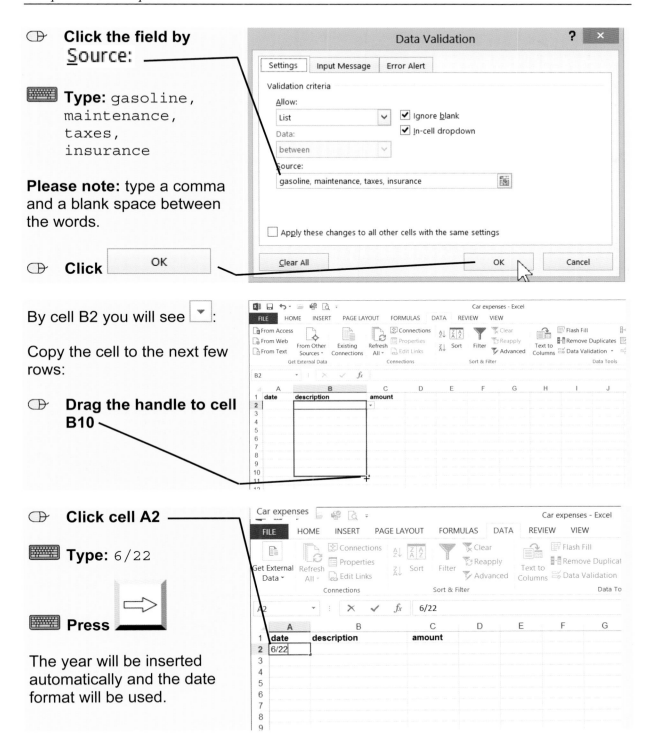

👆 **By cell B2, click** ▽

👆 **Click** gasoline

⌨ **Press** ➡

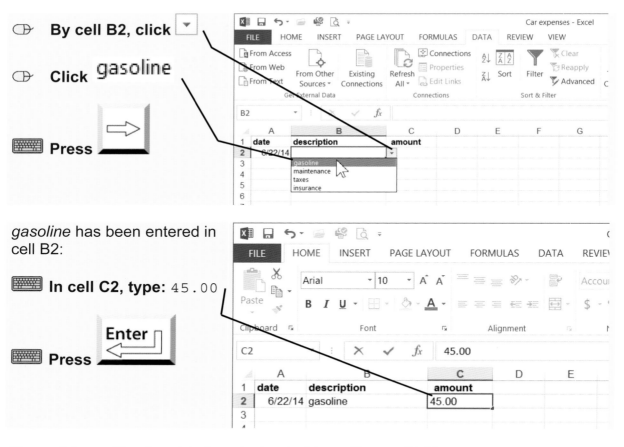

gasoline has been entered in cell B2:

⌨ **In cell C2, type:** 45.00

⌨ **Press** Enter ⬅

The cell formatting is set to two decimals. You will see: 45.00.

⌨ **Enter the data as shown in this example**

	A	B	C
1	date	description	amount
2	6/22/14	gasoline	45.00
3			39.00
4			32.00
5			86.50
6			47.00
7			

Sometimes it may be necessary to type your own description, for example, if an item is not shown in the list:

In cell A7, type: 7/10

In cell B7, type: fine

Press

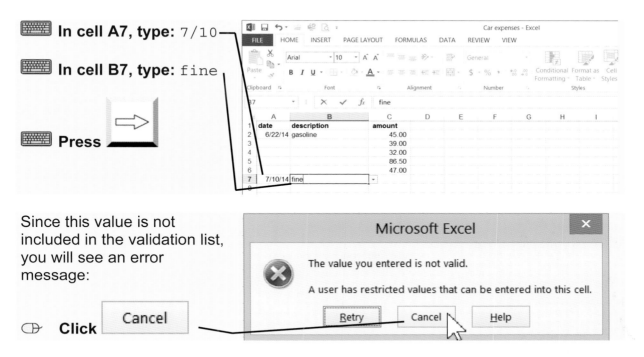

Since this value is not included in the validation list, you will see an error message:

Click Cancel

You can adjust the setting for these cells, so you will be able to enter other values yourself. You can do this for all the cells for which you have set the validation list:

Select cells B2 through B10 ℰℰ 10

If necessary, click the DATA **tab**

Click Data Validation

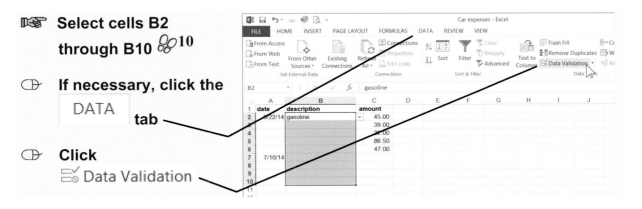

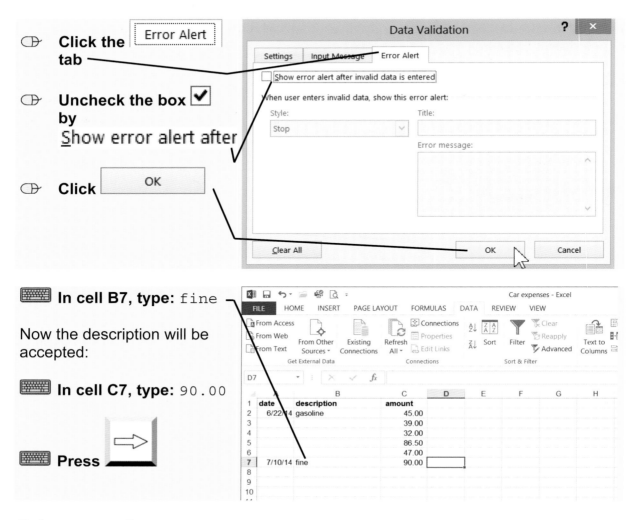

☞ **Click the** **Error Alert** **tab**

☞ **Uncheck the box** ☑ **by** Show error alert after

☞ **Click** OK

⌨ **In cell B7, type:** `fine`

Now the description will be accepted:

⌨ **In cell C7, type:** `90.00`

⌨ **Press** ⇒

Before you continue:

☞ **Save the workbook** 🦶🦶7

8.2 Turn a Table into a Validation List

If the dropdown lists are too long or prone to frequent changes, you can enter the items for the list in a worksheet. In this case you will be using a distance table to record the trips you have taken with city and distance data. You can turn this table into a validation list.

☞ **Open the *Distances* worksheet** 🦶🦶19

In order to use the cities in a dropdown list, the cells that contain the cities need to be labelled as a whole.

You will see some cities and distances:

☞ **Select cells A2 up to A10** 👣¹⁰

☞ **Click the *Name Box***

⌨ **Type:** `cities`

⌨ **Press** **Enter**

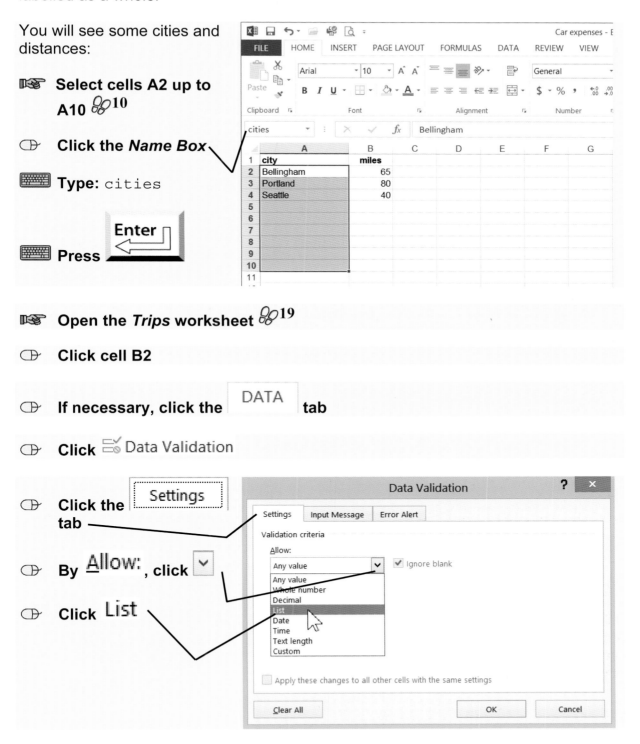

☞ **Open the *Trips* worksheet** 👣¹⁹

☞ **Click cell B2**

☞ **If necessary, click the** DATA **tab**

☞ **Click** ☑ Data Validation

☞ **Click the** Settings **tab**

☞ **By** Allow: **, click** ⌄

☞ **Click** List

☞ **Click the box by** Source:

⌨ **Type:** =cities

At the bottom of the window:

☞ **Click** OK

By cell B2 you will see ▼ :

Copy the cell to the next few rows, so you can add new cities later on:

☞ **Drag the handle to cell B20**

☞ **Click cell A2**

⌨ **Type:** 6/22

⌨ **Press** ⇨

The year will be entered automatically.

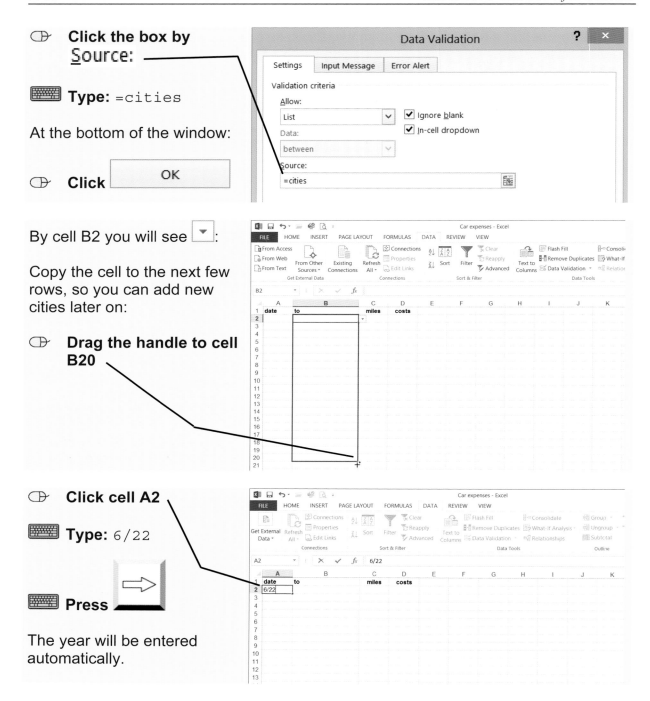

By cell B2, click ▼

 Click Portland

 Press ➡

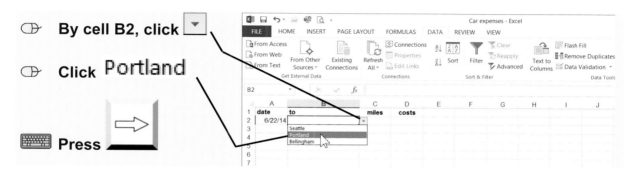

The city has been entered in the cell.

💡 **Tip**

Edit the dropdown list

You can add or delete cities on the *Distances* sheet. But make sure that the cities you add are entered within the area of cells that you have named *cities*.

8.3 Looking Up Distances

You could also create a validation list for the distances too, but then you would need to look up the correct distance yourself every time. It is more practical to let *Excel* look up the distance by using a search function. You can read more about the search function in *Chapter 7 Calculating with Time and the Search Function*. First, you will need to name the distances table:

☞ **Open the *Distances* worksheet** ✂19

☞ **Select cells A2 through B10** ✂10

 Click the *Name Box*

⌨ **Type:** distances

⌨ **Press** Enter

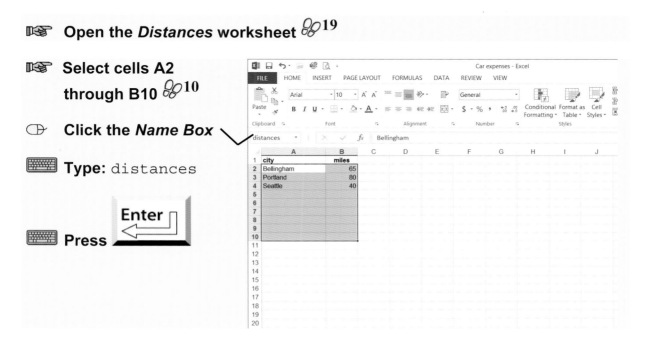

☞ **Open the *Trips* worksheet** 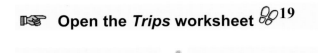¹⁹

👆 **Click cell C2,** 𝑓x

☞ **Open the *VLOOKUP* function** 👣³⁷

In this function you need to fill in four 'arguments'. By **Table_array** you indicate where the cities and distances are located:

By **Lookup_value** you enter the cell that contains the city for which you want to look up the distance:

👆 **Click cell B2**

If necessary you can move the window in order to click cell B2.

👆 **Click the field by Table_array**

Here you indicate where the cities and distances are located:

⌨ **Type:** distances

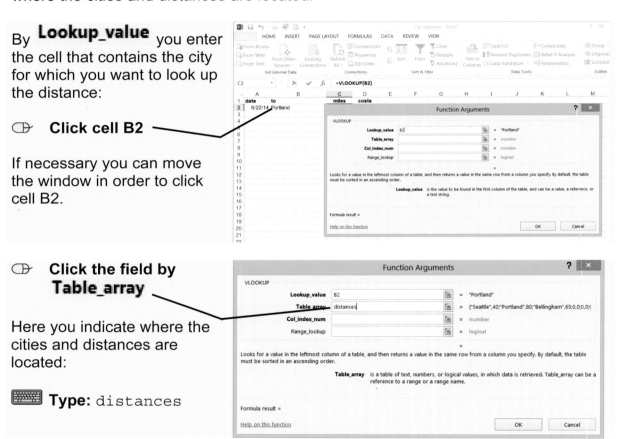

⊕ **Click the field by Col_index_num**

In the first column you will see the name of the city, and in the second column the distance.

⌨ **Type:** 2

⊕ **Click the field by Range_lookup**

⌨ **Type:** false

The name of the city needs to be an exact match.

⊕ **Click** OK

The distance has been found:

⊕ **Drag the handle to cell C20**

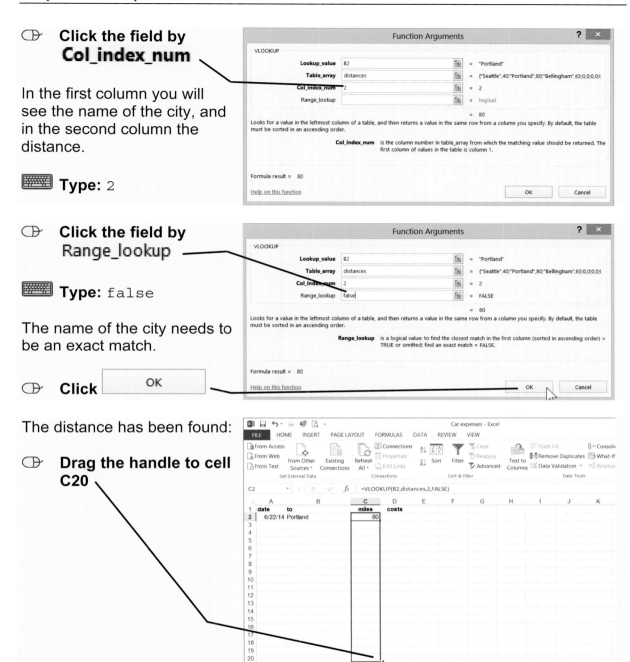

8.4 Nested Formulas

You will see lots of error messages. This is because there are not any cities entered in the other cells. Instead of these error codes you can insert a zero. You can do this by applying the search function only when column A contains a date on the same line:

☞ **Click cell C2**

You will see the formula
=VLOOKUP(B2,distances,2,FAL

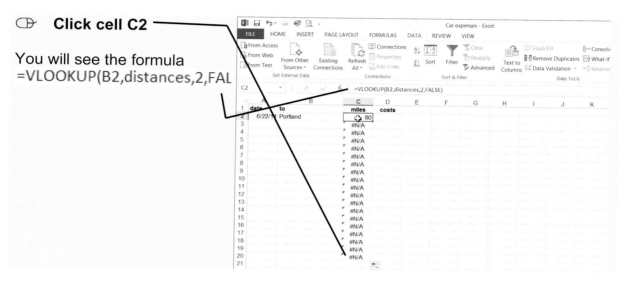

This formula should only be applied if column A contains a date.
You can use the *IF* function to achieve this. This is what the function looks like:

IF (condition; true; false)

Condition: This is the condition you want *Excel* to check.
                  *In this example: does column A contain a date? You are going to
                  check this with the condition A2>0.*

True: The action that needs to be performed if the condition is met.
                  *In this example: the distance needs to be looked up, so the search
                  function will be used.*

False: The action that needs to be performed if the condition is not met.
                  In this example: a zero needs to be filled in.

The formula is put between brackets and a comma ',' is inserted between the conditions.

Now you are going to build the *IF* formula and wrap it around the *search* function. This is called *nesting* a formula, and you can do this directly in the *Formula Bar*:

☞ **Click to the left of** `VLOOKUP`

Enter the condition:

⌨ **Type:** `if(a2>0`

Type the separator:

⌨ **Type:** `,`

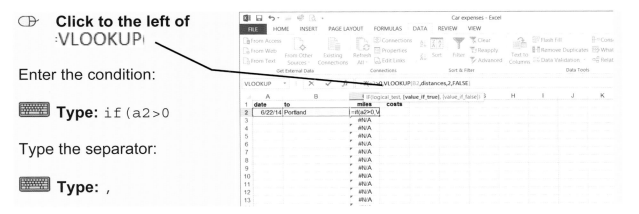

You can leave the *search* function where it is. This function is performed if the condition is met. Now you can expand the formula further and add the action that needs to be done if the condition is not met. This action is inserted at the end:

☞ **Click at the end of the formula**

Type the separator:

⌨ **Type:** `,`

You want to insert a zero if column A does not contain a date:

⌨ **Type:** `0`

To finish the formula:

⌨ **Type:** `)`

⌨ **Press** Enter

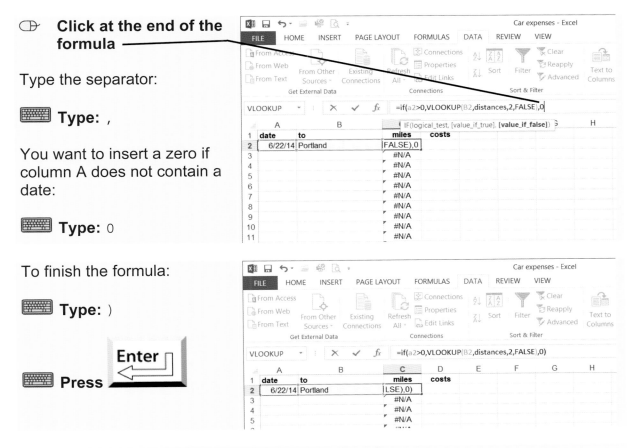

☞ **Copy the formula from cell C2 up to C20** ✂⁴

Now you will see zeroes instead of error messages.

8.5 Conditional Formatting

You can hide the zeroes with *Conditional Formatting*. You can also set the font color to white, if the cell contains a zero:

☞ **Click the** HOME **tab**

☞ **Click Conditional Formatting ▾ , Highlight Cells Rules , Equal To...**

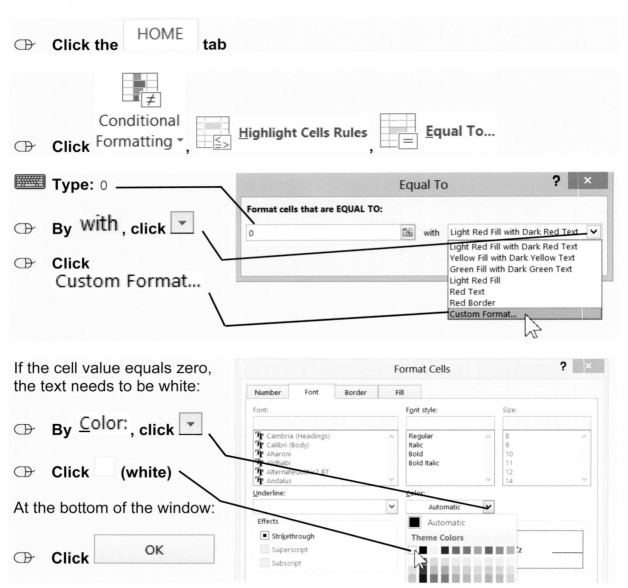

⌨ **Type:** 0

☞ **By with , click ▾**

☞ **Click Custom Format...**

If the cell value equals zero, the text needs to be white:

☞ **By Color:, click ▾**

☞ **Click ☐ (white)**

At the bottom of the window:

☞ **Click OK**

In the *Equal To* window:

⬡ **Click** OK

⬡ **Click cell C2**

Now the zeroes are hidden.

To test your changes you can fill in the second row:

⌨ **In cell A3, type:** 6/23

⌨ **Press** ⇨

You will see an error message in cell C3:

⬡ **By cell B3, click** ▼

⬡ **Click** Bellingham

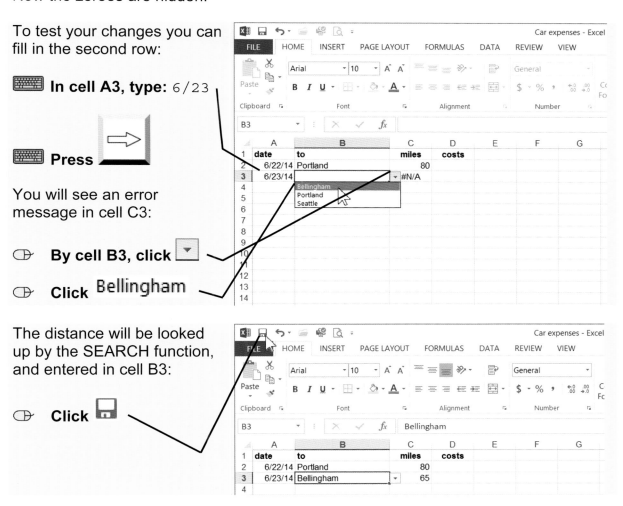

The distance will be looked up by the SEARCH function, and entered in cell B3:

⬡ **Click** 💾

 Please note:

On the *Distances* sheet you can add or delete cities with their distances. But make sure that the cities you add are included within the array of cells that you have given the table name 'distances'. And you also need to sort the cities in alphabetical order, if you want the search function to work properly.

8.6 Costs per Mile

After you have recorded the costs and trips made with your car, you can calculate how much your car costs per mile. To do this you can create a new worksheet:

By 📑 Insert, click ▼

Click Insert Sheet

At the bottom of the window you will see a new worksheet:

👉 **Name this worksheet** *Costs per mile* 🐾18

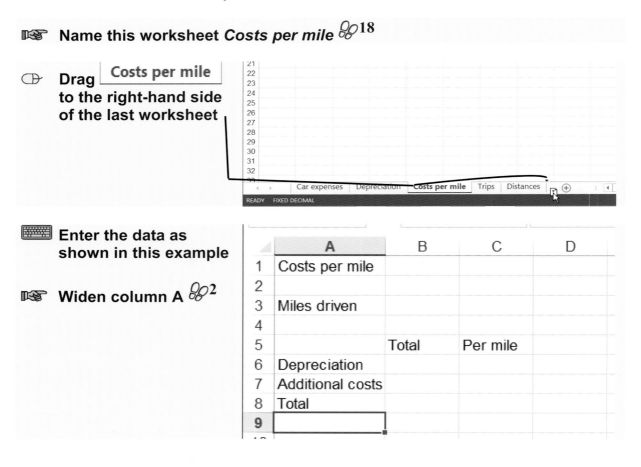

Drag | Costs per mile |
to the right-hand side
of the last worksheet

⌨ **Enter the data as
shown in this example**

👉 **Widen column A** 🐾2

	A	B	C	D
1	Costs per mile			
2				
3	Miles driven			
4				
5		Total	Per mile	
6	Depreciation			
7	Additional costs			
8	Total			
9				

You can set two decimals for the cells that will contain amounts:

☞ **Select cells B6 through C8** 🐾10

☞ **Click** 🔘 ← .0 / .00

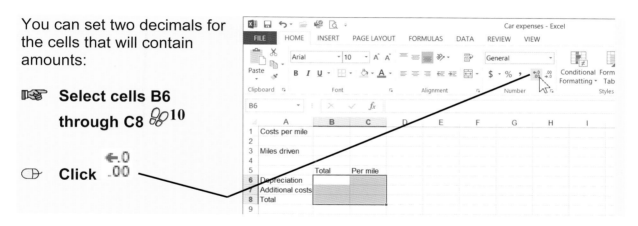

By *Miles driven* you can add up the mileage from the *Trips* worksheet:

☞ **Click cell B3**

☞ **Click Σ**

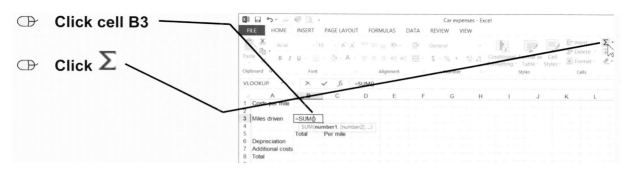

☞ **Open the *Trips* worksheet** 🐾19

☞ **Click** C

Column C will be added up.

⌨ **Press** Enter

You will see the total amount of miles you have driven. You can calculate the additional costs in the same way:

☞ **Click cell B7**

☞ **Click Σ**

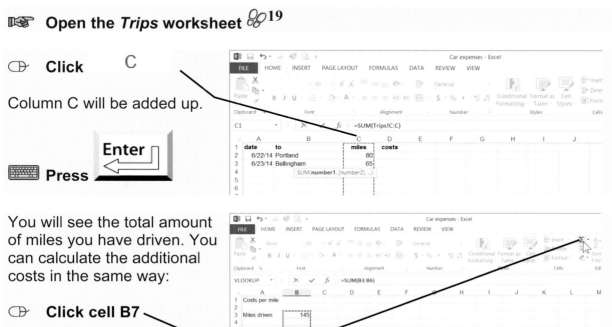

☞ **Open the *Car expenses* worksheet** 🐾**19**

🖱 **Click   C**

Column C will be added up:

⌨ **Press Enter**

Now the costs have been added up. You can find the depreciation values on the *Depreciation* worksheet:

🖱 **Click cell B6**

⌨ **Type:** =

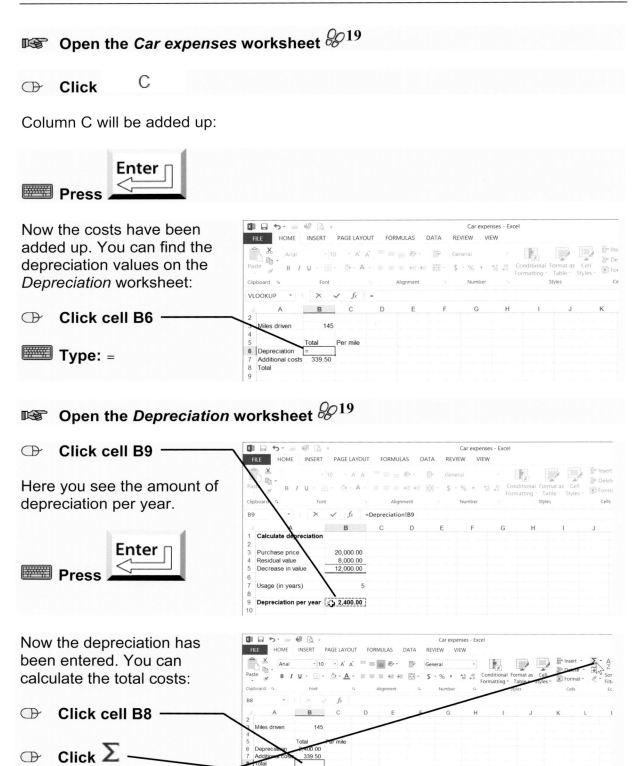

☞ **Open the *Depreciation* worksheet** 🐾**19**

🖱 **Click cell B9**

Here you see the amount of depreciation per year.

⌨ **Press Enter**

Now the depreciation has been entered. You can calculate the total costs:

🖱 **Click cell B8**

🖱 **Click** Σ

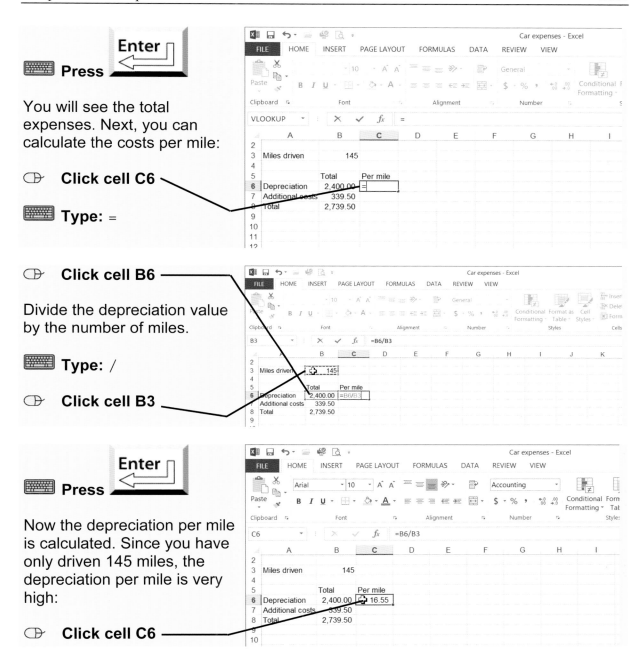

Press **Enter**

You will see the total expenses. Next, you can calculate the costs per mile:

Click cell **C6**

Type: **=**

Click cell **B6**

Divide the depreciation value by the number of miles.

Type: **/**

Click cell **B3**

Press **Enter**

Now the depreciation per mile is calculated. Since you have only driven 145 miles, the depreciation per mile is very high:

Click cell **C6**

In order to copy the formula in cell C6 to the next few rows, you will first need to create an absolute reference to the number of miles driven. If you do not do this, the reference will change when you copy it and the result will not be accurate.

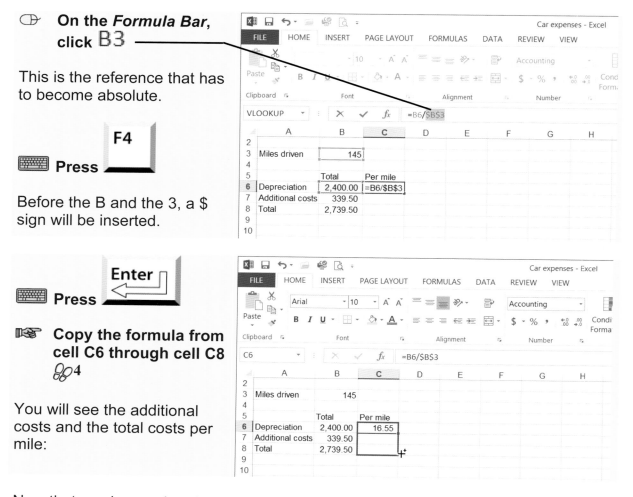

☞ **On the *Formula Bar*, click B3**

This is the reference that has to become absolute.

F4

⌨ **Press**

Before the B and the 3, a $ sign will be inserted.

Enter

⌨ **Press**

☞ **Copy the formula from cell C6 through cell C8** 𝒬𝒬4

You will see the additional costs and the total costs per mile:

Now that you know what the costs per mile are, you can calculate how much each trip costs:

☞ **Open the *Trips* worksheet** 𝒬𝒬19

☞ **Click cell D2** ——————

⌨ **Type:** =

☞ **Click cell C2** ——————

⌨ **Type:** *

☞ **Open the *Costs per mile* worksheet** 🦶¹⁹

☞ **Click cell C8** ——————

⌨ **Press** **Enter** ⏎

You will see the costs: ——————

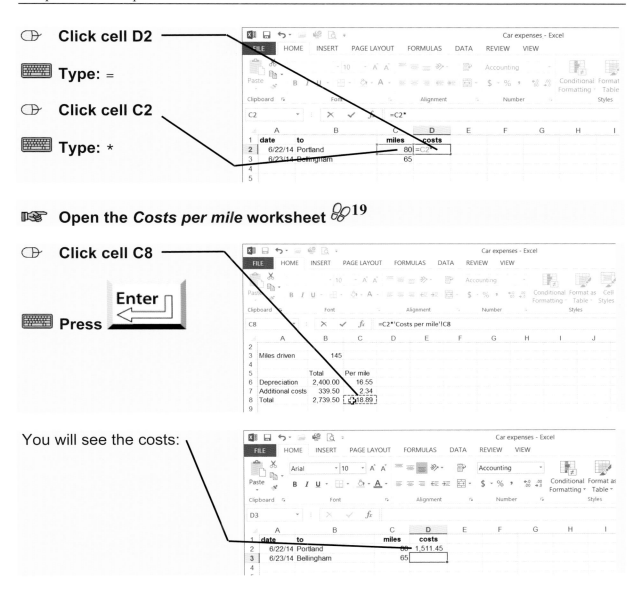

You can see that this appears to be a very expensive trip. This is due to the limited number of miles. This results in an extremely high value for the depreciation per mile. The more you drive, the lower the depreciation per mile will become.

You can also add your own trips to the *Trips* worksheet, for example, for occasional trips, or special journeys:

☞ **In row 4, enter:**
  7/31
  Vacation
  3000

⌨ **Press** ➡

Now the costs of the trip to Portland have become much lower.

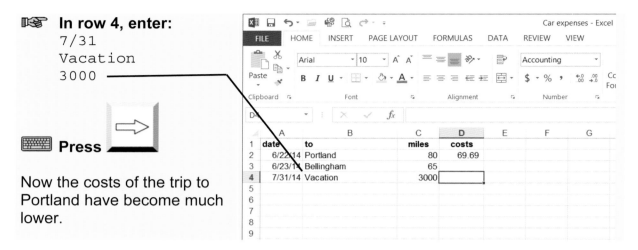

If you want to calculate the costs for the other trips, you will first need to make an absolute reference to the total costs:

👆 **Click cell D2**

👆 **In the *Formula Bar*, click C8**

This is the reference that needs to be made absolute.

⌨ **Press** F4

You will see the $ signs appear before the C and the 8.

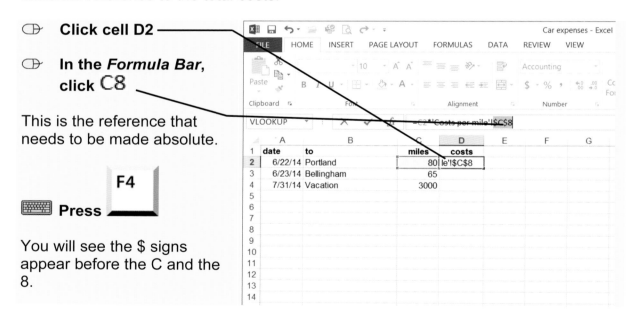

Press **Enter**

☞ **Copy the formula from cell D2 through D20** 🐾4

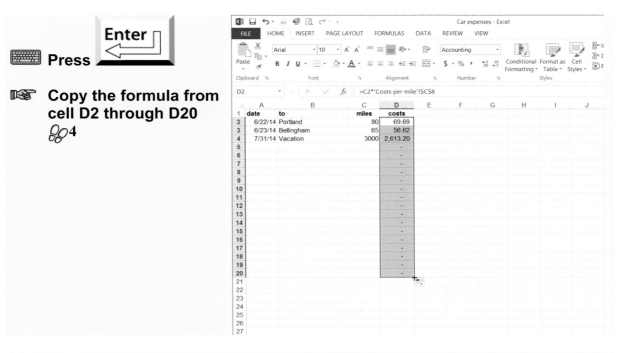

☞ **Save the workbook** 🐾7

☞ **Close *Excel*** 🐾11

In this chapter you have learned how to calculate how much your car will cost.

8.7 Exercises

Have you forgotten how to do something? Use the number beside the footsteps to look it up in appendix *B How Do I Do That Again?* at the end of this book.

☞   Open *Excel*. 🐾⁹

☞   If necessary, open a new workbook. 🐾¹²

☞   Enter the following data in the worksheet

	A	B	C	D	E
1	Compensation for Car Expenses				
2					
3	Per mile	0.25			
4	Max. compensation	$ 30.00			
5					
6		Distance	Compensation	Pay	
7	Trip 1	50			
8	Trip 2	30			
9	Trip 3	150			
10	Trip 4	20			

☞   In cell C7, type the formula =B7*B3

☞   Copy the formula from cell C7 through C10. 🐾⁴

☞   The results are wrong. You will see:

	A	B	C	D
6		Distance	Compensation	Pay
7	Trip 1	50	12.5	
8	Trip 2	30	900	
9	Trip 3	150	0	
10	Trip 4	20	#VALUE!	

In order to obtain the correct results, you will need to make an absolute reference to cell B3, in the formula:

☞   Click cell C7.

☞   In the *Formula Bar*, change the formula to =B7*B3 🐾⁵³

☞   Copy the formula from cell C7 through cell C10. 🐾⁴

☞ Set the currency notation for cells C7 through C10. 🦶23

In trip 3, the compensation has exceeded the maximum amount for compensation. In the *Pay* column you will see the amount that is due. This can never be higher than the maximum compensation:

☞ Click cell D7.

☞ Open the *IF* formula. 🦶39

☞ Fill in the formula like this:

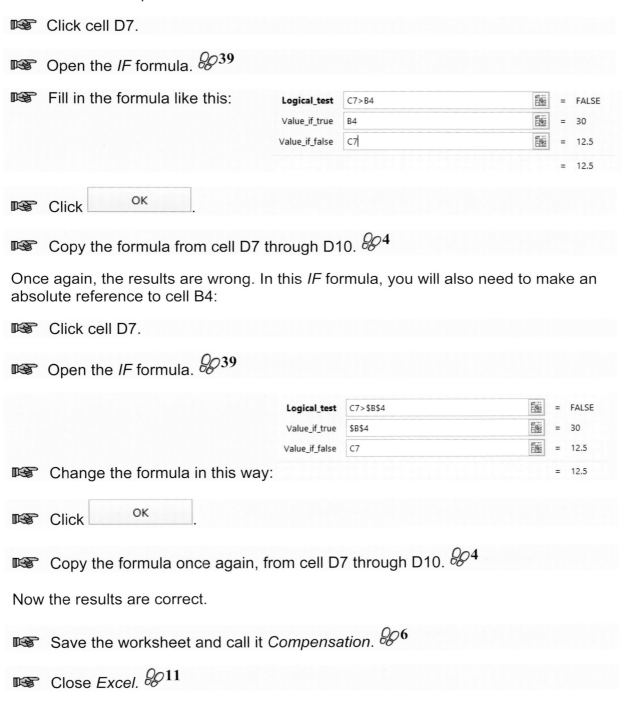

Logical_test	C7>B4		= FALSE
Value_if_true	B4		= 30
Value_if_false	C7		= 12.5
			= 12.5

☞ Click   OK   .

☞ Copy the formula from cell D7 through D10. 🦶4

Once again, the results are wrong. In this *IF* formula, you will also need to make an absolute reference to cell B4:

☞ Click cell D7.

☞ Open the *IF* formula. 🦶39

Logical_test	C7>B4		= FALSE
Value_if_true	B4		= 30
Value_if_false	C7		= 12.5
			= 12.5

☞ Change the formula in this way:

☞ Click   OK   .

☞ Copy the formula once again, from cell D7 through D10. 🦶4

Now the results are correct.

☞ Save the worksheet and call it *Compensation*. 🦶6

☞ Close *Excel*. 🦶11

8.8 Background Information

Dictionary

Absolute reference	In a formula, the absolute cell reference is the exact address of a cell, regardless of the position of the cell that contains the formula. An absolute cell reference is often used while calculating with constants, and uses the reference style A1.
Dropdown / validation list	A list with standard values that can be selected.
Function	Functions are predefined formulas that do calculations by using specific values, called arguments, in a specific order or structure.
Nesting	Sometimes, it is necessary to use a function as one of the arguments in another function. A certain function that is incorporated within another function is called a *nesting function*.
Validate	Check whether the data that is entered or selected meets certain conditions.

Source: Microsoft Excel Help

8.9 Tips

 Tip

Automatic dropdown list

If you have one-time only lists that often contain the same descriptions, you can use the automatic dropdown list option in *Excel*. To use the option:

Type the list ————

If you need to enter an item that is already in the list:

☞ **Right-click the blank cell below the list**

☞ **Click**
Pick From Drop-down List..

You will see a dropdown list:

☞ **Click the item of your choice**

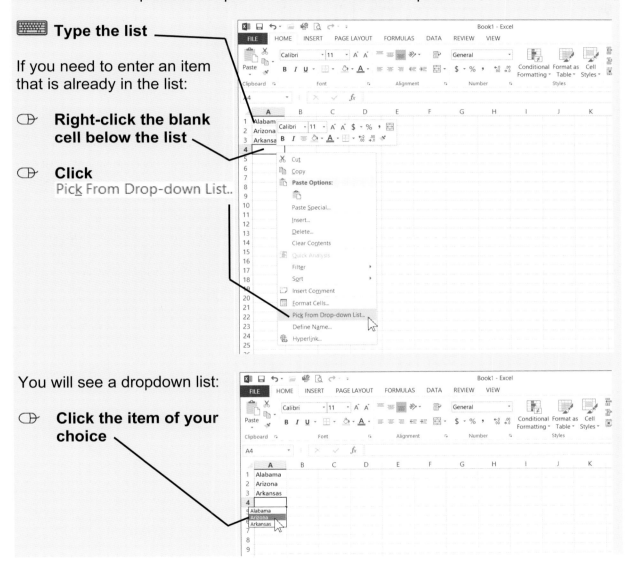

Tip

AutoComplete function

Even if you do not use any lists, it might not be necessary to type the descriptions you frequently use in full. After the first few letters, *Excel* will guess what you want to type:

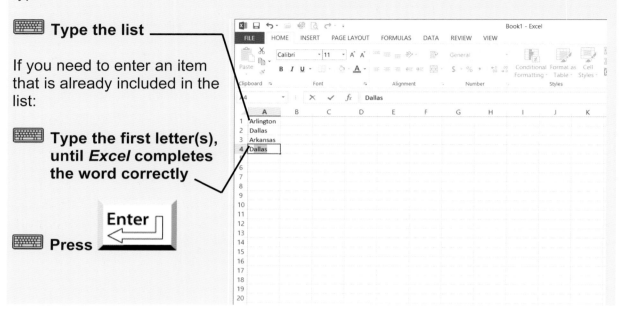

Type the list

If you need to enter an item that is already included in the list:

Type the first letter(s), until *Excel* completes the word correctly

Enter

Press

9. Subtotals and Pivot Tables

Spreadsheets are often used for entering large amounts of data. Once entered, the data can be sorted, compared, analyzed and summarized to discover trends or patterns or to gain insight into a financial situation. An example of this way of using *Excel* is a household recordkeeping book where you record all your expenses, but it could just as well be the financial administration of a club or a local business.

First, you enter the data from receipts, pay slips or bank statements. You can do this in random order or in chronological order. After that, you can sort, group and analyze the data. You will know exactly where the money has gone and perhaps discover ways of planning for the future.

In this chapter you will learn two methods of organizing randomly entered data in order to obtain useful information. You can create a data summary or use the data to create charts and reports to represent your data graphically.

In this chapter you will learn how to:

- create a summary with subtotals;
- create pivot tables;
- recalculate pivot tables;
- create a chart from a pivot table;
- set a report format for pivot table.

 Please note:

In order to perform all the tasks in this chapter, you will need to have copied the practice files to your computer. In *Appendix A Downloading the Practice Files* you can read how to download the practice files from the website accompanying this book.

9.1 Classifying

Once you have entered your data in a spreadsheet it will need to be organized. When you organize your data it is important to classify your information. By classifying you will be arranging the data under different headings. You can practice doing this using the example shown below.

☞ **Open *Excel*** 🦶⁹

☞ **Open the *Summary of expenses* workbook** 🦶²²

👆 **If necessary, click** Enable Editing

A summary of expenses could look like this example:

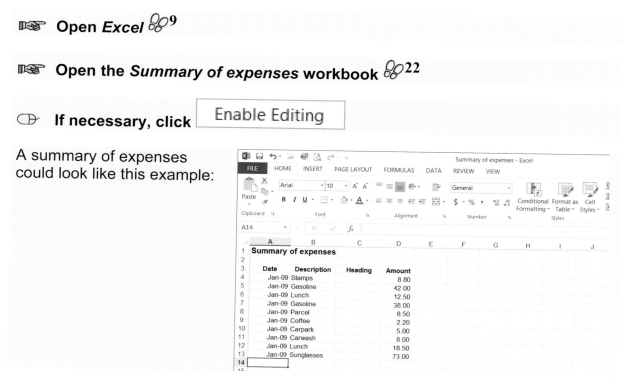

In order to view the expenses more clearly, they should be classified (or grouped) under a specific heading. You can do this easily by using the headings from the *Headings* worksheet and creating a dropdown list for them:

☞ **Open the *Headings* worksheet** 🦶¹⁹

☞ **Select cells A1 through A10** 🦶¹⁰

☞ **Give these cells the name *headings*** 🦶²⁴

☞ **Open the *Expenses* worksheet** 🦶¹⁹

☞ **In cell C4, create a dropdown list that is linked to the *headings* table** ✂️⁴⁰

☞ **Copy the formula from cell C4 up to cell C13** ✂️⁴

☞ **Select the headings according to this example**

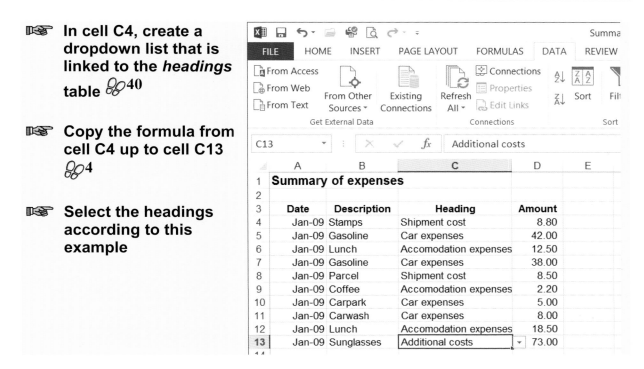

9.2 Calculate Subtotals

If you want to know how much you have spent per heading, first you need to sort the expenses by their headings:

 Please note:

You need to have selected a cell in the *Heading* column.

☞ **Sort the *Heading* column in ascending order** ✂️⁴⁶

The expenses have been sorted according to their heading. To display the totals per heading, you need to calculate the subtotals:

☞ **Click the** DATA **tab**

☞ **Click** 🔢 Subtotal

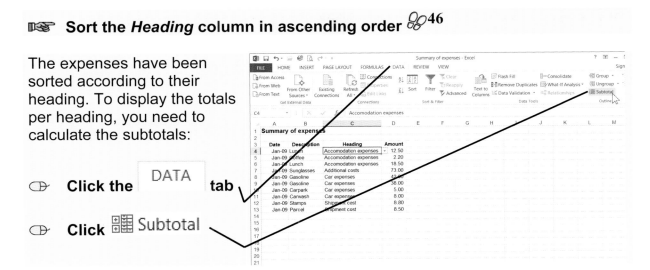

You will see a window with various questions:

By the question regarding **At each change in:** you need to choose when a subtotal has to be calculated. In this case, we will use the *Heading* column:

☞ **By At each change in:** , **click** ⌄

☞ **Click Heading**

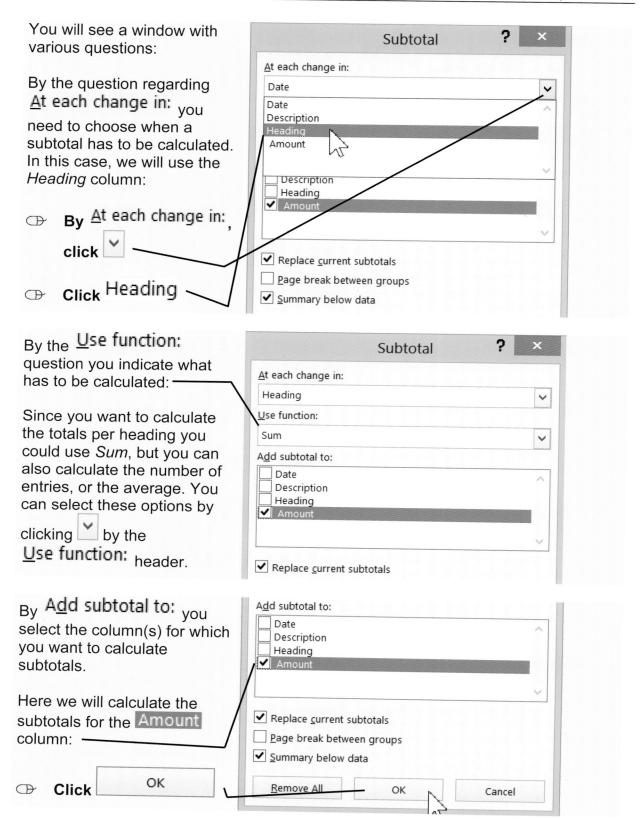

By the **Use function:** question you indicate what has to be calculated:

Since you want to calculate the totals per heading you could use *Sum*, but you can also calculate the number of entries, or the average. You can select these options by clicking ⌄ by the **Use function:** header.

By **Add subtotal to:** you select the column(s) for which you want to calculate subtotals.

Here we will calculate the subtotals for the **Amount** column:

☞ **Click** **OK**

Please note:

If you want to calculate the *Sum*, you can only calculate subtotals for columns that contain numerical data. If you do not select *Sum* but instead you select *Number*, for instance, you will also be able to calculate subtotals for non-numerical columns.

Also, keep in mind that multiple columns may have been checked, columns that you might not see in the list. Use the scroll bar to find out which other columns have been checked as well.

You will see the overview with the subtotals per heading.

If the worksheet is rather long, you will only see the first part. By collapsing the detail rows into a group only the summary row will be visible:

☞ **Click**

Now you will only see the grand total.

This feature is called the *outline mode* in *Excel*. To view a specification per heading:

☞ **Click** 2

You will see the groups with the subtotals:

You can hone down further and view a specification for each heading:

☞ **By a heading, click**

You will see all the rows that make up these expenses:

By clicking ⎯ , the specification is closed again.

☞ **Click** ⬚3

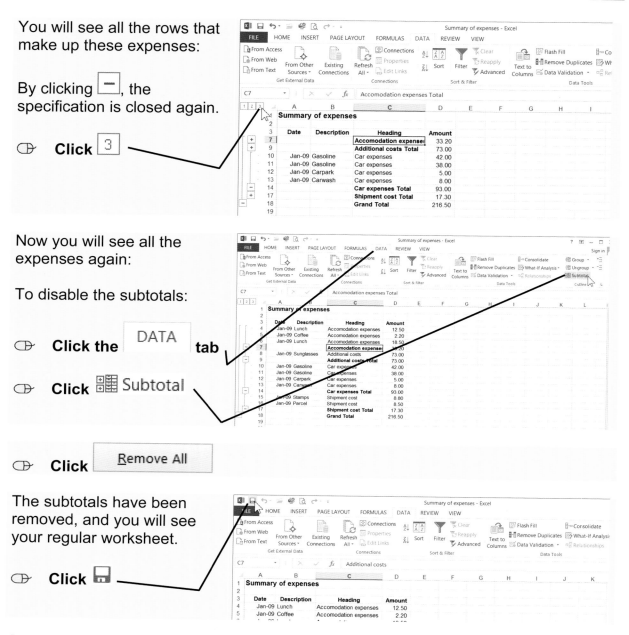

Now you will see all the expenses again:

To disable the subtotals:

☞ **Click the** DATA **tab**

☞ **Click** ⊞ Subtotal

☞ **Click** Remove All

The subtotals have been removed, and you will see your regular worksheet.

☞ **Click** 💾

☞ **Please note:**

Any changes to your expenses should only be entered in the worksheet in this form. If you edit the worksheet with the subtotals, the subtotals will no longer be accurate.

9.3 Creating Pivot Tables

Another way of summarizing large amounts of data is by using a pivot table. What is different about the worksheet with the subtotals is that *Excel* can place a pivot table on a new worksheet. The original table stays intact. Any changes to the table will also be reflected in the pivot table. You can create a pivot table like this:

 Please note:
You need to select one cell in the table for which you want to create the pivot table.

☞ **Click the tab** — INSERT

☞ **Click** PivotTable

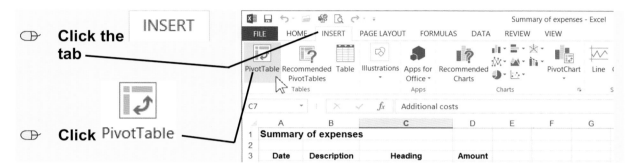

The table for which the pivot table will be created, has been selected:

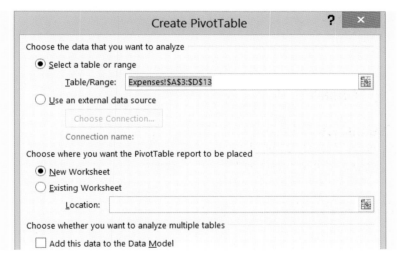

 HELP! The wrong table has been selected.
Is more than one table selected, or perhaps the wrong table? Then click
Cancel and check whether one of the cells within the table has been selected.

If necessary, you can select the entire table yourself. ✂**10**

The location for the pivot table is a new worksheet:

☞ **Click** OK

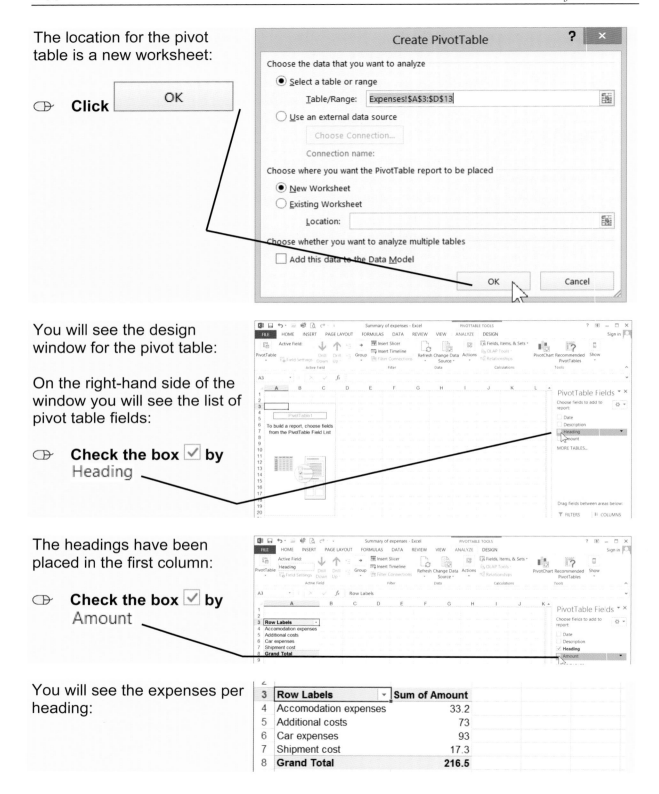

You will see the design window for the pivot table:

On the right-hand side of the window you will see the list of pivot table fields:

☞ **Check the box ✓ by** Heading

The headings have been placed in the first column:

☞ **Check the box ✓ by** Amount

You will see the expenses per heading:

Row Labels	Sum of Amount
Accomodation expenses	33.2
Additional costs	73
Car expenses	93
Shipment cost	17.3
Grand Total	**216.5**

If anything changes in the summary of expenses, you can decide whether you want these changes to be reflected in the pivot table.

☞ **Open the *Expenses* worksheet** 🐾¹⁹

⌨ **In cell D7, type:**
173.00

⌨ **Press** Enter

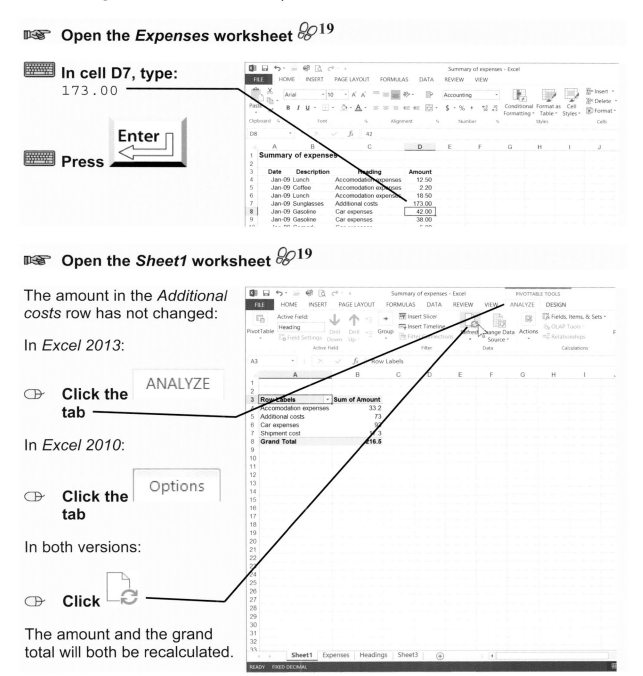

☞ **Open the *Sheet1* worksheet** 🐾¹⁹

The amount in the *Additional costs* row has not changed:

In *Excel 2013*:

☞ **Click the** ANALYZE **tab**

In *Excel 2010*:

☞ **Click the** Options **tab**

In both versions:

☞ **Click** 🔄

The amount and the grand total will both be recalculated.

9.4 Charts and Reports of Pivot Tables

You can easily create charts and reports from your pivot tables. A chart will be placed on a new worksheet and you can edit the chart as usual, by changing the chart type, background colors, and labels, for example.

You will see the recalculated figures:

Click PivotChart

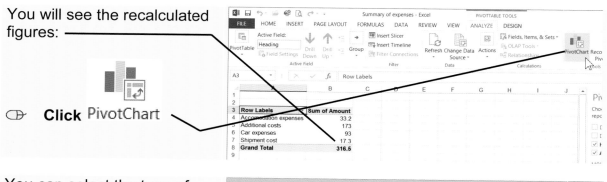

You can select the type of pivot chart. The column option has already been selected:

At the bottom of the window:

Click OK

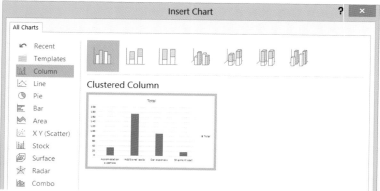

Now you will see the chart.

If you no longer need the chart, it is best to remove it:

Click the chart

Press Delete

You can hone down a little further and display the details for a specific amount:

👉 **Double-click the amount of the car expenses**

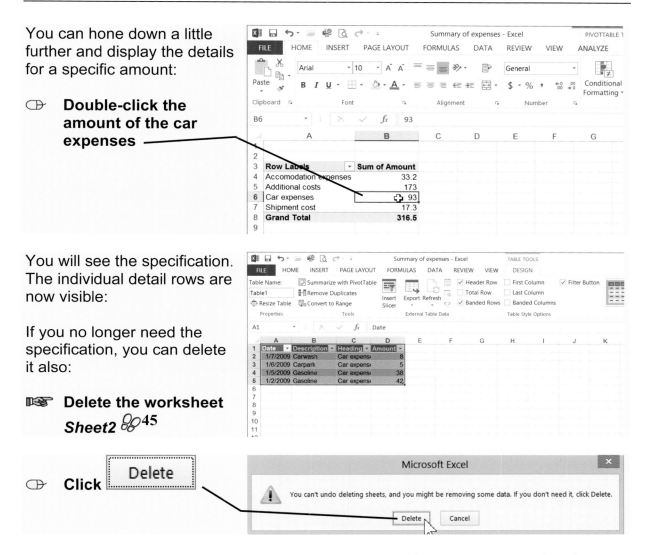

You will see the specification. The individual detail rows are now visible:

If you no longer need the specification, you can delete it also:

👉 **Delete the worksheet Sheet2** 🦶⁴⁵

👉 **Click** `Delete`

You can edit a pivot table, just like other regular cells. If you want to use the pivot table for a report, you can improve the formatting of the numbers:

👉 **Select cells B4 up to B8** 🦶¹⁰

👉 **If necessary, click the** `HOME` **tab**

👉 **Click** `.00`

Now the amounts will have two decimals:

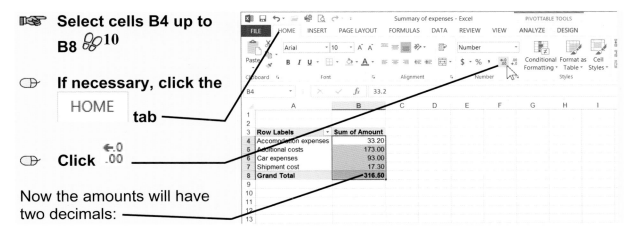

You can print a pivot table in report form. You can choose from a large number of standard formats:

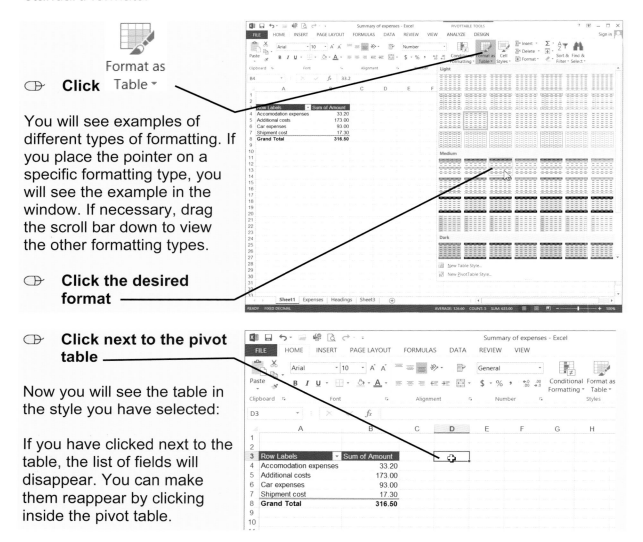

☞ **Click** Format as Table ▾

You will see examples of different types of formatting. If you place the pointer on a specific formatting type, you will see the example in the window. If necessary, drag the scroll bar down to view the other formatting types.

☞ **Click the desired format** ——

☞ **Click next to the pivot table** ——

Now you will see the table in the style you have selected:

If you have clicked next to the table, the list of fields will disappear. You can make them reappear by clicking inside the pivot table.

You can also decide to hide the headings in the pivot table. For example, when there are a lot of headings, or when you want to display only certain headings that relate to this report. Here is how you select the headings:

☞ By Row Labels, click ▼

All the headings are selected:

☞ **Uncheck the box ☑ by (Select All)**

☞ **Check the box ☑ by Car expenses**

☞ **Check the box ☑ by Accomodation expenses**

☞ **Click** OK

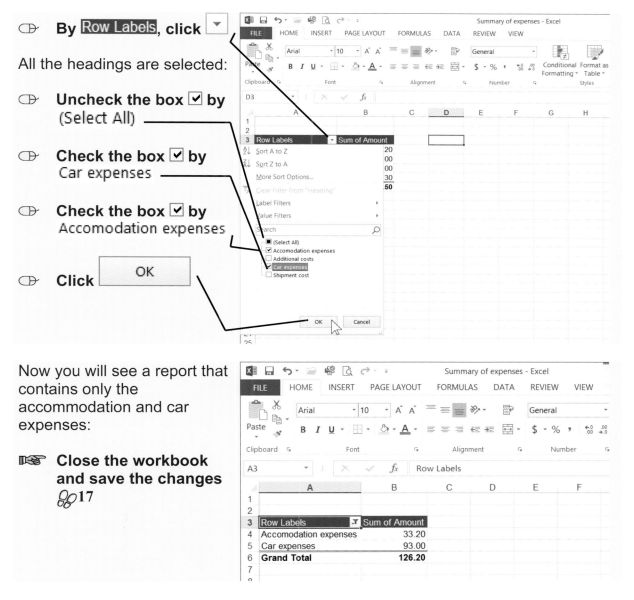

Now you will see a report that contains only the accommodation and car expenses:

☞ **Close the workbook and save the changes** ✂17

Pivot tables can be a powerful tool. They allow you to view data in a way that makes large amounts of data understandable. You can learn more about them in the following chapter.

☞ **Close *Excel*** ✂11

9.5 Exercises

Have you forgotten how to do something? Use the number beside the footsteps to look it up in appendix *B How Do I Do That Again?* at the end of this book.

☞ Open *Excel.* $\mathscr{QQ}^9$

☞ If necessary, open a new workbook. $\mathscr{QQ}^{12}$

☞ Enter these data in *Sheet1*:

	A	B	C	D	E
1	Beginner				
2	Advanced				
3	Junior				

☞ Give column A a name and call it *type.* $\mathscr{QQ}^{24}$

In *Excel 2013*:

☞ Add a worksheet. $\mathscr{QQ}^{73}$

In *Excel 2010*:

☞ Go to *Sheet2.* $\mathscr{QQ}^{19}$

☞ Enter these data in *Sheet2*:

	A	B	C	D	E
1	**Name**	**Type**	**Points**		
2	Hank		5		
3	Peter		2		
4	Carly		3		
5	John		3		
6	Ivy		4		
7	Mario		1		

☞ Use the data validation option to create a dropdown list in cell B2, in order to select the type used in *Sheet1.* $\mathscr{QQ}^{40}$

☞ Copy the formula from cell B2 up to B7. ✂️**4**

☞ Enter the types by using the dropdown list:

	A	B	C	D	E
1	**Name**	**Type**	**Points**		
2	Hank	Advanced	5		
3	Peter	Junior	2		
4	Carly	Advanced	3		
5	John	Beginner	3		
6	Ivy	Advanced	4		
7	Mario	Beginner	1		

☞ Save the document and call it *Points*. ✂️**6**

☞ Sort the overview by *type*. ✂️**46**

☞ Create an overview with the subtotals of the points per *type*. ✂️**55**
You will see this:

	A	B	C	D	E	F
1	**Name**	**Type**	**Points**			
2	Hank	Advanced	5			
3	Carly	Advanced	3			
4	Ivy	Advanced	4			
5		**Advanced**	12			
6	John	Beginner	3			
7	Mario	Beginner	1			
8		**Beginner 1**	4			
9	Peter	Junior	2			
10		**Junior Tot**	2			
11		**Grand Tot**	18			
12						

☞ Delete the subtotals. ✂️**57**

☞ Click the overview and create a pivot table. ✂️**58**

☞ Arrange the pivot table like this:
  Type by ▥ COLUMNS *(Excel 2013)* / ▦ Column Labels *(Excel 2010)*
  Name by ≡ ROWS *(Excel 2013)* / ▦ Row Labels *(Excel 2010)*
  Points by Σ VALUES *(Excel 2013)* / Σ Values *(Excel 2010)*

If necessary, drag the labels to the desired option, see the screen shot below:

☞ Now the pivot table will look like this:

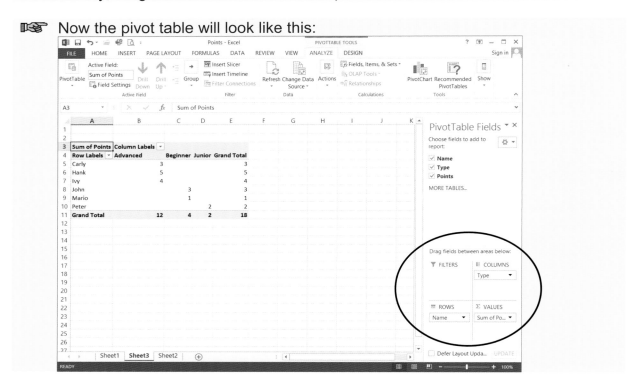

☞ Go to *Sheet2.* 🦶¹⁹

☞ Change the number of points by Carly to 9.

☞ Update the pivot table. 🦶⁶⁰

☞ Save the document. 🦶⁷

☞ Close *Excel.* 🦶¹¹

9.6 Background Information

Dictionary

Pivot chart	You can use a pivot chart report to visualize summarized data from a pivot table. You can use it the report to make comparisons, detect patterns and relationships, and discover trends.
Pivot table	Pivot tables are used to summarize, analyze, explore and present your data. A pivot table is a way to extract data from a long list of information and present it in a more meaningful and understandable format.

Source: Microsoft Excel Help

When do you create a pivot table or use subtotals?

You can use both pivot tables and subtotals to create an overview of grouped or summarized data. Both functions have their own characteristics:

Subtotals

- In order to create subtotals, you will need to sort the table first. This can be a disadvantage, since the original table cannot always be restored.
- It is better not to change any data in the worksheet that contains the subtotals. Changes will not always be applied correctly. Instead, you will need to delete the subtotals first, update the data, sort the table once more and set the subtotals all over again.
- It is easy to display or hide details within the headings, in an overview with subtotals. You can also print such an overview.
- Subtotals are a snapshot in time. If you no longer need them, you can delete them and recalculate them next time.

Pivot tables

- Can be created on a separate worksheet, which means the original table stays intact and can be used as normal. This means you can also save a pivot table, and create multiple pivot tables based on the same data source, if necessary.
- You can display specifications of individual headings, but they will each be put on a new worksheet. You cannot create automatic specifications of multiple headings on a single worksheet.
- You can easily turn a pivot table into a pivot chart.
- A pivot table contains only the data that is important to you.

Generally speaking, subtotals are better suited to create simple (temporary) overviews, while pivot tables are more suitable for creating complex overviews.

10. Tabular Account Book

In the previous chapter you have created a summary of expenses. The next step is to create a more complete accounting book in which you can keep a record of all your revenues and expenses. In this chapter you will be creating a tabular accounting book with a separate column for each type of revenue or expense. This will provide direct insight into your revenues and expenses under those headings. The advantage of a spreadsheet is that it has a large number of columns, so you can keep track of a large number of items. This type of account booking is often used in clubs and small companies.

Usually an accounting book is created for a certain period of time, for example, a month, a quarter or a year. Although *Excel* would probably let you keep track of a much longer period of time in a single accounting book, it is recommended that you limit the period to smaller segments. Otherwise it is harder to keep a clear picture of your data.

You can recap all your income and expenses over a longer period of time using the consolidating function. Consolidating means combining various worksheets that have the same formatting into a larger total overview. More information about consolidating can be found in the *Background Information* of this chapter.

In this chapter you will learn how to:

- set up and edit a tabular accounting book;
- apply *Conditional formatting* with formulas;
- create a recapitulation of the expenses;
- create a pivot table with multiple merge ranges;
- merge different periods with a pivot table.

 Please note:

In order to perform all the tasks in this chapter, you will need to have copied the practice files to your computer. In *Appendix A Downloading the Practice Files* you can read how to download the practice files from the website accompanying this book.

10.1 A Tabular Account Book

In an accounting book you keep track of both revenues and expenses in tabular form. The individual headings will vary per company or club. You will see a number of possible options in the example that will be used in this chapter. You can easily adapt these headings to fit your own situation.

☞ **Open** *Excel* ❦⁹

☞ **Open the workbook called** *Accounting book* ❦²²

⊕ **If necessary, click** $\boxed{\text{Enable Editing}}$

You will see the accounting book. It is partially completed.

You still need to calculate the daily balance:

⊕ **Click cell H5**

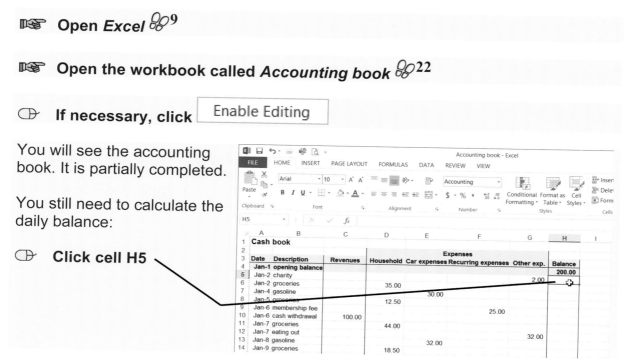

The balance on this line is: previous balance + revenues - expenses. You can convert this basic accounting rule into a formula:

⌨ **Type:** =

Start with the previous balance:

⊕ **Click cell H4**

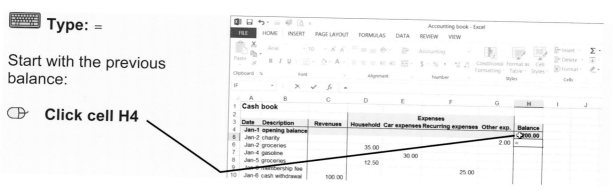

The revenues need to be added to this figure:

Type: +

Click cell C5

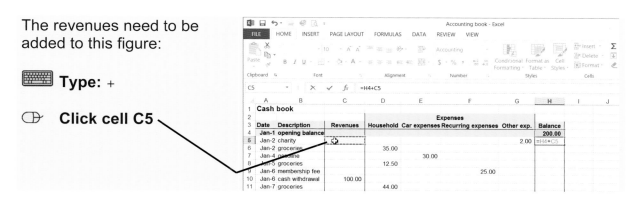

The expenses will be subtracted from the opening balance and the revenues. Because this involves multiple cells, you need to use the *Sum* function. You cannot use the Σ button however, you will need to enter the function yourself:

Type: - sum

Type: (

Drag across cells D5 through G5

Type:)

Now the formula is =H4+C5-sum(D5:G5).

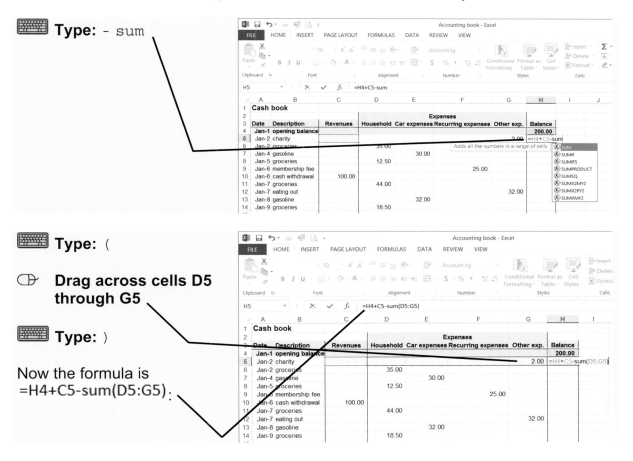

Press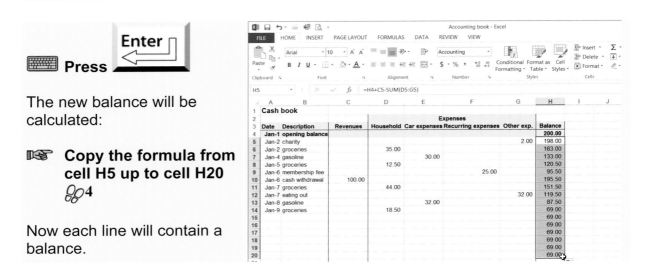

The new balance will be calculated:

 Copy the formula from cell H5 up to cell H20 ⌨4

Now each line will contain a balance.

💡 **Tip**

Check the balance

Here you have calculated the theoretical balance. If you would like to find out whether you have recorded any incorrect amounts or have created any other irregularities in your cash balance, you will need to compare this balance with the actual money you have in cash at regular intervals.

10.2 Conditional Formatting with Formulas

Each line contains a balance, even if the other cells have not been filled in yet. In order to hide the balance if there are no entries on a line, you can use *Conditional formatting*. The method resembles the conditional formatting option you previously used, but in this case, the formatting is dependent on the formatting of another cell. If the balance is identical to the balance on the previous line, nothing has been calculated. You can hide the balance on the 'blank' line. You can do this by displaying the balance in white letters.

To display a white balance if the balance is identical to the previous line:

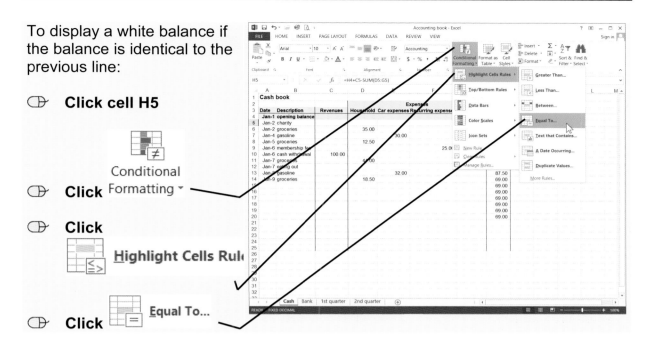

☞ **Click cell H5**

☞ **Click** Conditional Formatting ▾

☞ **Click** Highlight Cells Rule

☞ **Click** Equal To...

If cell H5 equals cell H4, the formatting needs to be applied.

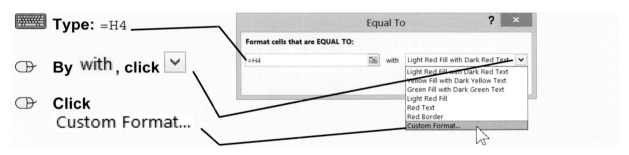

⌨ **Type:** =H4

☞ **By** with **, click** ☑

☞ **Click** Custom Format...

🖐 **Please note:**
Do not fill in the cell by clicking H4. If you do this, the cell reference will automatically be made absolute, and then the conditional formatting will not work properly.

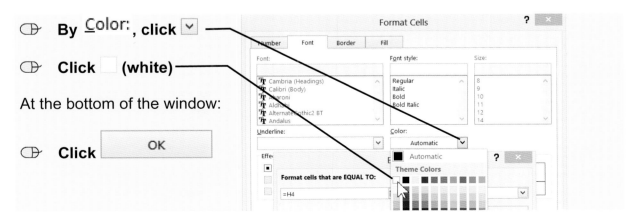

☞ **By** Color: **, click** ☑

☞ **Click** ☐ (white)

At the bottom of the window:

☞ **Click** OK

In the next window:

☞ **Click** OK

☞ **Copy the formula from cell H5 up to H20** ✏4

☞ **Click cell H5**

Now the balances on the blank lines will no longer be visible:

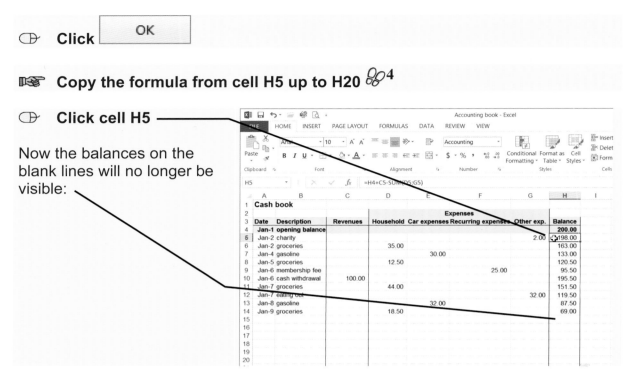

As soon as you enter an amount on a new line, you will see the balance:

☞ **Click cell A15**

⌨ **In cell A15, type:** 1/10

⌨ **In cell B15, type:** parking

⌨ **In cell E15, type:** 1.50

⌨ **Press** ➡

You will see the new balance:

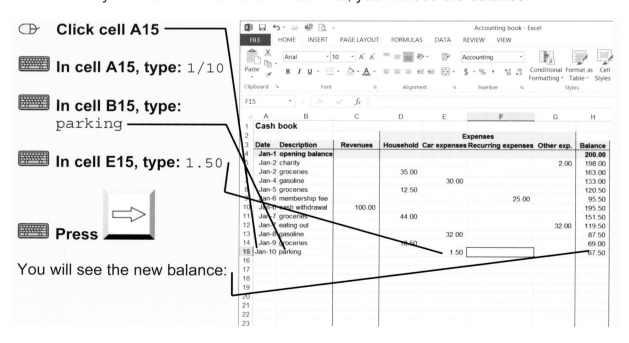

You can easily edit the column headings, for example, by changing their name. If you need more column headings, you just add a new column:

👉 **Right-click**
   G

👉 **Click** Insert

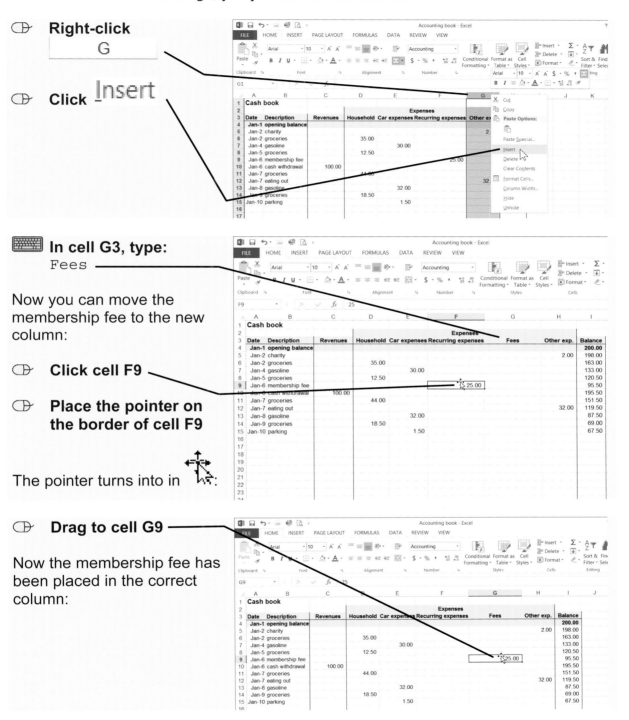

⌨️ **In cell G3, type:**
   Fees

Now you can move the membership fee to the new column:

👉 **Click cell F9**

👉 **Place the pointer on the border of cell F9**

The pointer turns into in ✛:

👉 **Drag to cell G9**

Now the membership fee has been placed in the correct column:

Please note:

Do not add new columns before or after the last expenses column. These new columns will not be included in the calculation of the balance. If you do want to include these columns, you will need to adjust the calculation formula of the balance.

10.3 Create a Recap

You can create a periodical recap of your expenses in cash and through your bank account. But if you have more than one bank account it is harder to know exactly how much you spend for certain items without pulling them all together into a recap. You can recap activities over a period of time, for instance, per month or per quarter.

☞ **Open the *Bank* worksheet** 𝒢𝒢¹⁹

You will see the revenues and expenses per bank transaction. These revenues have already been included in the recap of the first quarter.

☞ **Open the *1ˢᵗ quarter* worksheet** 𝒢𝒢¹⁹

You will see the totals of the expenses paid through your bank account. Now you need to add the amounts of the individual headings in the cash worksheet, so you will know what has been paid in cash:

⊕ **Click cell B2**

⊕ **Click Σ**

☞ **Open the *Cash* worksheet** 𝒢𝒢¹⁹

⊕ **Click ___ D ___**

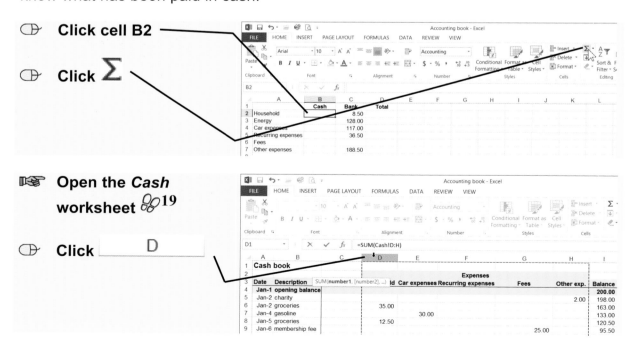

Because the cells D2 up to H2 have been merged, the columns D up to H will be selected at once. But you just need to use only column D:

☞ **Click the *Formula Bar*, next to H**

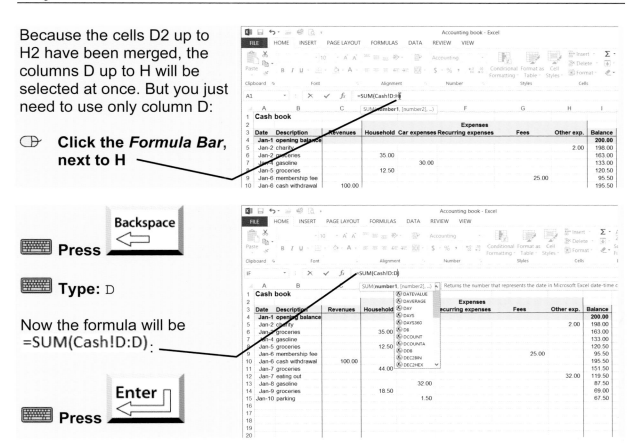

Press Backspace

Type: D

Now the formula will be =SUM(Cash!D:D):

Press Enter

You will see that the total amount spent on the household is shown:

☞ **In the same way, calculate the totals for:**
   Car expenses
   Recurring expenses
   ***Fees*, and**
   Other expenses

Please note: you need to adjust the *Sum* formula each time.

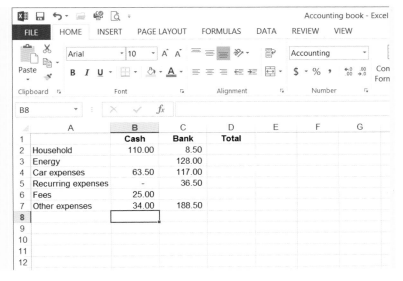

	A	B	C	D	E	F	G
1		Cash	Bank	Total			
2	Household	110.00	8.50				
3	Energy		128.00				
4	Car expenses	63.50	117.00				
5	Recurring expenses	-	36.50				
6	Fees	25.00					
7	Other expenses	34.00	188.50				
8							

Finally, you can calculate the combined total expenses of the cash and bank worksheet, for each separate heading:

⊕   **Click cell D2**

⊕   **Click Σ**

⌨   **Press** Enter ⏎

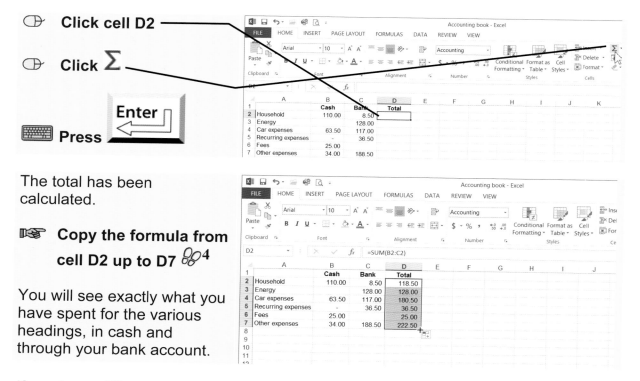

The total has been calculated.

☞   **Copy the formula from cell D2 up to D7** ✂️**4**

You will see exactly what you have spent for the various headings, in cash and through your bank account.

If you have different types of revenues, you can create a summary of these revenues in the same way.

10.4 Consolidating with Pivot Tables

If you have created recaps over different periods, you can merge them with a pivot table. In this example you will see a recap of the second quarter.

Please note:

All the recaps need to be arranged in exactly the same way, in order to combine them in a pivot table.

☞   **Open the 2ⁿᵈ *quarter* worksheet** ✂️**19**

You will see the expenses from second quarter. In order to create this type of pivot table, you will need to use the *PivotTable and PivotChart Wizard*. You can add this wizard to the *Quick Access* toolbar.

☞ **Add the *PivotTable and PivotChart Wizard* command to the *Quick Access* toolbar** **1**

HELP! I cannot find the PivotTable and PivotChart Wizard.

You will find the *PivotTable and PivotChart Wizard* command by All Commands.

You will see the command on the *Quick Access* toolbar:

⊕ **Click**

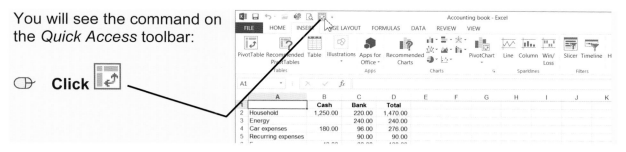

You will be creating a pivot table from multiple *Excel* lists:

⊕ **Click the radio button ⦿ by**
Multiple consolidation

⊕ **Click** Next >

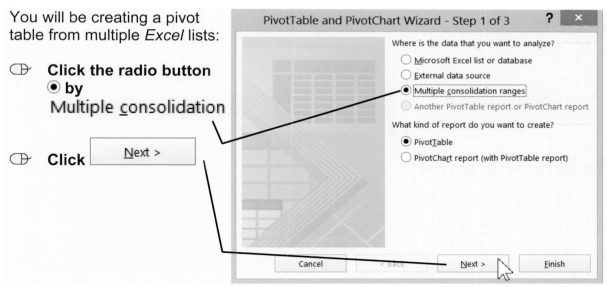

You do not need to change anything in the next window:

⊕ **Click** Next >

Select the tables you want to include in the pivot table:

Click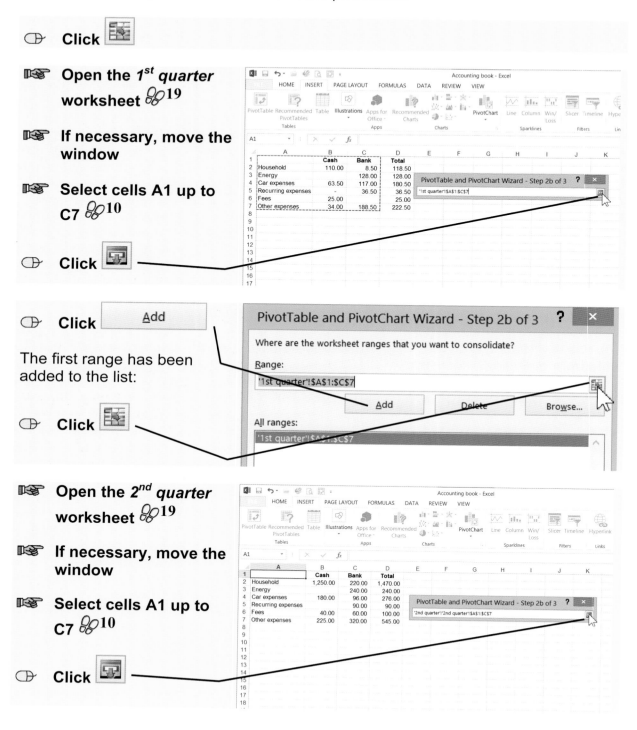

Open the *1st quarter* worksheet ✂19

If necessary, move the window

Select cells A1 up to C7 ✂10

Click

Click   Add

The first range has been added to the list:

Click

Open the *2nd quarter* worksheet ✂19

If necessary, move the window

Select cells A1 up to C7 ✂10

Click

Click [Add]

Click [Next >]

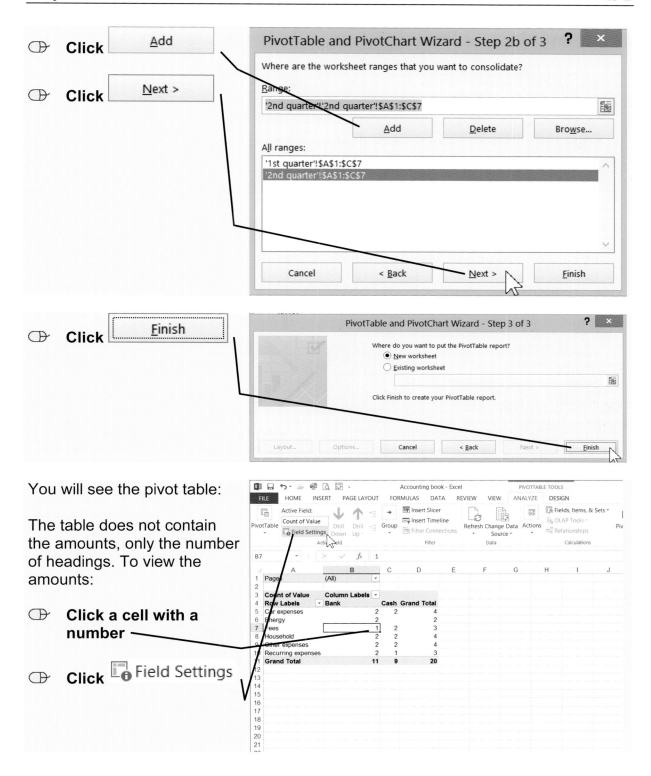

Click [Finish]

You will see the pivot table:

The table does not contain the amounts, only the number of headings. To view the amounts:

Click a cell with a number

Click Field Settings

Click Sum

You can also set the number format right away:

Click Number Format

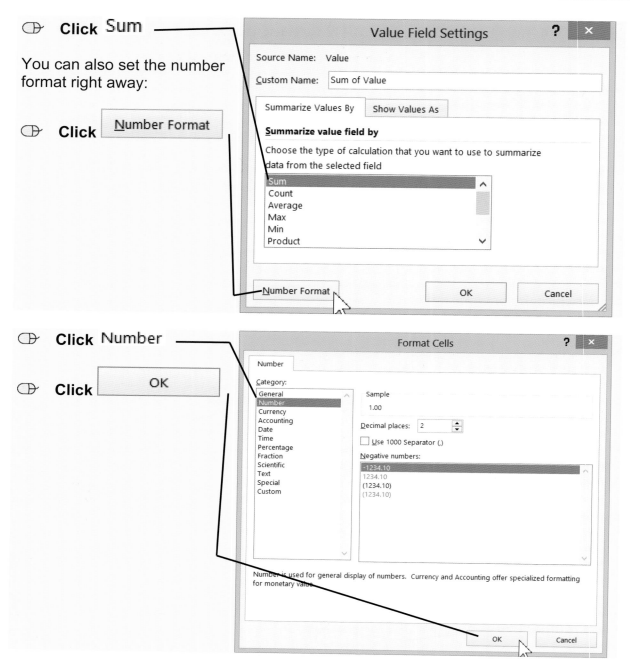

Click Number

Click OK

In the next window:

Click OK

You will see the amounts for each quarter, and for each heading, subdivided between cash and bank expenses:

You can also view just the first or the second quarter:

By (All), click ▼

Click Item2, OK

Now you will only see the amounts for the second quarter:

You can also display just the cash or the bank figures:

By **Column Labels**, click ▼

Uncheck the box ☑ by (Select All)

Check the box ☑ by Cash

Click OK

Now you will only see the cash expenses from the second quarter:

To display the first quarter as well, once again:

By Item2, click ▼

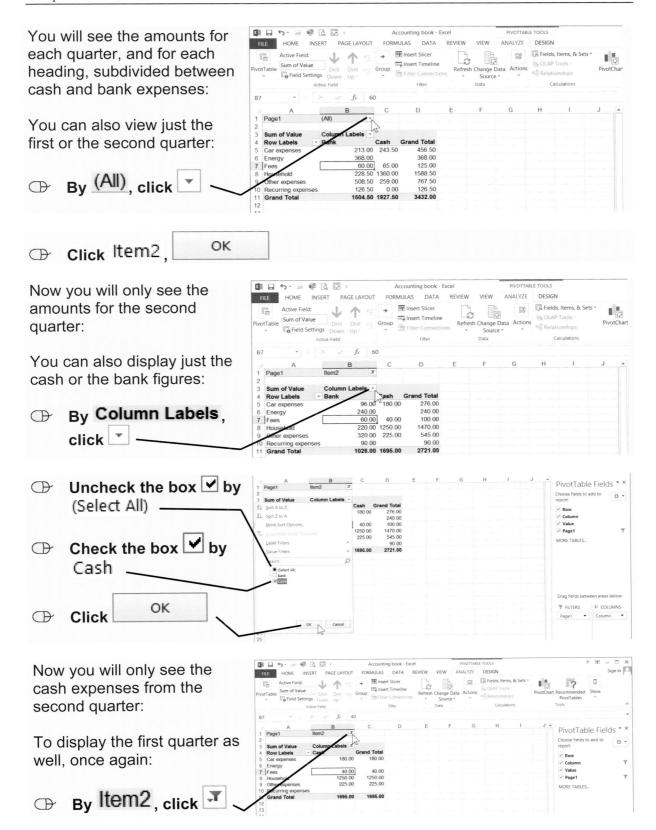

🖰 **Click** (All) , [OK]

To display the bank figures again:

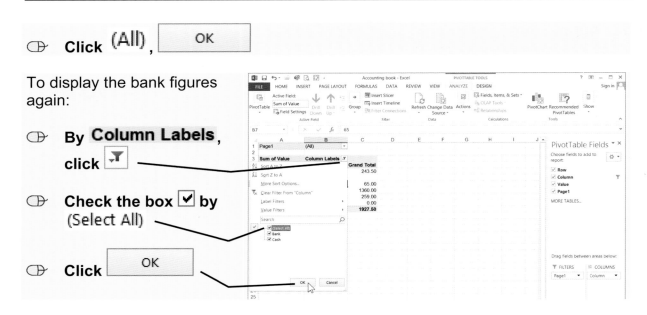

🖰 **By Column Labels,** click 🔽

🖰 **Check the box** ☑ **by** (Select All)

🖰 **Click** [OK]

If you are using a more complex workbook, the number of worksheets can become quite large. Enter clear names for all the worksheets, so you will quickly be able to find them, and arrange them in a logical order. You will see all the totals:

☞ **Change the name of** *Sheet1* to *Recap* 🐾18

☞ **Move the** *Recap* **worksheet to the end** 🐾65

☞ **Save the workbook** 🐾7

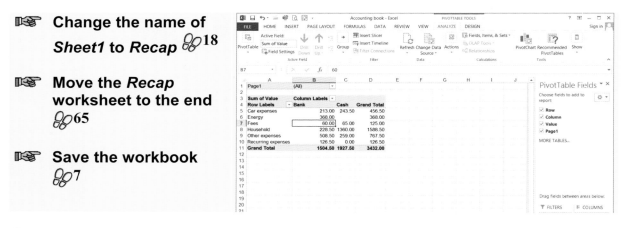

🡢 **Please note:**

If you have changed any amounts in your cash or bank books, you will need to recalculate the pivot table by clicking 🗋🔄 on the [ANALYZE] tab (*Excel 2013*) / [Options] tab (*Excel 2010*).

☞ **Close** *Excel* 🐾11

In this chapter you have learned how to work with an accounting book.

10.5 Exercises

Have you forgotten how to do something? Use the number beside the footsteps to look it up in appendix *B How Do I Do That Again?* at the end of this book.

☞ Open *Excel*. 🐾⁹

☞ If necessary, open a new workbook. 🐾¹²

☞ Enter the following data in *Sheet1*:

	A	B	C	D	E	F
1	cash book					
2	Date	Description	Revenues	Household	Car	Cash in hand
3	1/1/2014	Opening balance				75.00
4	1/2/2104	Gasoline			50.00	
5	1/3/2014	Groceries		40.00		
6	1/3/2014	Bank withdrawel	100.00			
7	1/4/2014	Parking			10.00	
8	1/4/2014	Groceries		35.00		
9	1/5/2014	Groceries		10.00		
10	1/5/2014	Clothes		40.00		

☞ In cell F4, type the formula =F3+C4-D4-E4

☞ Copy the formula from cell F4 up to F10. 🐾⁴

☞ Select cells F3 up to F10. 🐾¹⁰

☞ Set a conditional formatting for these cells, in order to display the cells with negative numbers with a red background. 🐾⁶⁶

In *Excel 2013*:

☞ Create a new worksheet. 🐾⁷³

In *Excel 2010*:

☞ Go to *Sheet2*. ♀♀19

☞ Enter these data in *Sheet2*:

	A	B	C	D
1	**Recap**			
2	Revenues			
3	Household			
4	Car			

☞ Click cell B2.

☞ Use the *Sum* formula to calculate the total amount of the revenues on *Sheet1*. ♀♀74

☞ Calculate the sum total of the household and car in the same way. ♀♀74

☞ Save the document and call it *Cash overview*. ♀♀6

☞ Close *Excel*. ♀♀11

10.6 Background Information

Dictionary

Consolidating   Combining different overviews that are arranged in the same way to create a total overview. For example, for different time periods, products, branches, etcetera.

Tabular account book   A cash or a bank book in which the revenues and/or expenses are grouped by headings or labels, in order to quickly gain an insight in the types of revenues/expenses.

Source: Microsoft Excel Help

Consolidating
By consolidating data you can create an overview of a larger entity. If you consolidate a number of periods (months, quarters, years), you will be able to look at the figures over a longer period of time. Although in most cases, you will need to consolidate consecutive periods, in order to get meaningful figures.

You can also consolidate the figures for:
- branches
- districts
- countries
- salespersons
- products or product groups

After you have consolidated the figures, you will have a better overview of the totals that encompass larger entities. If necessary, you can split up the figures again, as you have learned in this book.

If you want to consolidate figures with pivot tables, all the summaries you use need to be arranged in exactly the same way. In order to achieve this, you may need to adapt the arrangement of some of the summaries, for example, by adding an extra row or column that is not used in that particular summary, but is used in the other summaries.

10.7 Tips

 Tip

View details

You can use the *Pivot table* toolbar to display the details of an amount in the pivot table. The details will be placed on a new worksheet:

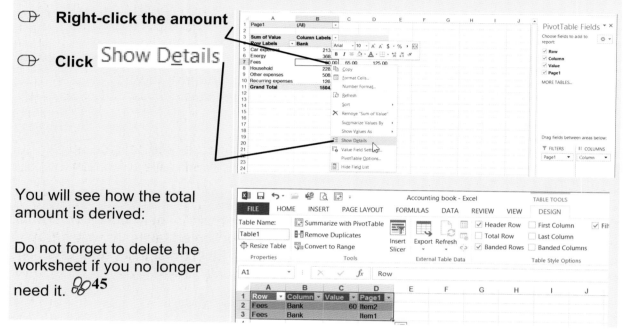

Right-click the amount

Click Show De_t_ails

You will see how the total amount is derived:

Do not forget to delete the worksheet if you no longer need it. 🐾45

 Tip

Adjust the pivot table with the menu

Instead of using the *Pivot table* toolbar you can also change the properties by right-clicking:

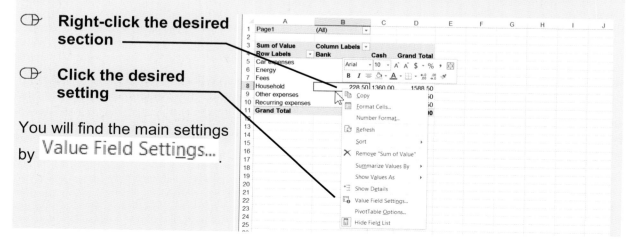

Right-click the desired section

Click the desired setting

You will find the main settings by Value Field Settin_g_s... .

11. More Functions and Macros

Microsoft Excel has dozens of functions that can help you solve complex problems. Up till now, you have used just a few of these functions. In this chapter you will learn how to work with a few more functions. You may not need to use these functions on a daily basis, but it is useful to know how they work. Once you know this, you can begin to use these other functions.

Did you know that you can use *Excel* to draw lots, for a lottery or a match? For this purpose, the list used needs to be unsorted. In this chapter you will learn how to put sorted data back into a list with random order.

Also, you will learn how to use the *COUNT* function to count all the cells containing numbers within a selected area (or just the opposite: the blank cells). This function is very suitable for creating work schedules.

Do you need to perform a number of tasks on a regular basis? Then you can create a macro for these tasks. A macro is very handy for complicated tasks, or when they need to be done by less experienced users. By using a key combination you can automatically perform the tasks that go with a certain command.

In this chapter you will learn how to:

- use the *RAND* function;
- use this function to draw lots;
- count cells with *COUNT*;
- use a multiple sorting command;
- create a macro;
- run macros.

 Please note:

In order to perform all the tasks in this chapter, you will need to have copied the practice files to your computer. In *Appendix A Downloading the Practice Files* you can read how to download the practice files from the website accompanying this book.

11.1 Organize a Lottery with Excel

Microsoft Excel can sort data in different ways. But how do you do the exact opposite? How do you turn a sorted list into a randomly ordered list again, for a lottery, for instance? There is no specific function for this, but via a small workaround you will be able to achieve this without too much difficulty.

☞ **Open *Excel*** 👣⁹

☞ **If necessary, click** | Enable Editing |

☞ **Open the *Horseracing* practice file** 👣²²

You will see the worksheet, with a list of competitors. The horses have been listed in alphabetical order by their names. In order to determine the starting order for the race, a draw needs to be made. First, you need to let *Excel* assign a number between zero and one to each horse. For this you can use the *RAND* function:

☞ **Click** *fx*

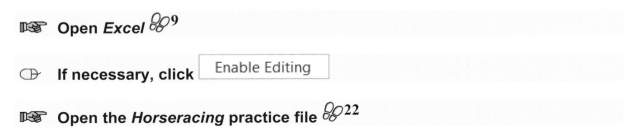

Since you already know which function you are looking for, you can enter its name directly:———

⌨ **Type:** rand

☞ **Click** | Go |

The function has been found and selected. If you want to know more about this function before you start, you can click <u>Help on this function</u>.

☞ **Click** | OK |

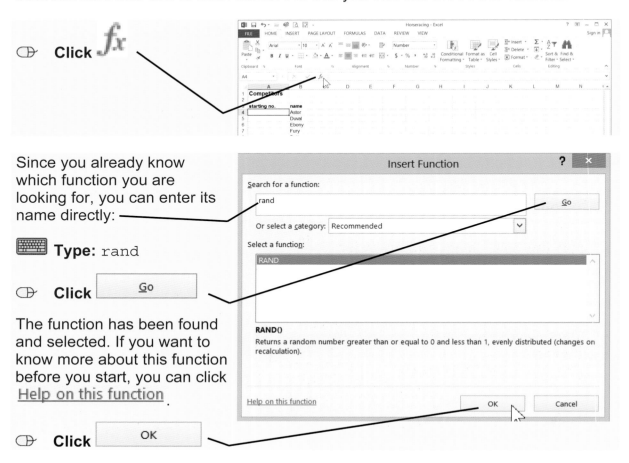

You do not need to enter any other data to use this function:

⊕ **Click** OK

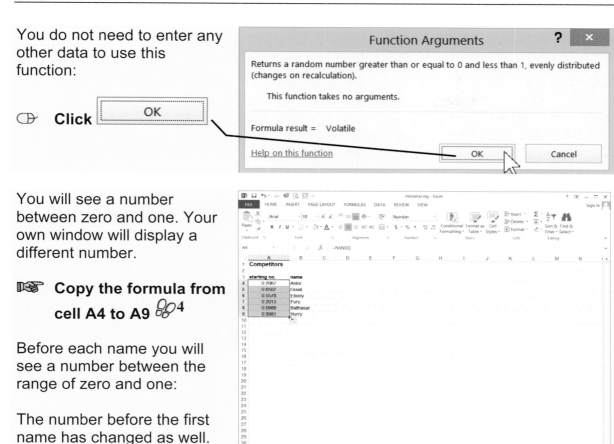

You will see a number between zero and one. Your own window will display a different number.

☞ **Copy the formula from cell A4 to A9** ৶4

Before each name you will see a number between the range of zero and one:

The number before the first name has changed as well.

By sorting the names according to this number, you can determine a random starting order.

☞ **Select cells A4 through B9** ৶10

☞ **Sort the cells in ascending order** ৶46

In *Excel 2010* you might see this window:

⊕ **Click** a **radio button** ⦿ **next to** Continue with the curr

⊕ **Click** Sort

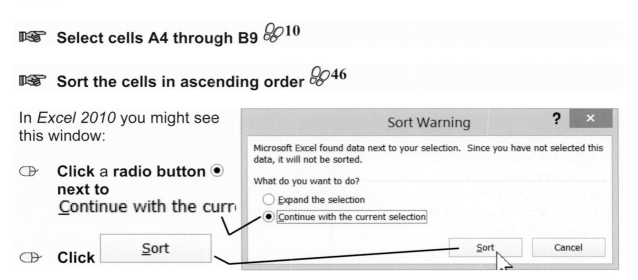

Now the names have been sorted:

Please note: in your own window, a different starting order will be displayed.

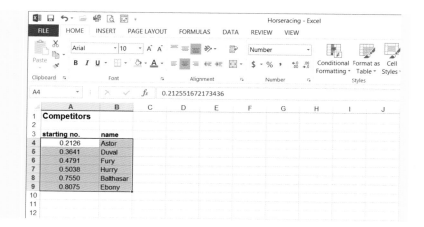

 Please note:

Once again, the numbers before the names have changed. Every time you change anything in these cells, *RAND* will calculate a new value. If you sort the list for a second time, the order will change once more, and you will also see different numbers.

Now you can replace the numbers by starting numbers:

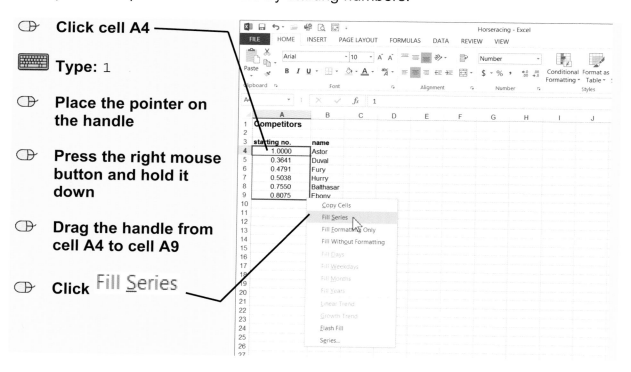

Click cell A4 ——

Type: 1

Place the pointer on the handle

Press the right mouse button and hold it down

Drag the handle from cell A4 to cell A9

Click Fill Series

Now you will see the starting numbers: —————

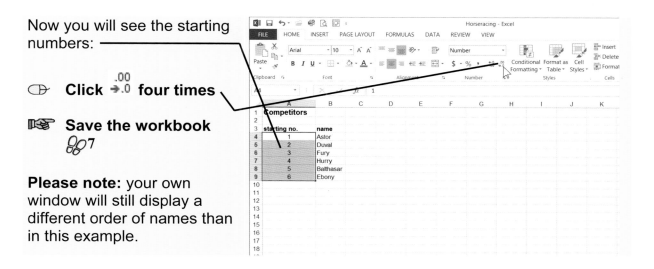

👉 **Click** .00 →.0 **four times**

👉 **Save the workbook** 👣7

Please note: your own window will still display a different order of names than in this example.

11.2 Counting Numbers

Now that the starting order has been established, you can fill in the schedule for the competition.

👉 **Open the *Day 1* worksheet** 👣19

The names need to be copied from the list of competitors.

⌨ **In cell A5, type:** =

👉 **Open the *Competitors* worksheet** 👣19

👉 **Click cell B4**

⌨ **Press** Enter

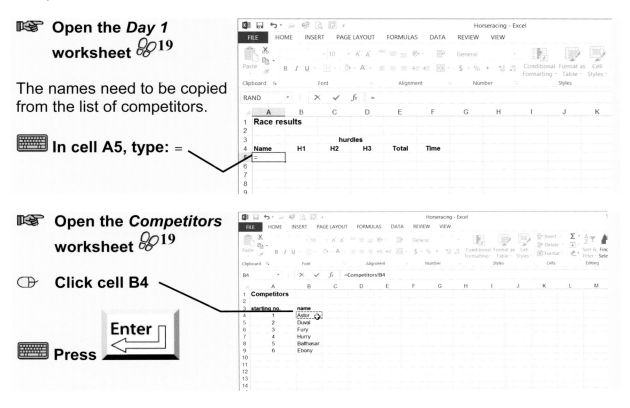

The first name has been filled in:

☞ **Copy the formula from cell A5 to A10** 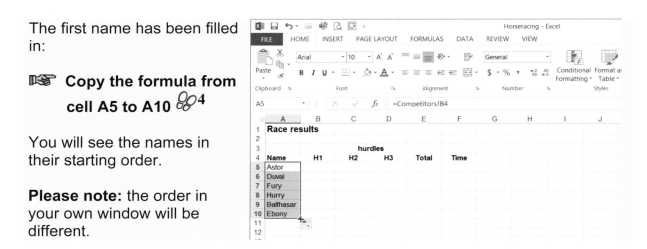⁴

You will see the names in their starting order.

Please note: the order in your own window will be different.

Since the event is comprised of two races on two days, you can copy this sheet to the second day:

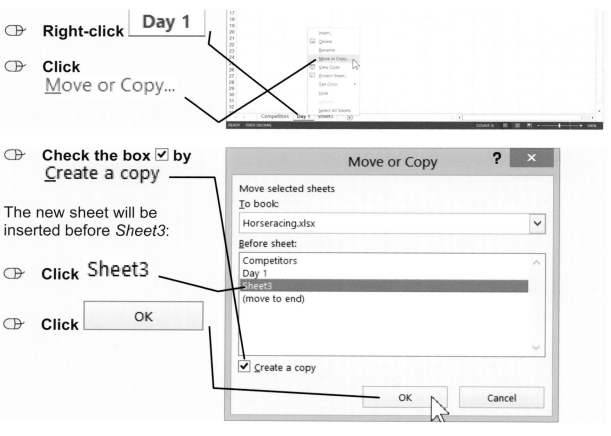

⊕ **Right-click** Day 1

⊕ **Click** Move or Copy...

⊕ **Check the box ☑ by** Create a copy

The new sheet will be inserted before *Sheet3*:

⊕ **Click** Sheet3

⊕ **Click** OK

The copy is called Day 1 (2).

☞ **Name the sheet *Day 2*** ⁱ⁸

Now the schedule is finished, you can fill it in during or after the race. This is how you do it:

- For each failed hurdle, you fill in a 0 (zero).
- By 'Total', the number of failed hurdles is counted.
- The time the competitors need to complete the course is also recorded.
- The competitor with the lowest number of failed hurdles wins the race.
- If multiple competitors have the same number of failed hurdles, then the competitor with the fastest time wins the race.

The end result is achieved by adding up the results of both days.

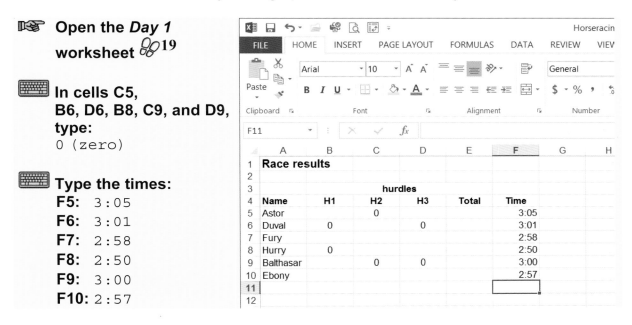

☞ **Open the *Day 1* worksheet** ✂19

⌨ **In cells C5, B6, D6, B8, C9, and D9, type:**
0 (zero)

⌨ **Type the times:**
F5: 3:05
F6: 3:01
F7: 2:58
F8: 2:50
F9: 3:00
F10: 2:57

In order to count the number of failed hurdles per horse, you use the *COUNT* function:

👉 **Click cell E5**

👉 **Click** *fx*

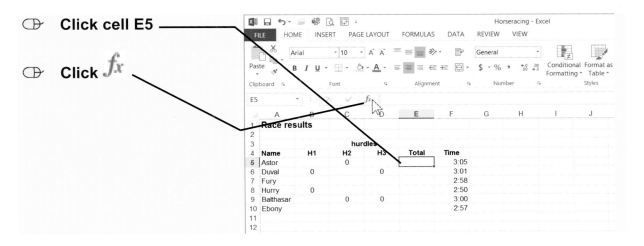

☞ **Select the** All **category** 🐾67

⊕ **If necessary, drag the scroll bar downwards**

⊕ **Click** COUNT

The *COUNT* function counts the number of cells that contain a number.

If you want to know more about this function before using it, you can click Help on this function.

⊕ **Click** OK

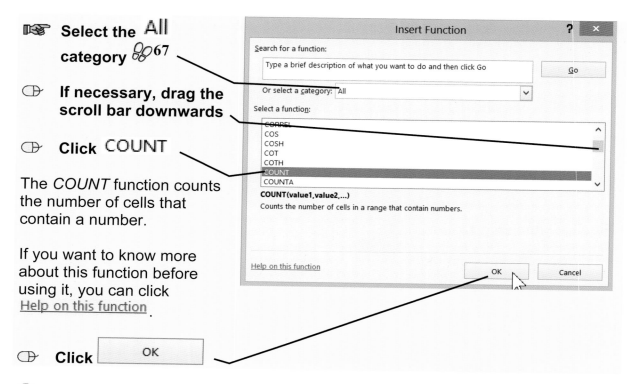

💡 **Tip**

Counting empty cells

With the *COUNTBLANK* function you can count the number of empty cells in a selected area.

Select the cells for which you want to count the number of zeroes:

⊕ **If necessary, move the window**

⊕ **Drag across cells B5 up to D5**

The cells will be filled in:

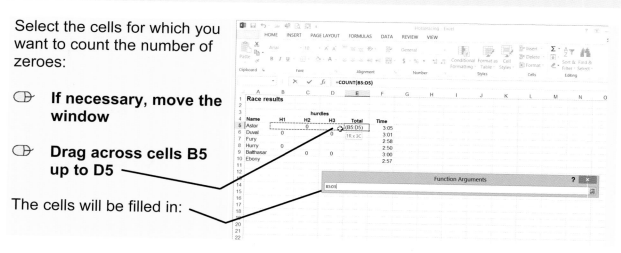

Click [OK]

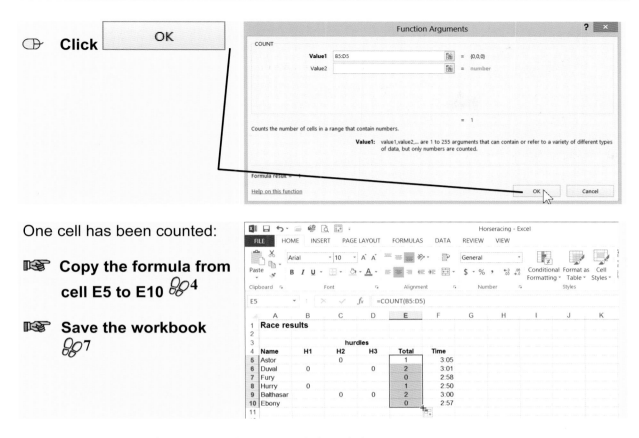

One cell has been counted:

☞ **Copy the formula from cell E5 to E10** 👣4

☞ **Save the workbook** 👣7

You can copy this formula to the second day right away:

In the top left corner of the window:

Click [copy icon]

☞ **Open the *Day 2* worksheet** 👣19

Click cell E5

Click [paste icon]

Please note: the total for each horse will still be zero, since no failed hurdles have been filled in yet.

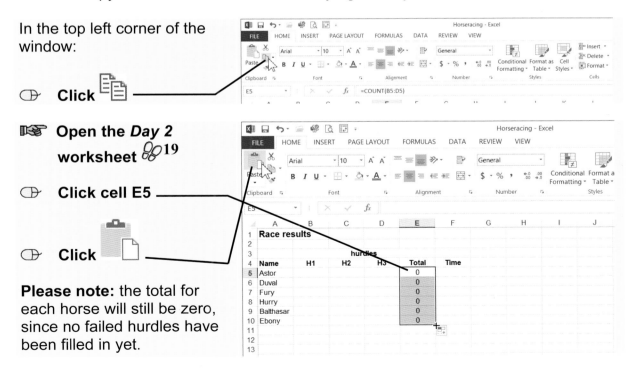

In cells C5,
D7, C8, B9, C9, and
C10, type: 0 (zero)

Fill in the times:
F5: 3:00
F6: 2:57
F7: 2:49
F8: 2:52
F9: 3:10
F10: 2:52

Save the workbook

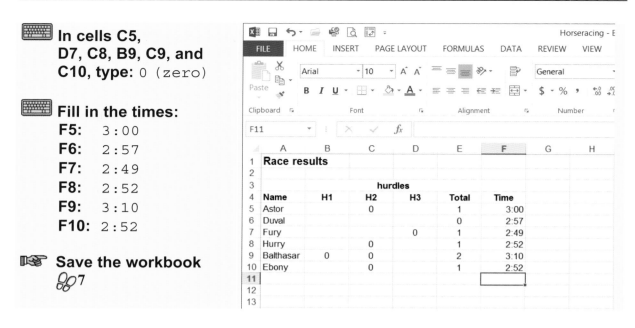

11.3 The Final Result

In order to obtain the final result, you need to add up the results of the individual days. You can do this on a separate sheet:

Open the *Sheet3* worksheet

First, you copy the name of the horse from *Day 1*:

In cell B4, type: =

Open the *Day 1* worksheet

Click cell A5

Press Enter

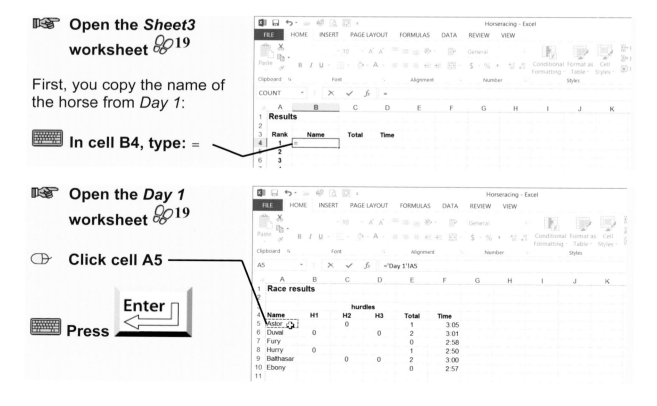

The first name has been entered:

🖰 **Click cell C4**

⌨ **Type: =**

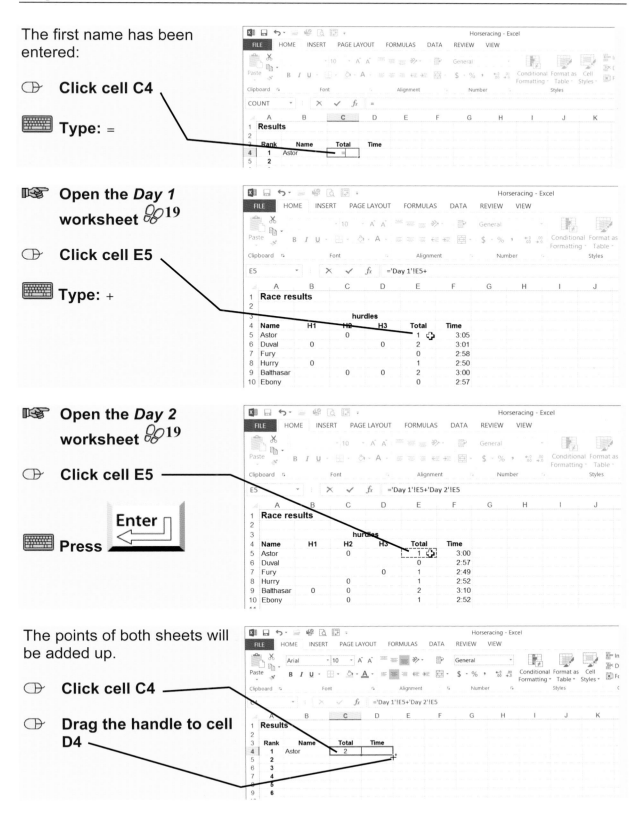

👉 **Open the *Day 1* worksheet** 🐾¹⁹

🖰 **Click cell E5**

⌨ **Type: +**

👉 **Open the *Day 2* worksheet** 🐾¹⁹

🖰 **Click cell E5**

⌨ **Press** Enter

The points of both sheets will be added up.

🖰 **Click cell C4**

🖰 **Drag the handle to cell D4**

The times have been added up as well, but the formatting is not correct:

☞ **Click cell D4**

☞ **Right-click cell D4**

☞ **Click** Format Cells...

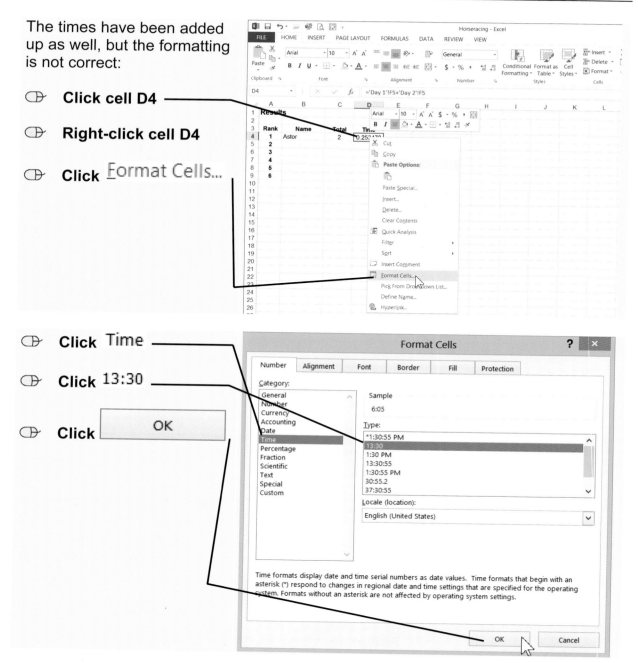

☞ **Click** Time

☞ **Click** 13:30

☞ **Click** OK

🖐 **Please note:**

Up till this point, you have filled in the hours and minutes in this exercise as time units. As long as the total does not exceed 24 hours, this is not a problem. From 24 hours on, *Excel* will start calculating in days. Then the total time will not be accurately displayed. If you want to enter the time in the correct format, you need to type 0:03:05 instead of 3:05, or 0:02:58 instead of 2:58.

You will see the time. Now you can copy the formula to the next rows:

☞ **Select cells B4 up to D4** 👣10

☞ **Drag the handle from cell D4 to cell D9**

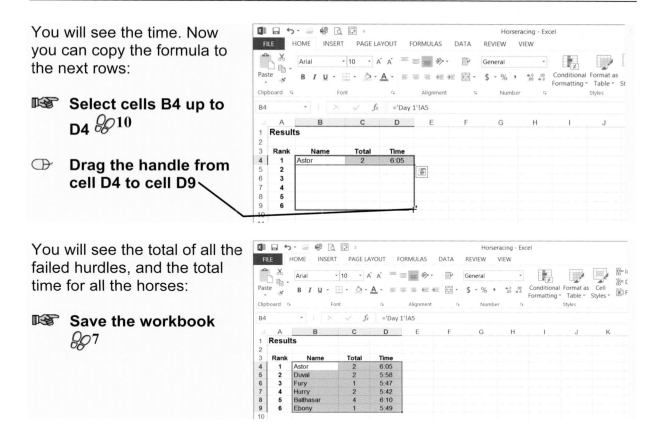

You will see the total of all the failed hurdles, and the total time for all the horses:

☞ **Save the workbook** 👣7

11.4 Sorting List on Multiple Fields

After the results have been combined, the final result can be determined. You can do this by sorting the results list by the number of penalty points, and the time.

You can do these things in the *Sort* window. If you only use the $\frac{A}{Z}\downarrow$ or $\frac{Z}{A}\downarrow$ button, the twofold sorting command (total and time) will be more complicated. Also, the ranking list in column A (from 1 up to and including 6) will be included in the sort command. First, you need to select the area you want to sort:

☞ **Select cells B4 up to D9** 👣10

☞ **Click the** DATA **tab**

☞ **Click** Sort

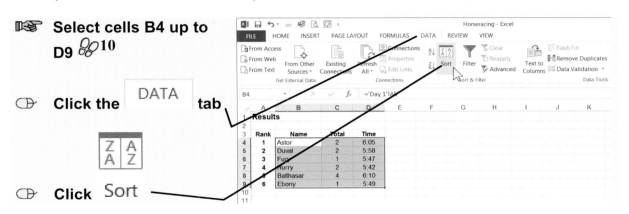

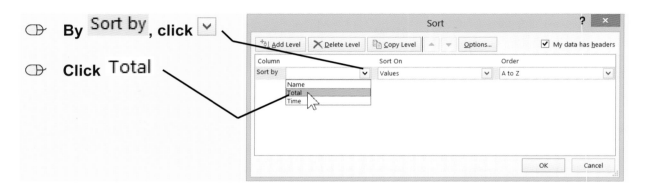

By **Sort by**, click ∨

Click **Total**

The horse with the lowest number of penalty points wins, so the total needs to be sorted in ascending order. This is similar to using the $^{A}_{Z}\downarrow$ button. If the number of points is equal, the time is taken into consideration. The shorter the time, the better the horse has run. So the time needs to be sorted in ascending order too:

To add a sorting level:

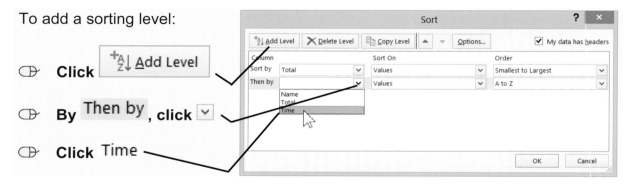

Click **Add Level**

By **Then by**, click ∨

Click **Time**

Please note:
You are telling *Excel* to perform the sort commands in order of relevance. In this case, the points are considered first, and in the second instance the time is considered. If you sort the results by time first, and then by number of penalty points, you will get a different order.

The sorting levels have been entered. Extra sorting levels are not required:

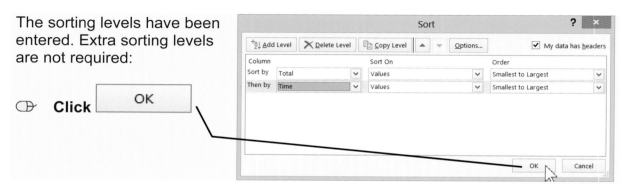

Click **OK**

You will see the sorted lists with all the results:

Please note: the names in your window will be in a different order, since the starting order of your horses is different too.

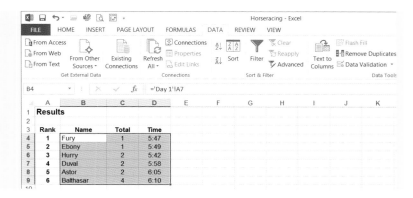

11.5 Creating a Macro

It is important that you sort your data correctly. If intermediate rankings need to be created at regular intervals, or if the results are recorded by someone who does not have sufficient knowledge of *Excel*, you can create a macro for a particular sorting task. Then, the sorting task can be done by pressing a key combination. In *Excel*, this is a combination of **Ctrl** plus a letter key. You can also place a button on the *Quick Access* toolbar for this key combination.

In this section you are going to create a macro with a key combination. Here is how you create a macro:

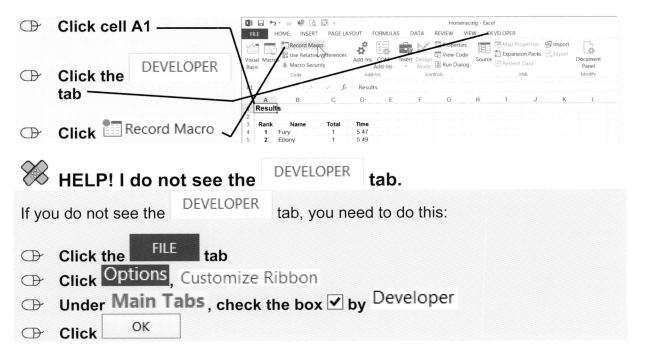

Click cell A1

Click the DEVELOPER tab

Click Record Macro

HELP! I do not see the DEVELOPER tab.

If you do not see the DEVELOPER tab, you need to do this:

Click the FILE tab

Click Options, Customize Ribbon

Under Main Tabs, check the box ☑ by Developer

Click OK

Enter an easily identifiable
name for the macro:

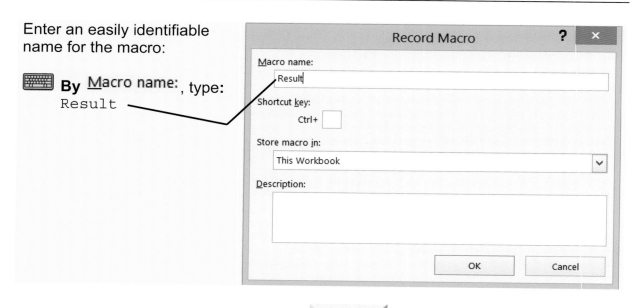

⌨ **By** <u>M</u>acro name: , **type:**
    `Result`

Next you can select the key combination **Ctrl** plus the letter **R** (for result).

👉 **Please note:**

If you use this key combination, any other existing function for **Ctrl** + **R** will be overwritten in this workbook.

⌨ **By** Ctrl+, **type:** `r`

The macro will be saved in
This Workbook :

🖱 **Click** OK

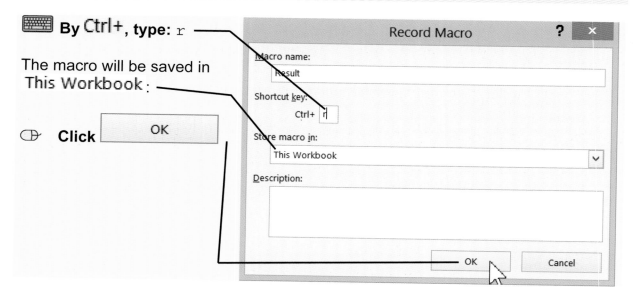

From this moment on, your actions will be recorded, until you end the macro. While you are recording, you will see this symbol ☐ (*Excel 2013*) / ■ (*Excel 2010*) in the bottom left corner of the status bar, and also READY ☐ (*Excel 2013*) / Ready ■ (*Excel 2010*) window. You can move this, but do not close the toolbar.

☞ **Select cells B3 up to D9** 🐾 **10**

👉 **Click the** DATA **tab**

👉 **Click** Sort

👉 **By** Sort by **, click** ☑

👉 **Click** Total

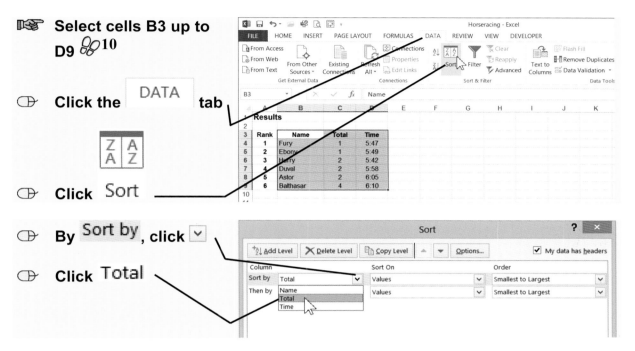

🐦 **Please note:**

Because you just did this particular sorting task, the Total option will still be selected. If you open the worksheet the next time, or if you have already done a different sorting task, some other name may be selected. That is why you need to select Total once again, to make this macro run smoothly.

👉 **By** Then by **, click** ☑

👉 **Click** Time

This item needs to be reselected as well.

👉 **Click** OK

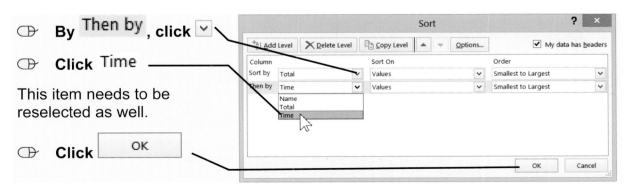

In the bottom left corner of the window:

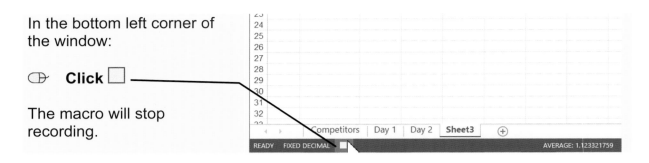

☞ **Click** ☐

The macro will stop recording.

11.6 Using a Macro

When you are using this worksheet, you can sort the results at any given moment by pressing **Ctrl** and the letter **R**. Since the results had already been sorted, nothing has changed. In order to check if the macro runs correctly, you can change a result on the *Day 1* worksheet:

☞ **Open the *Day 1* worksheet** 👣19

☞ **Click cell B8**

⌨ **Press** **Delete**

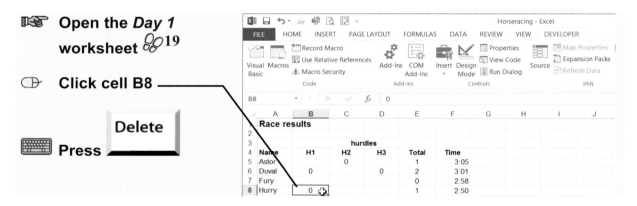

This horse has made no mistakes. In your own window, row 8 will probably contain a different name. Remember the name of the horse on row 8 (in your window).

☞ **Open the *Sheet3* worksheet** 👣19

☞ **Click a cell**

The penalty points have been adjusted, but the sorting order has not yet been adjusted (notice the time):

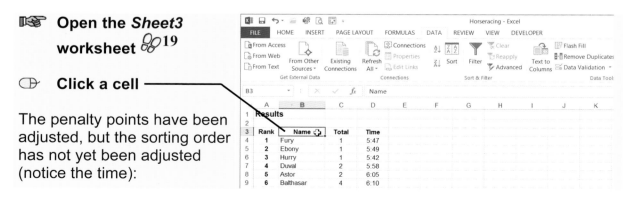

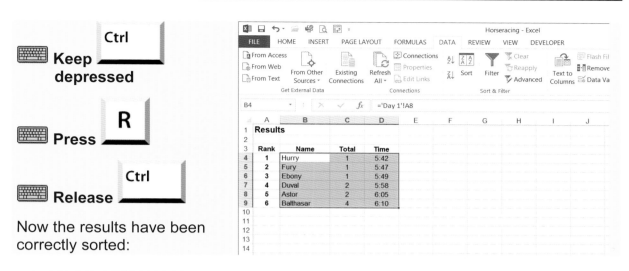

Keep **Ctrl** **depressed**

Press **R**

Release **Ctrl**

Now the results have been correctly sorted:

☞ **Change the name of *Sheet3* to *Results* 🐾18**

☞ **Save the workbook 🐾7**

You will be asked whether you want to save this workbook with or without the macros. You can save it with the macros, if you want to use them again later on.

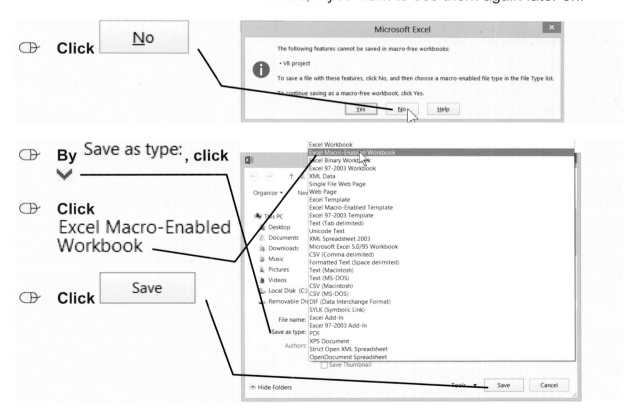

☞ **Click** No

☞ **By** Save as type: **, click** ⌄

☞ **Click** Excel Macro-Enabled Workbook

☞ **Click** Save

This macro can be used for the entire workbook, but will only function correctly if you are using the *Results* worksheet.

☞ **Close** *Excel* ¹¹

11.7 Visual Steps Website and Newsletter

By now we hope you have noticed that the Visual Steps method is an excellent method for quickly and efficiently learning more about tablets, computers, other devices and software applications. All books published by Visual Steps use this same method.
In various series, we have published a large number of books on a wide variety of topics including *Windows*, *Mac OS X*, the iPad, iPhone, Samsung Galaxy Tab, Kindle, photo editing and many other topics.

On the **www.visualsteps.com** website you can click the Catalog page to find an overview of all the Visual Steps titles. Each title gives you an extensive description and allows you to preview the full table of contents and a sample chapter in PDF format. In this way, you can quickly determine if a specific title will meet your expectations. All titles can be ordered online and are also available in bookstores in the USA, Canada, United Kingdom, Australia and New Zealand.
Furthermore, the website offers many extras, among other things:
• free computer guides and booklets (PDF files) covering all sorts of subjects;
• frequently asked questions and their answers;
• information on the free Computer Certificate that you can acquire at the certificate's website **www.ccforseniors.com**;
• a free email notification service: let's you know when a new book is published.

There is always more to learn. Visual Steps offers many other books on computer-related subjects. Each Visual Steps book has been written using the same step-by-step method with short, concise instructions and screen shots illustrating every step.

Would you like to be informed when a new Visual Steps title becomes available? Subscribe to the free Visual Steps newsletter (no strings attached) and you will receive this information in your inbox.
The Newsletter is sent approximately each month and includes information about
• the latest titles;
• supplemental information concerning titles previously released;
• new free computer booklets and guides;
• contests and questionnaires with which you can win prizes.
When you subscribe to our Newsletter you will have direct access to the free booklets on the **www.visualsteps.com/info_downloads** web page.

11.8 Exercises

Have you forgotten how to do something? Use the number beside the footsteps to look it up in appendix *B How Do I Do That Again?* at the end of this book.

☞ Open *Excel.* 👣⁹

☞ If necessary, open a new worksheet. 👣12

☞ Enter the following data in the worksheet:

	A	B	C	D	E	F	G
1	Schedule						
2		John	Hank	Peter	Gary	Casey	Number
3	Monday	x		x		x	
4	Tuesday	x	x	x	x		
5	Wednesday		x	x	x	x	
6	Thursday	x			x		
7	Friday		x	x		x	

There are five employees that work in various shifts. Every day, a minimum of three working employees is required.

☞ Click cell G3.

☞ Open the *COUNTBLANK* function. 👣68

☞ Select cells B3 up to F3. 👣10

☞ Click OK .

However, in this case you do not want to know how many empty cells there are, but instead you want to know how many times an 'x' is entered. That is 5 minus the number of empty cells:

☞ Change the formula to: =5-COUNTBLANK(B3:F3) . 👣26

☞ Copy the formula from cell G3 up to G7. 👣4

☞ Set a conditional formatting for the cells that contain a number lower than 3; they need to have a red background. 𝒮𝒮66

You will see a red background for the Number cell of Thursday.

☞ Save the worksheet and call it *Schedule*. 𝒮𝒮6

☞ Close *Excel*. 𝒮𝒮11

11.9 Background Information

Dictionary

Macro	A set of instructions that are recorded and triggered by a special key combination or button. The goal of a macro is to automate frequently used tasks.
Multiple level sorting	Sorting a list of data by more than one item, for example: first by date, and then by name.
Visual Basic	Programming language for writing macros.

Source: Microsoft Excel Help

Absolute or relative references in macros
You can use absolute or relative references in macros.

In the case of a relative reference, the cursor starts moving from the selected cell. If cell A1 is selected and you use the cursor keys to move the cursor to cell A3 while recording a macro, a relative reference requires you to move the cursor downwards two rows. If you have selected cell B5 and you run the macro, the cursor will move downwards two rows there as well, and end up in cell B7. So, the spot where the cursor will move to will depend on the cell where the macro is started.

With an absolute reference, the macro will always move the cursor to the cell that has been defined, regardless of the cell that is selected at that moment.

When you are recording a macro you need to choose between relative or absolute references.

To enable the relative or absolute reference:

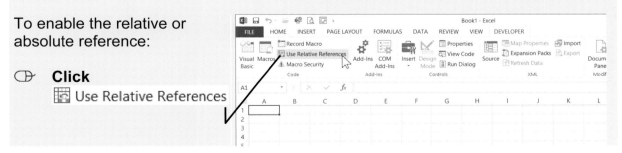

☞ **Click**
🔲 Use Relative References

11.10 Tips

 Tip

Change or delete a macro

Making adjustments to a recorded macro is only a good idea if you are acquainted with the *Visual Basic* programming language. If a macro does not function correctly, you can simply delete it and record it again. This is how you delete a macro:

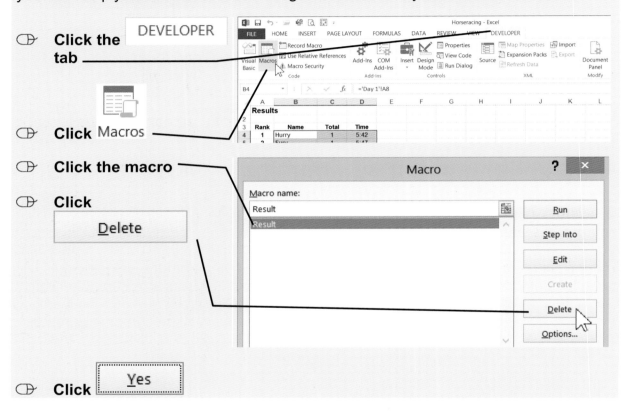

☞ **Click the tab** DEVELOPER

☞ **Click** Macros

☞ **Click the macro**

☞ **Click** Delete

☞ **Click** Yes

 Tip

Set macro security

If the security settings in *Excel* are set to high alert, the macros will not be loaded when you open a workbook that contains macros. If you are certain that you are using reliable files, you can reduce the security settings to a lower level:

If you see this warning when you open a workbook:

☞ **Click** Enable Content

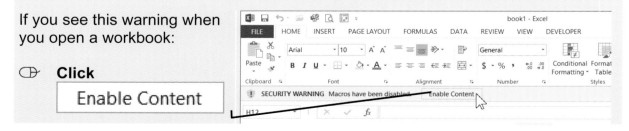

Appendix A. Downloading the Practice Files

In this appendix, we explain how to download and save the practice files from the website accompanying this book. Downloading means you are transferring files to your own computer.

☞ **Open *Internet Explorer*** ⬭⬭**69**

☞ **Open the www.visualsteps.com/excel2013 web page** ⬭⬭**70**

Now you will see the website that goes with this book. You can download the practice files from the *Practice files* page:

⊕ **Click Practice files**

⊕ **Right-click**
[Practice files Excel 2013

You will see a menu:

⊕ **Click Save target as...**

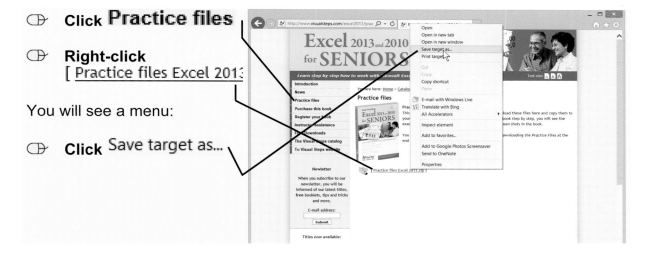

The *Practice files Excel 2013.zip* folder is a compressed folder. You can save this folder in the (*My*) *Documents* folder.

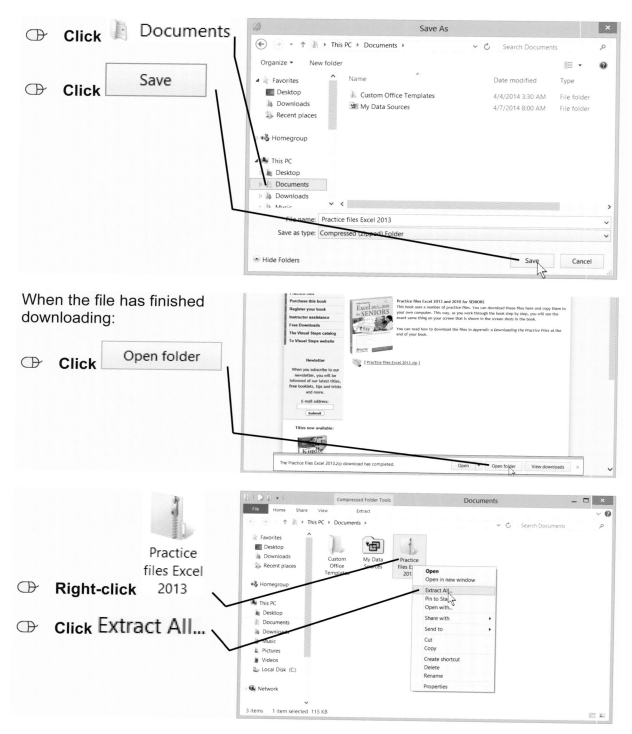

Click 📁 Documents

Click Save

When the file has finished downloading:

Click Open folder

Right-click Practice files Excel 2013

Click Extract All...

Extract the files:

⊕ **Uncheck the box** ☑ **by**
Show extracted files wh

⊕ **Click** Extract

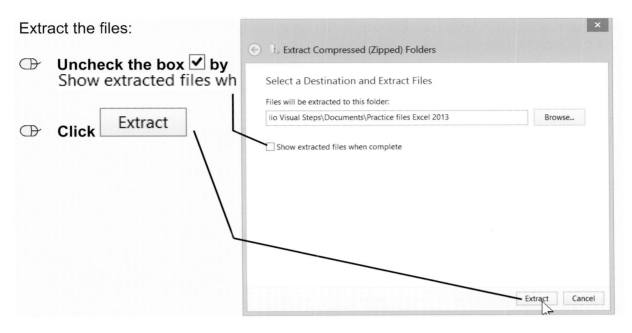

Now the *Practice files Excel 2013* folder has been saved in the (*My*) *Documents* folder:

You can delete the compressed folder:

⊕ **Right-click** Practice files Excel 2013

⊕ **Click** Delete

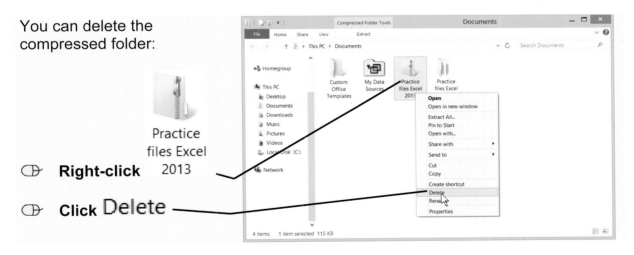

In *Windows 8.1*, the folder will be deleted at once. In *Windows 7* and *Vista* you will see the *Delete folder* window:

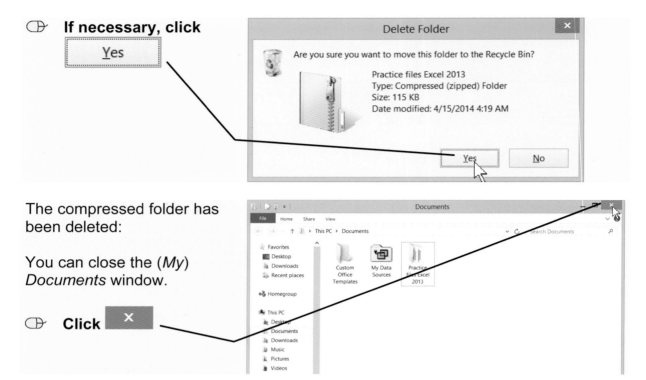

☞ **If necessary, click**

[Yes]

The compressed folder has been deleted:

You can close the (*My*) *Documents* window.

☞ **Click** [×]

☞ **Close** *Internet Explorer* 𝒪𝒪**11**

Appendix B. How Do I Do That Again?

The actions and exercises in this book are marked with footsteps: 👣1
In this appendix you can look up the numbers of the footsteps and read how to execute certain operations.

👣1 **Add a button to the *Quick Access* toolbar**
- On the right side of the *Quick Access* toolbar, click ▼
- Click the button you want to add

If applicable:
- Click More Commands...
- By Choose commands from:, select the All Commands option
- Drag the scroll bar down
- Click PivotTable and PivotChart Wizard
- Click Add >>
- Click OK

👣2 **Adjust the column width**
- Place the pointer between the column headings
- Press the mouse button and hold it down, then drag to the left or right until the desired width is reached

👣3 **Enter a formula**
- Click the cell where the formula is to be inserted
- Type: =
- Click the cell that contains the first number
- Type: +, -, * or /
- Click the cell that contains the second number
- Press

👣4 **Copy formulas**
- Click the cell that contains the formula
- Place the pointer on the handle ✛
- Press the mouse button and hold it down, then drag the handle across the cells to which you want to copy the formula

👣5 **Adding up with *Sum***
- Select the desired cells
- If necessary, click the HOME tab
- Click Σ

6   **Save a new workbook**

- Click 🖫

Only in Excel 2013:

- Click 📁 Documents

In both versions:

- By **File name:** , type the name for your file

- Click | Save |

7   **Save an existing workbook**

- Click 🖫

8   **Close *Excel* without saving**

- Click ✕

- Click | Don't Save |

9   **Open *Excel***

In Windows 8.1, from the Start screen:

- **Click** Excel 2013

In Windows 7 and Vista:

- **Click**

- **Click** ▶   All Programs

- **Click** 📁 Microsoft Office

- **Click** 📊 Microsoft Excel

10   **Select cells**

One cell:
- Click the cell

Multiple cells:
- Drag the pointer across the cells you want to select

- If necessary, select the other cells you want to use, while pressing | **Ctrl** |

One column:
- Click the column header

Multiple columns:
- If necessary, click the other columns you want to use, while pressing | **Ctrl** |

One row:
- Click the row number

Multiple rows:
- If necessary, click the other rows you want to use, while pressing | **Ctrl** |

11   **Close *Excel* or close a window**
- Click ✕

12   **Open a new workbook**
- Click the [FILE] tab

- Click [New]

- Click Blank workbook

Only in Excel 2010:

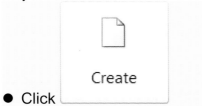

● Click

13 Go to another page
● At the bottom of the window, click ▶

14 Change the font size
● Select the desired cell(s) or text

● By 11, click ▼

● Click the desired font size

15 Add a chart title
When the chart title is not shown in Excel 2013:
● Click +

● Click Chart Title

● Click ▶

● Click Above Chart

In Excel 2010:
● Click the Layout tab

● Click Title ▼

● Click

Above Chart
Display Title at top of chart area and resize cha

To change the name:

● Double-click

● Type the name of the chart

● Click the chart area outside the text box

16 Undo the last action
● Click ↩

17 Close workbook and save changes
● Click the  FILE tab

● Click Close

To save changes:
● Click Save

18 Change name of worksheet
● Right-click the worksheet

● Click Rename

● Type the name

● Press

19 Open another worksheet
● At the bottom of the window, click the name of the worksheet

20 Fetch numbers from another worksheet
● Click the cell in which you want to insert the number

● Type: =

● Click the other worksheet

- Click the cell you want to insert

- Press 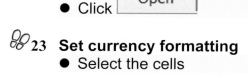 Enter

21   Close workbook, do not save changes

- Click the **FILE** tab

- Click **Close**

Do not save changes:

- Click **Don't Save**

22   Open a workbook

- Click the **FILE** tab

In Excel 2013:

- Click **Open Other Workbooks**

- Click **Documents**

- Click **Computer**

- Click the desired workbook

- Click **Open**

In Excel 2010:

- Click **Open**

- Click the desired workbook

- Click **Open**

23   Set currency formatting

- Select the cells

- Click **$**

24   Name cells

- Select the cells

- Click the *Name Box*

  A1 ▾

- Type the name

- Press **Enter**

25   Create ranges

- Place the pointer on the handle

- Press the left mouse button

- Drag to the last cell

26   Change a formula

- In the *Formula Bar*, click f_x

Or:

- Click the formula in the *Formula Bar*

- Change the formula

- Press **Enter**

27   Change the cell formatting

- Right-click the cell

- Click **Format Cells...**

- Change the formatting of the cell

- Click **OK**

28 Open print preview

- Click the FILE tab

- Click Print

Or:

- Click ⌕ in the *Quick Access* toolbar

29 Enlarge or reduce the print preview

- Click Page Setup

- By Adjust to: , click the arrows ▲▼ until you have the desired size

- Click OK

30 Display the grid

- Click Page Setup

- Click the Sheet tab

- Check the box ☑ by Gridlines

- Click OK

31 Close print preview

In Excel 2013:

- Click ←

In Excel 2010:

- Click the File tab

32 Set the print area

- Select the area you want to print

- Click the PAGE LAYOUT tab

- Click Print Area ▾

- Click Set Print Area

33 Clear the print area

- Click the PAGE LAYOUT tab

- Click Print Area ▾

- Click Clear Print Area

34 Hide a column/row

- Select the columns/rows you want to hide

- Click the HOME tab

- Click Format ▾

- Click Hide & Unhide

- Click Hide Columns or Hide Rows

35 Display (unhide) columns/rows

- Click Format ▾

- Click Hide & Unhide

- Click Unhide Columns or Unhide Rows

🐾36 Insert a column
- Click the column to the left of which you want to insert the new column
- Click the HOME tab
- By ⊞ Insert ▾, click ▼
- Click Insert Sheet Columns

🐾37 Open the *VLOOKUP* function
- Click *fx*
- By Or select a category:, click ▼
- Click Lookup & Reference
- Click VLOOKUP
- Click OK

🐾38 Print
- In the *Quick Access* toolbar, click 🖶

🐾39 Open an *IF* formula
- Click *fx*
- Type: if
- Click Go
- Click OK

🐾40 Create a linked dropdown (validation) list
- Click the DATA tab
- Click ⊟ Data Validation
- By Allow:, click ▼
- Click List
- By Source:, type: = followed by the name of the list
- Click OK

🐾41 Select two columns
- Select the first column
- Select the second column while pressing **Ctrl**

🐾42 Change the color
- Select the object
- Right-click the object

In Excel 2013:

- Click Fill

In Excel 2010:
- By 🖌, click ▾

In both versions:
- Click the desired color

🐾43 Select columns
All the columns:
- Click one of the desired columns

Select one column:
- Click one of the desired columns

- Click the column you want to select once more

44 Select chart area
- Click the area you want to select

45 Delete worksheet
- Right-click the name of the worksheet

- Click Delete

46 Sort in ascending order
- Click a cell in the column

- Click the HOME tab

A
Z
Sort &
- Click Filter ▾

- Click Sort A to Z

47 Sort in descending order
- Click a cell in the column

- Click the HOME tab

A
Z
Sort &
- Click Filter ▾

- Click Sort Z to A

48 Enable the *Filter* function
- Click the HOME tab

A
Z
Sort &
- Click Filter ▾

- Click Filter

49 Filtering
- If necessary, enable the *Filter* function 48

- In the column heading of the column you want to filter, click ▾

- Check the box ✔ by the desired category

- Click OK

50 Display full list
- In the column heading of the column that has been filtered, click ▾

- Check the box by (Select All)

- Click OK

51 Custom filter
- If necessary, enable the *Filter* function 48

- In the column heading of the column you want to filter, click ▾

- Click Number Filters

- Click a condition

- Type the value

- Click   OK

𝄞52 Add a merge field
- If necessary, click the
  MAILINGS tab

- Click   Insert Merge Field ▾

- Click the merge field

- Click   Insert

- Click   Close

𝄞53 Make cells absolute
- Click the cell that contains the formula

- In the *Formula Bar*, click the desired cell reference

- Press   F4

- You will see $ signs in the formula

- Press   Enter

𝄞54 Enable thousands separator
- Select the desired cells

- Click the   HOME tab

- Click   ˒

𝄞55 Create subtotals
- Click the overview

- Click the   DATA tab

- Click   Subtotal

- Choose the settings

- Click   OK

𝄞56 Delete cell content
- Select the desired cell(s)

- Press   Delete

𝄞57 Delete subtotals
- Click the overview

- Click the   DATA tab

- Click   Subtotal

- Click   Remove All

𝄞58 Create a pivot table
- Click the overview

- Click the   INSERT tab

- Click   PivotTable

- Click   OK

59 **Close *Word*, do not save document**
In Word 2013:

- Click ✕

- Click [✕]

Save changes?

- Click [Don't Save]

60 **Update pivot table**
- Click the pivot table

- Click the [ANALYZE] tab
(*Excel 2013*) / [Options] tab
(*Excel 2010*)

- Click 🗐

61 **Open the *Excel Options* window**
- Click the [FILE] tab

- Click [Options]

62 **Align cells**
- Select the desired cell(s)

- Click:
  ≡ (align left)
  ≡ (center)
  ≡ (align right)

63 **Bold, italics, underlined**
- Select the desired cell(s)

- Click:

B (**bold**)

I (*italics*)

U̲ (underlined)

64 **Place chart on a separate sheet**
- Click the [DESIGN] tab

- Click Move Chart

- Click the radio button by New sheet:

- Click [OK]

65 **Move worksheet**
- Click the name of the worksheet

- Drag the name to the desired location

66 **Conditional formatting**
- Select the cell(s)

- Click the [HOME] tab

- Click Conditional Formatting ▾

- Click Highlight Cells Rules

- Select the condition

- Type the value

● By with , click ☑

● Select the desired formatting

● Click [OK]

67 Select a command/function from a dropdown list
● By the dropdown list, click ☑

● Click the command/function

68 Open the COUNTBLANK function

● Click *fx*

● By Or select a category: , click ☑

● Click Statistical

● Click COUNTBLANK

● Click [OK]

69 Open *Internet Explorer*
In Windows 8.1, from the Start screen:

● Click Internet Explorer

In Windows 7 and Vista:

● Click

● Click ▶ All Programs

● Click 🅮 Internet Explorer

70 Go to a website
● Click the address bar

● Type the web address

● Press

71 Create a chart
● Click the [INSERT] tab

● Select the desired chart

72 Open a *Word* document
● Click Blank document

In Word 2010:

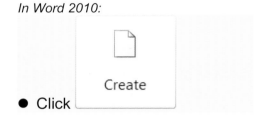

● Click

73 Add a worksheet
● Click ⊕

74 Calculate the sum total of data on other sheets
● Click the [HOME] tab

● Click Σ

● Click the other sheet

● Select the desired cells or column

Appendix C. Index

Word 2013 and 2010 for Seniors

Microsoft's well-known text editing program *Word* is user-friendly and offers a wide range of features and built-in functions for many different uses.

LEARN STEP BY STEP HOW TO WORK WITH WORD

The book *Word 2013 and 2010 for SENIORS* will teach the basics of working with documents, from creating and editing to formatting text. You will also learn some of the more advanced features such as working with tables, merging documents and adding table of contents, indexes and other source references. This fully illustrated book features step by step instructions that will let you learn *Word* at your own pace. This is a practical book for the office, school or home!

Please note: In order to work with this book, you need to own *Word 2013* or *Word 2010* and have it already installed on your computer or have a subscription to Office 365, the online version.

Author: Studio Visual Steps
ISBN 978 90 5905 110 2
Book type: Paperback, full color
Nr of pages: 312 pages
Accompanying website: www.visualsteps.com/word2013

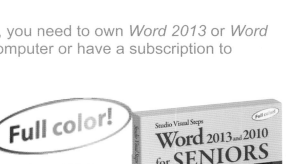

You will learn how to:
- write, edit and format text
- insert images and tables
- work with styles and themes
- add headers, footers and captions
- add a table of contents and an index
- work with letters, envelopes and address labels
- merge documents

Suitable for:
Microsoft Word 2013 and *Word 2010*
Windows 8.1, *7* or *Vista*

Windows 8.1 for SENIORS

GET STARTED QUICKLY WITH WINDOWS 8.1

The computer book *Windows 8.1 for SENIORS* is a great computer book for senior citizens who want to get started using computers. The book walks you through the basics of the operating system *Windows 8.1* in an easy step-by-step manner.

Use this learn-as-you-go book right alongside your computer as you perform the tasks laid out in each chapter. Learn how to use the computer and the mouse and write letters.

This book also teaches you how to surf the Internet and send and receive e-mails. Be amazed at how fast you will start having fun with your computer with the new skills and information you will gain!

Author: Studio Visual Steps
ISBN 978 90 5905 118 8
Book type: Paperback, full color
Nr of pages: 368 pages
Accompanying website: www.visualsteps.com/windows8

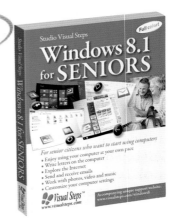

You will learn how to:
- become comfortable and enjoy using your computer
- write letters and memos on the computer
- send and receive messages by e-mail
- explore the World Wide Web
- customize your computer settings

Suitable for:
Windows 8.1 on a desktop or laptop computer

Digital Photo Editing with Picasa for SENIORS

Picasa, a very popular and free photo editing program, is one of the best choices for managing and editing your digital photos.

> **LEARN ALL ABOUT PHOTO EDITING WITH PICASA**

In this book you will get acquainted step by step with some of the many things you can do with photos. You can sort and arrange your photos into albums. Edits can be applied manually or automatically. The contrast, color and exposure in a photo can be adjusted. It's possible to rotate photos, eliminate scratches or blemishes and remove red eyes. You can add effects or even text to a photo and create something unique to print or send. *Picasa* also gives you the option to make collages, view slideshows or create movies from your photos. A great way to share photos with family and friends!

In this book you will work with practice photos. Once you have become familiar with the sorting and editing options available in *Picasa* you can start to work with your own photo collection. At the end of the book you will also learn how to import photos from a digital camera or other device to your computer.

With *Picasa* and this book you will have everything you need to manage, edit and share your photos.

Author: Studio Visual Steps
ISBN 978 90 5905 368 7
Book type: Paperback, full color
Nr of pages: 272 pages
Accompanying website:
www.visualsteps.com/picasaseniors

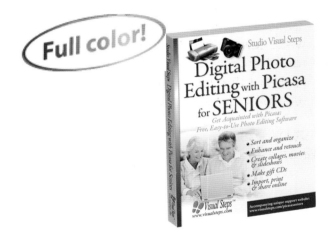

You will learn how to:
- sort and organize photos in albums
- enhance and retouch photos
- create collages and make gift CDs
- create movies and slideshows
- print and share photos online
- import photos

Suitable for:
Windows 8.1, 7 and Vista

iPad for SENIORS

This comprehensive and invaluable book shows you how to get the most out of an iPad with *iOS 7*. The iPad is a user friendly, portable multimedia device with endless capabilities.

LEARN HOW TO WORK WITH THE IPAD WITH IOS 7

This book teaches you how to use the built-in apps to surf the Internet, write emails, jot down notes and maintain a calendar. Other apps discussed show you how to listen to music, take pictures and make video calls.

The book also guides you on how to use the App Store, where you can download other interesting applications free of charge or for a small fee. There are hundreds of thousands of apps to add extra functionality to your iPad.

Each chapter of this book is broken down into small, concise, well-illustrated step-by-step instructions that can be followed at your own pace. With a large-print type and an extensive index, this is the best resource for anyone that wants to get to know their iPad.

Author: Studio Visual Steps
ISBN 978 90 5905 339 7
Book type: Paperback, full color
Nr of pages: 320 pages
Accompanying website:
www.visualsteps.com/ipadseniors

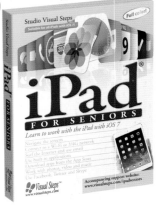

You will learn how to:
- navigate the screens
- connect to a Wi-Fi or 3/4G network
- surf the Internet and use email
- use built-in applications
- download apps from the *App Store*
- work with photos, video and music
- use *Facebook*, *Twitter* and *Skype*

Suitable for:
iPad 2, the new iPad (3rd and 4th generation), iPad Air, iPad mini and iPad mini 2 with *iOS 7*